CHINESE CINEMA

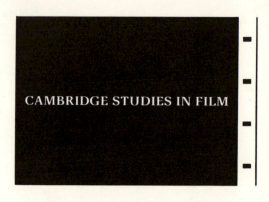

CAMBRIDGE STUDIES IN FILM

GENERAL EDITORS

Henry Breitrose, *Stanford University*
William Rothman

ADVISORY BOARD

Dudley Andrew, *University of Iowa*
Garth Jowett, *University of Texas at Houston*
Anthony Smith, *Director, British Film Institute*
Colin Young, *Director, The National Film School*

OTHER BOOKS IN THE SERIES

Sergei Eisenstein, *Nonindifferent Nature: Film and the Structure of Things*
(trans. by Herbert Marshall)
Vlada Petrić, *Constructivism in Film: The Man with the Movie Camera*
Paul Swann, *The British Documentary Film Movement, 1926–1946*

CHINESE CINEMA

Culture and Politics since 1949

PAUL CLARK

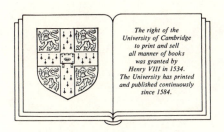

The right of the
University of Cambridge
to print and sell
all manner of books
was granted by
Henry VIII in 1534.
The University has printed
and published continuously
since 1584.

CAMBRIDGE UNIVERSITY PRESS

CAMBRIDGE

NEW YORK   NEW ROCHELLE   MELBOURNE   SYDNEY

Published by the Press Syndicate of the University of Cambridge
The Pitt Building, Trumpington Street, Cambridge CB2 1RP
32 East 57th Street, New York, NY 10022, USA
10 Stamford Road, Oakleigh, Melbourne 3166, Australia

© Cambridge University Press 1987

First published 1987

Printed in the United States of America

Library of Congress Cataloging-in-Publication Data
Clark, Paul, 1949–
Chinese cinema.
(Cambridge studies in film)
Bibliography: p.
Includes index
1. Moving-pictures – China – History.   I. Title.
II. Series.
PN1993.5.C4C58   1988   791.43'0951   87–26785

British Library Cataloguing-in-Publication Data
Clark, Paul
Chinese cinema : culture and politics
since 1949. – (Cambridge studies in film).
1. Moving-pictures – China – History
I. Title
791.43'0951   PN1993.5.C6

ISBN 0 521 32638 9

Contents

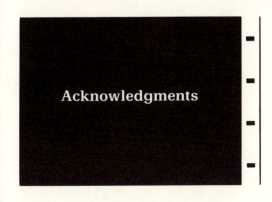

Acknowledgments

Somewhat like making a movie, writing a book depends on the cooperation and support of a number of people. Three friends in particular have contributed to the completion of this study: Bonnie McDougall first suggested I look more closely at Chinese films; Tony Rayns and Chris Berry generously shared their enthusiasm for the subject. Marco Müller added his interest. The hospitality of John Morgan made possible a research visit to China. I greatly appreciate the kind assistance extended to me in China during this and subsequent visits by filmmakers and others – they know who they are, even if I do not name them here. I alone must naturally take full responsibility for the opinions expressed in the book.

Benjamin Schwartz and Patrick Hanan had the generosity to allow me to embark on this project as a doctoral dissertation at Harvard and the patience to await its completion. Joseph Fletcher was an inspiring teacher who encouraged breadth in historians. The staff of the Harvard–Yenching Library made working there as pleasant as it was productive.

This study would not have been possible without the financial support of a Frank Knox Memorial Fellowship at Harvard, a New Zealand University Grants Committee Postgraduate Scholarship, an NCR East Asia Traveling Fellowship, a Teaching Fellowship in Chinese in the Department of East Asian Languages and Civilizations at Harvard, and a Postdoctoral Fellowship from the East–West Center.

Mary Bitterman and colleagues in the Institute of Culture and Communication at the East–West Center have given much appreciated support. Henry Breitrose and William Rothman were ideal editors. William Worger brought a well-trained historian's eye and an old friend's attentive skepticism to the manuscript in its earliest stages.

The encouragement given by these people has contributed immeasurably to this study. The faults in what follows would be measurably greater without their generosity.

Introduction

China is one of the oldest continuous civilizations; film is the most modern of the arts. Until the belated rise of television in the 1980s, film was the major medium of mass communication in the People's Republic, and it remains of exceptional importance. However, there has been no full-length scholarly study of film in China after 1949, despite the significance of the subject. The presumption seems to be that, in such a politicized culture, film has been simply a political tool in the hands of the national leadership. In this view there is little to learn from the history of Chinese filmmaking after 1949. At a time when a "new wave" of Chinese filmmakers has begun to take the art in unprecedented directions, this book hopes to suggest otherwise. What has happened to the newest art in the oldest culture illuminates much about both the nation and the medium.

When the leaders of the Communist Party stood in Tiananmen Square in Beijing in October 1949 and proclaimed their political leadership of the Chinese nation, they might have gone further and claimed leadership of Chinese civilization and culture as well. As for all rulers of China, leadership entailed more than political responsibilities. Moreover, as Chinese communists, the new leaders cherished pretensions that also went beyond politics. They believed that to succeed fully, they should take their revolution further and reshape the culture of the nation. The political revolution they proclaimed that autumn day would stimulate a remaking of society, which in turn would effect a cultural revolution.

Yet transforming Chinese culture would be as difficult as the war which the Party had just won. The nation (and the culture) was riven by divisions between regions, and among ethnic groups, classes, languages, and levels of development. A nineteenth-century invention, Marxism, had helped put these men and women on the podium in Tiananmen Square. A twentieth-century invention – film – offered the new leaders a means to overcome the cleavages in an ancient civilization.

For the victors of 1949, the new medium presented two advantages that performing arts such as opera and literary forms like novels did not have.

1

The Party leaders could reach the widest possible audiences with a message presented on film, and could do so without any intermediary between producers and viewers. Wide, though usually literate, audiences might be reached through other media, including radio, newspapers, and literature. But these means of relaying the cultural aspirations of Party central to the population lacked the immediacy offered to both the literate population and others by the combination of sound and moving images on a screen. A film made under Party auspices in a studio in Beijing could be shown throughout the nation. At the center, film was more amenable to manipulation by the Party leadership because of the technological complexity and capital-intensive nature of the medium. At the periphery, the sort of abuse local opera troupes or art galleries could cause to a supposedly standardized cultural artifact in its performance or display was less possible with film. In this way Party and audiences could be directly linked in a new, mass, nationwide culture.

In creating this new culture, the national leadership and the artists on whom they depended could draw upon two different revolutionary, cultural, and political inheritances. One was a more autochthonous heritage closely associated with the wartime Party headquarters in the interior town of Yan'an. It drew heavily on folk traditions, severely modified to conform with Party ideology. In contrast, the alternative cultural tradition grew out of the Westernized, cosmopolitan coastal cities, notably Shanghai. Its cultural inspiration was to a large extent foreign and its political stance reformist or revolutionary, but not necessarily Marxist. Urban protests on May 4, 1919, against the allocation of former German-held Chinese territory to Japan in the Treaty of Versailles had given a name to the whole intellectual and social upheaval characterized by a rejection of tradition and an embracing of reformist, Westernized ideas in early Republican China. May Fourth literature was one of the distinctive components of this modern, Shanghai-centered, cultural heritage. Before 1949 most Chinese filmmakers were part of this cultural strain. They had had little exposure to the more remote, though in many ways more Chinese, Yan'an alternative.

Chinese cultural history since 1949, and filmmaking as a major part of this history, has been dominated by three themes: the expansion of mass national culture, relations among Party, artists, and audiences, and tensions between Yan'an and Shanghai.

The new national culture was to appeal to mass audiences; not just those in the interior or the urban educated, but to all within the purview of Chinese culture. The Party was determined to gain and retain control over what artists created and, more important, what audiences read, listened to, or watched. Balancing the claims to cultural competence of Party cadres, artists, and heterogeneous audiences was not easy. Too much control by Party authorities, drawing upon a Yan'an-derived style of cultural leadership, could lead not to a cultural revolution, but to a cultural sterility that would satisfy none of the three parties involved. Artists, many of whose attitudes owed more to Shanghai and May Fourth than to Yan'an and the war, might not satisfy Party or perceived audience demands if not carefully directed. But even a greatly circumscribed art required artists to create it, a factor particularly obvious in a medium as specialized and expensive as film. Audiences, the largest, most differentiated, and weakest of these three groups, overall had less in common with the other two groups than Party leaders and artists, who as educated shapers of the culture had much in common.

A study of film offers an effective means of illuminating these themes in modern Chinese cultural history. Film was the most "popular" element in the new mass culture, with the potential to reach the widest possible audience. Moreover, film could reach audiences in an unadulterated form and was most readily controllable by Party censors. But film was also one of the newest cultural media in China: It was closely associated with social and geographical elements that enjoyed the least trust of a leadership whose views of their political and cultural responsibilities had been shaped by backgrounds rather different from those of most experienced filmmakers. These tensions and potentials created a cultural battlefield on which many men and women would struggle for four decades.

CHAPTER 1

Film and Chinese society before 1949

On a typical night in Shanghai in the mid-1930s, Chinese of relatively modest means could choose from a wide variety of diversions. They might spend the evening in a multistoried entertainment center, such as the New World near the eastern end of Bubbling Well Road in the British concession, moving, as the fancy took them, from floor to floor and theater to theater. They could watch more than a half dozen regional opera styles performed by members of the resident troupes. An exhibition of Siamese twins or a magician's act might pass the time after dinner before settling down to see a film. More often than not (in fact, eight times out of ten), the feature would be a Hollywood movie, preceded perhaps by shorts on recent Chinese events: a flood in Sichuan Province, a new airmail service in Yunnan, or a former warlord's funeral in Beijing. As the lights dimmed for the main show, Chinese titles would appear, projected to the sides of the screen to accompany the English dialogue of Janet Gaynor, Lillian Harvey, or Paul Muni.

All this seems to have little connection with Chinese film history after 1949. However, as much as the victors of that year hoped for a break with the past—in culture as in other fields—history was not so easily rejected. The development of film in China before 1949 established patterns and problems that have characterized Chinese film history to the present. Most obviously, those who made the locally produced movies in the People's Republic remained to a remarkable extent the same people who had made them during the two decades before 1949. As for viewers, at the start of the 1950s film had a long way to go if it was to achieve its potential as a mass medium.

Audiences, filmmakers, and industry management of the 1930s were all somewhat dissimilar from the post-1949 ideal. The leaders of the Communist Party had early recognized the propaganda promise of film and established an organization to guide progressive filmmakers in Shanghai. The Film Group was an important subdivision of the League of Left-Wing Writers during the period before the War of Resistance to Japan (1937–45). Many of the most prominent writers, directors, and actors in Chinese film were members and leaders of the Film Group. Their experience in film work, while extensive, was in an environment hostile to the Party. The transition to state management after 1949 was not easy, for both the artists and for those who remained in positions of cultural leadership in the 1950s. Their earlier experience had been as insurgents and infiltrators in a system geared to making money and under a hostile government. After 1949, the former insurgents became the controllers of the system.

Most of the prominent filmmakers in the 1950s and 1960s had started work in film before 1949, not infrequently under Party auspices. The artists' backgrounds, however, like those of their audiences, did not match the post-1949 ideal. Filmmakers in the 1930s and 1940s were urban, lower-middle-class (petit-bourgeois) intellectuals whose tastes and outlooks were shaped by the May Fourth movement. While the May Fourth critique of Chinese tradition and its opening up to foreign influence formed the background to the emergence of the Chinese Communist Party, Mao Zedong as early as 1942 rejected the unreconstructed May Fourth petit-bourgeois intelligentsia, labeling them "heroes without battlefields." The Party's "heroes" in filmmaking were expected to abandon their elitist backgrounds and make a thoroughgoing adaptation to a proletarian world outlook. Here too the transition from making urbane comedies and melodramas to producing socialist drama was not easy.

Film audiences in the 1930s and 1940s had a lot in common with film artists. Before the War of Resistance to Japan, and to a considerable extent after the Japanese surrender, audiences were confined to segments of society inhabiting the most Westernized parts of China, notably Shanghai and the other treaty ports. Their styles of living were very different from those of the majority of Chinese. After 1949 filmmakers were expected to reach a far wider audience, and making films accessible to this huge new audience required more than merely providing projection facilities.

The films made and seen before 1949 by the relatively tiny segment of society also had a rather special appeal. The May Fourth nexus is again significant, for foreign – namely Western – influences were as important in the tastes of filmmakers and audiences as they were for readers of May Fourth prose and poetry. In the case of film, the non-Chinese influences were greater than for the rest of May Fourth literature and art, with the possible exception of spoken drama (*huaju*). The other forms of the so-called new writing promulgated after 1915 in vernacular language, in what became the May Fourth New Literature movement, had strong parallels, if not direct links, with existing literary forms. The use of the vernacular in prose narrative, for example, had a long pedigree.

Like film, modern spoken drama could not draw on a tradition of dramatic performance, for theater in earlier times, and in modern times in other areas, had strongly stylized features, with singing given a prominent place. Naturalistic spoken drama was therefore something of an acquired taste in twentieth-century China, its performers and audiences remaining a narrow, Western-educated intelligentsia. In contrast, vast audiences simultaneously enjoyed a range of traditional Chinese theatrical genres, from festival "sprout songs" (*yangge*) performances in the northwest to metropolitan professional opera troupes.[1]

Given these similarities in the social position of modern drama and film in early twentieth-century China, filmmakers were often involved in spoken drama production. Particularly in the 1930s, writers for the screen also wrote for the stage, directors worked in both forms, and actors overlooked any division between the two arts.

Not withstanding these generalizations, in the 1930s Chinese film art made major contributions to world cinema history. Many film artists, chiefly those associated with the Communist Party or of a leftist persuasion, made successful efforts to expand film's audience and its relevance to the Chinese experience in the twentieth century. The films they made in the last four years of the 1940s marked a brief period in which film was perhaps the dominant artistic mode in the continuing May Fourth meditation on the condition of modern China.

Beginnings to the 1930s

The achievement of the late 1940s came after a half-century of activity, for films reached China in August 1896, when the first films to be projected in the celestial empire were presented as part of a teahouse variety show in Shanghai. As elsewhere in the world, the items shown were of novelty interest, as the Qianlong emperor's clocks had been a century and a half before. The early audiences for these films were undifferentiated from those who came to see and hear the rest of the program, and seem to have included foreigners as well as Chinese.

Having begun, significantly, in Shanghai, film showings took some years to reach Beijing, the capital of the Qing (1644–1911) Empire. Western cameramen had filmed some of the aftermath of the Yihetuan (Boxer) uprising in Beijing and the empress dowager had been given a private screening, although she rapidly lost interest when she almost went up in flames because of the projector. The first public film show – with its usual mixture of maharajas, bellydancers, and circus acts – took place in the capital in 1902, a full six years after variety audiences in Shanghai first enjoyed a film.

It was in Beijing, however, that Chinese entrepreneurs first started to make films for local audiences and in the hope of profiting from the popularity of the new gadget. The proprietors of the Fengtai photoshop in Liulichang, a district famous for its antique dealers, were the first in a long history of film businessmen. Between 1905 and 1908, the Fengtai cameramen recorded a local equivalent of the exotica of the foreign news-reels — scenes from Beijing Opera performed by some of the most famous actors of the day. How these silent performances were received, possibly with live musical "dubbing," has not been recorded. Perhaps the sheer novelty of the projection of a distinctly Chinese image on a screen was satisfying enough.[2]

The owners of the Fengtai photoshop moved in 1909 to Shanghai, where the first cinema in China had opened a year earlier. From then on until the 1980s, this most cosmopolitan of cities was China's undisputed film capital. Other businessmen were not slow to see the moneymaking possibilities of the foreign novelty. Most of the films shown, however, were not local products, but imports from the United States, France, and elsewhere. Moreover, many of the people who worked in the new Shanghai film companies were foreign nationals, who had the necessary technical expertise. Some companies were in fact joint ventures. At this stage few companies lasted very long, even if the involvement of the Western Powers in World War I and the consequent decline in Western film production promised some hope for Chinese-produced films finding a market.[3]

Filmmaking efforts in the 1920s were undercapitalized and overambitious. At least 164 production companies were established between 1921 and mid-1930, mostly in Shanghai, but also in Guangzhou (Canton), Tianjin, Beijing, and Dalian. Less than one-third (53) of them actually made any films during the decade. By July 1930 scarcely more than a half dozen of these companies were still active. Levels of production were also erratic: Between 1921 and 1922, when one source reports that 140 new production companies were registered, a mere six films were made. More than fifty films appeared in 1926 and again in 1927, and in the following two years slightly fewer films were released.[4]

This Chinese production should be put into proper perspective. In the 1920s, and indeed well into the 1950s, most of the films shown in China were foreign-made. In 1929, for example, less than 50 Chinese films were produced. The market in which they competed included an estimated 450 imported films (90 percent of them American). Similarly, Chinese companies in 1933 made 67 films (14 of which were silent), and 500 American and 100 other films were imported. Eighty-eight percent of all films shown in 1936 were foreign-made.[5]

In some respects the foreign and Chinese films did not directly compete, but appealed to different audiences. In Guangzhou, for example, only four of the fifteen theaters in the city in 1929 showed exclusively Chinese films. Two other theaters showed up to fifty percent Chinese films, six theaters about one-third Chinese, and three exhibited only foreign films. Three years later, foreign films were shown in six Guangzhou theaters, three of which were in department store roof gardens which featured other variety entertainment in conjunction with films, in the manner of the first film shows in a Shanghai teahouse thirty years earlier. Twelve other Guangzhou theaters showed Chinese films and second-run Western movies to a poorer audience.[6] As elsewhere, ticket prices were usually lower for Chinese films, which seem to have attracted a less financially comfortable and less Westernized clientele than did American features.

Given the overwhelming preponderance of foreign films, most Chinese viewers needed help in understanding and responding to the movies. In the days before the general introduction of sound movies, Chinese filmgoers often depended on a narrator who at least translated the English titles on the screen. The announcer-narrator usually sat on a platform in the rear of the theater or stood on a balcony, presumably in order to be heard by those in the cheaper seats. Those in the forward seats paid more and may have been more familiar with the foreign-language titles and with the story and mores they saw on the screen. Locally produced documentaries were frequently captioned in both English and Chinese, but the main feature was most often in need of a narrator or translator. These modern versions of the traditional storyteller were the rule in the 106 picture theaters in the whole of China in 1927. All these theaters, counted in an American commercial report, were situated in 18 major, mostly treaty-port, cities where the presence of a non-Chinese community guaranteed at least foreign patronage.[7] In the sound-film decade that followed, the narrator gave way to written plot summaries available to patrons in the theater foyer, and to projected titles in the theater.

Films seem to have appealed to Chinese audiences at different, although simultaneous, levels. The expectations viewers brought to films were a mixture of Westernized tastes or interest in the exotic with the more customary interests they found in other literary genres of modern or ancient vintage. *Sister Flowers* (*Zimei hua*, 1933), for example, was a popular feature made at the Mingxing studio by progressive and leftist artists associated with the Communist Party.[8] Hu Die (known also as Butterfly Wu) stars in a dual role as twin sisters, one a modern, Westernized city type and the other a more traditional village girl. They are separated as infants and grow up in these very different circumstances. The attraction for viewers of seeing a Shanghai "starlet" in the technically ambitious double-exposure photography is added to a type of story little different from the "mandarin duck and butterfly" style of middle-brow fiction generally dismissed as vulgar by May Fourth literati. A common motif in these popular novels was the contrast between modern and traditional characters, not infrequently women, or between two different styles of life.[9] In *Sister Flowers* the twin sisters are coincidentally brought together in the city as adults when one comes to serve as wet nurse for the baby of the other. The former accidentally kills the infant, but the film ends with the family reunited.[10]

A contemporary left-wing critic's ambivalent view that the film "on the one hand expresses the reality of social inequality, and on the other, is a noxious sermon on behalf of the petit-bourgeois backward fantasy of social harmony"[11] may be hyperbolic, but it sums up the dual character of the film, and indeed of the filmmakers' task. In order to attract an audience interested in love stories with happy endings, progressive filmmakers were obliged to appeal to the tastes already served by popular novels and magazines, and by Western films.

Three Shanghai Girls (*Shanghai hua*, 1926) was perhaps a more typical film, which the writer of a 1927 U.S. Department of Commerce report on the Chinese film market described in detail. Exhibited in the summer of 1926, the film was apparently a vehicle to promote the sales of certain modern products. The emphasis was on the unusual and modern, in the homes, workplaces, modes of transport, and love mores of the principal characters. Titles were provided in English and Chinese, and the screenings were accompanied by Western music.[12]

As the mixture of reformist and conventional elements in *Sister Flowers* suggests, Chinese intellectuals had long recognized the potential of film as a medium not simply of commerce (despite examples like *Three Shanghai Girls*) or entertainment, but as a vehicle for intellectual, moral, and political uplift. Activists in the Communist Party were not alone in seeing this potential. The Commercial Press (Shangwu yinshu guan), a major element in the dissemination of May Fourth culture in the 1920s and 1930s, had set up a film production unit as early as 1917. The unit made short fiction films, newsreels, educational films, travelogues, and other documentaries. Its most valuable contribution was filming Mei Lanfang (1894–1961), Beijing Opera's most eminent twentieth-century actor, in scenes from two operas in 1920. The directors of the Commercial Press abandoned film production in 1926, however, because they found that competing with other film companies required making popular films of little educational value, an activity that did not sit well with the high purposes of the press.[13] The inherently popular mass nature of film's audience apparently made film difficult to adapt to the customary notions of the moral, uplifting purpose of literature held by Chinese intellectuals of either a May Fourth or more orthodox bent. Communist Party cultural leaders and filmmakers continued after 1949 to wrestle with this tension between education and entertainment.

Prewar leftist filmmakers

The Communist Party set up its first film organization as part of a front organization in literary circles in 1932. The League of Left-Wing Writers' establishment of a Film Group (Dianying zu) indicated a recognition of the popular potential of film as a political tool. The existence of a corps of progressive intellectuals in professional film ranks made it possible to contemplate setting up a Communist organization among filmmakers.

Such progressive May Fourth intellectuals began their association with film work from the start of the 1930s, when the Lianhua Film Company hired a number of May Fourth writers and artists and produced several relatively "serious" films on contemporary social problems. The Lianhua management must have felt that a market for sound films existed or could be created among educated Chinese, who seem in the mid-1920s to have drifted away from silent films as a vulgar medium.[14]

These shifts in the early 1930s towards social consciousness, seen in changes in personnel at Lianhua and the Communist Party decision to organize among filmmakers, arose from the reverberations of Japanese aggression. The Japanese Imperial Army's invasion and seizure of Northeast China in 1931, and the bombing in 1932 of Shanghai itself by Japanese planes, caused a general reorientation in Chinese intellectual and cultural life. Changes in film circles formed one part of this intellectual transformation.

But it would be easy, from the perspective of Chinese film history after 1949, to exaggerate the importance of these changes in the early 1930s. The Communist Party and progressive filmmakers did not dominate the film industry; nor did those artists who were later called "progressive" or "leftist" necessarily subscribe to Communist ideology or the Party leadership.[15] The introduction of sound films struck most people in the industry as an opportunity not for revolutionary or patriotic consciousness-raising, but for increased profits. The concentration in the rest of this chapter on left-wing or progressive filmmaking should not obscure the broader context in which these efforts were made. Most films (that is, at least three of every four features) remained foreign, chiefly American. In major cities they were screened not with an announcer-narrator competing with the sound track (when the theater was equipped for sound), but with side titles, as is usual for opera arias. A high proportion of Chinese-made films, although it would seem only occasionally a majority, continued in the pattern established in the previous decade. Screen versions of the "mandarin duck and butterfly" style of popular fiction became more sophisticated with the advent of sound, but their melodramatic, stereotyped content and emotions were little changed.

Audiences' tastes, however, seemed to be changing, and in the same general direction as was the case for intellectuals, Communist or otherwise. The predicament of the nation under the threat of further invasion by the Japanese, then firmly ensconced in the Northeast, had a not unexpected effect in galvanizing social and political concern. The fact that progressive film artists were able to produce films during the decade was an indication of these audience changes. The very nature of the film medium – its capital-intensive scale – meant that members of the

Communist-dominated Film Group and others could do little without the blessing or at least acquiescence of capitalists in control of the studios in Shanghai. The owners gave progressive filmmakers work, perceiving that there was an audience, and hence profits, for more socially responsible and even politically conscious films.

The first and major studio influenced by members of the Communist Party's newly organized Film Group was the most successful studio of the 1920s, Mingxing. Founded in 1922, Mingxing was not new territory for the writers and artists of the Film Group. The playwright Hong Shen (1894–1955) had joined the studio in 1925, and in 1931, in the rush to produce China's first talkie, wrote the script of *Sing-song Girl Red Peony* (*Genü hong mudan*), a sound-on-disk feature. After the 1932 bombing of Shanghai, the owners of Mingxing and their chief rivals at the Lianhua studio led an anti-Japanese boycott, realizing that there were balance-sheet advantages in the upsurge of patriotic sentiment. This reorientation of studio leadership coincided with the setting up of the Film Group. Its leader, Xia Yan (1900–   ) became head of a new script team at Mingxing and was joined there by other young left-wing artists. Mingxing became, in effect, a training ground for a generation of artists who dominated filmmaking into the 1950s and 1960s. As a result of this influx of progressive talent, Mingxing films began to feature more stories of the ordinary life of city dwellers and peasants.[16]

Lianhua, the other major film company of the 1930s, proved more difficult for the Film Group to infiltrate, despite the presence there of progressive artists like Sun Yu (1900–   ) and Shi Dongshan (1902–55). The chief obstacle was the founder of Lianhua, Luo Mingyou, who had close ties with the Blue Shirt faction of the ruling Guomindang party led by Jiang Jieshi (Chiang Kai-shek). But Luo's chief financier controlled the second of the three studios that made up the Lianhua enterprise. The financier's personal rivalry with Luo enabled the Film Group to secure a strong influence in this studio. Paradoxically, the other parts of the Lianhua company produced right-wing features until, in August 1936, the Left gained control of the whole company.

This success of left-wing filmmakers is an early indication of one feature of the art medium that worked in favor of those active in it. The specialization of film ensured that artists were assets vital to the prosperity of any enterprise in the capital-intensive industry. Owners' dependence on such specialists helps explain leftist influence in film studios in the 1930s. Having been dismissed from Mingxing in 1934 because of censorship problems, Xia Yan simply moved to Lianhua, although he retained close ties with former colleagues at Mingxing.

Three other film companies infiltrated by the Communist-controlled Film Group included the Yihua, Diantong, and Xinhua companies. The Guomindang Blue Shirt faction was the instrument of right-wing reaction to these developments. Blue Shirt thugs destroyed the Yihua company's facilities in 1933, the year after its founding. When production resumed in 1934, the films were less socially committed in order to avoid further trouble from the authorities. Like Mingxing and Lianhua, Yihua was forced to close in 1937 by the Japanese occupation of the Chinese parts of Shanghai. Diantong, actually acquired by the Left in 1934, produced *March of Youth* (*Qingnian jinxingqu*). The playwright Tian Han (1898–1968) finished the draft of the script before being arrested. Xia Yan produced a shooting script, but had to flee to Japan before the film was finished. Nie Er (1912–35), whose score included the "March of the Volunteers," later adopted by the Eighth Route Army and as the Chinese national anthem, also fled to Japan before the film was released. The Xinhua Film Company, founded in 1935 by a member of the Blue Shirt rightists, like other right-wing companies in the 1930s, included some leftist artists. Xinhua was unique among the Shanghai companies discussed here in continuing after 1937, during the "orphan island" period of Japanese occupation. It closed in 1942. Leftist filmmakers had meanwhile dispersed to the Guomindang- or Communist-controlled regions of China.

Three classic progressive films

Three films from the 1930s illustrate the level of artistic achievement of leftist filmmakers who remained prominent in the following three decades. Although the films may not have been typical, they epitomize some of the themes and concerns of more ordinary features made by progressive artists before the War of Resistance to Japan.

The film version of Mao Dun's short story *Spring Silkworms* (*Chuncan*), produced by the Mingxing company in 1933, was the first direct screen adaptation of a May Fourth major work. Xia Yan himself, as usual using a pen name for the sake of the censors, did the film adaptation, which had musical accompaniment and titles. Three features of the film are noteworthy: The foremost is the considerable emphasis given in the story to the centrality of work and the details of that work. Mao Dun's original story is a portrait of economic decline in the Zhejiang countryside outside Shanghai as foreign (Japanese) imports undermined native silk production. To preserve this theme so faithfully on the screen, and to add the details of silkworm raising that are possible in a visual medium, makes *Spring Silkworms* a milestone in the development of Chinese, and indeed world, cinema.[17]

The second feature of *Spring Silkworms* is more typical of films made by progressive artists in the 1930s. This is the usually indirect, but clearly understood, reference to the Japanese threat to China's territorial and economic integrity. Apparently the original version included explanatory maps and cartoons making explicit the connection between Japanese disruption of Shanghai silk manufacturing and the decision of local silk cocoon buyers in the film not to buy the bumper harvest of the Tong family which the film has so carefully detailed.[18] The third notable feature of *Spring Silkworms* is even more characteristic of contemporary films, and also seems to weaken the impact of the other two features. Most versions of the sound track are made up of popular Western classical music. The joys and trials of the Zhejiang peasant heroes are accompanied by Polish mazurkas and marches. The incongruity is a reminder of the foreign associations of the film medium, which a progressive film like *Spring Silkworms* shared with more mainstream and far less distinguished works.

The striking feature of *The Goddess* (*Shennü*, Lianhua, silent, 1934) is not so much the subject matter—prostitution was an urban phenomenon portrayed in other contemporary Chinese and imported movies, and indeed in popular fiction such as that of the "mandarin duck and butterfly" school—as the direct treatment of the subject. Again, as in *Spring Silkworms*, the centrality of work is emphasized. A more usual treatment of prostitution in film and fiction was indirect and had strong moralistic overtones. In *The Goddess*, however, the prostitute (played by Ruan Lingyu, China's Garbo and the most popular actress of the day, shortly before her suicide) is the central character. The film chronicles her efforts to give her illegitimate son a good education in the face of society's condemnation of his mother's profession. Upon finding that the school fees, which she has carefully saved from her earnings, have been stolen, she kills the thief, her pimp, and is taken to prison. The prostitute in the film symbolizes all women and their struggle in an unjust world. It is the uniqueness of the film's approach to its subject matter that makes *The Goddess* a major contribution to both Chinese and world film history.[19]

The Highway (*Dalu*) was made in 1934 at Lianhua by the writer-director Sun Yu, with some help from Xia Yan and the Communist-controlled Film Group. Sun Yu was one of the few persons working in the Shanghai film world who had had professional training. From 1923 to 1926 Sun had attended the University of Wisconsin Drama School and film scripting classes at Columbia University.

The Highway reflects the hand of a self-conscious film artist. It follows the trials of a gang of six young men, all bearing surnames shared with the actors who played them, from unemployment in Shanghai to work on a strategic highway in the countryside. The silence of the film is broken by songs, particularly the road-making song, which the workers sing together, and by a curious device, a series of percussion sounds, when one of the four men playfully taps the nose, chest, and forehead of a gang comrade. Sun Yu and his colleagues frankly regarded this device as an experiment. Its function in the film is to underline the most striking feature of *The Highway*, the emphasis on physicality and brotherly friendship. The bonds between the members of the road gang are paralleled by those between two young women who work in a roadside eatery near the work site. In an extraordinary scene, the women discuss their feelings for the four gang members while one sits in the other's lap and they caress each other. Physicality takes on new emphasis in a long sequence in which the men bathe naked in a river and jest with the two girls, who boldly observe them from the bank.

The second notable feature of *The Highway* is much less unusual but perhaps more significant in the context of Chinese film history. The film carries an anti-Japanese and united front message, carefully constructed to avoid the condemnation of Jiang Jieshi's censors when first released in the New Year of 1935. A local landlord and traitor, realizing that the soon-to-be-completed highway will be of strategic importance in resisting an unspecified enemy, seizes two members of the road gang. One of them is killed while effecting an escape with the help of the two women. Shortly thereafter, one of the women is mortally wounded in an enemy air attack on the highway. The survivors complete the road accompanied by the superimposed shades of their fallen comrades.[20]

Filmmakers and the War of Resistance to Japan

When full-scale war with Japan began in mid-1937, more patriotic appeals superseded the anti-Japanese allusions of films like *The Highway*. Although until at least 1945 Chinese filmmaking was split into three parts—Chongqing, Hong Kong, and Shanghai—the war years were a transition period during which the connections between Chinese society and film, which are evident in the movies of the late 1940s, began to grow stronger.

Such growth would seem unlikely in Chongqing, the wartime capital, under the direct control of either the Nationalist government apparatus or the Guomindang Propaganda Department.[21] But the popularizing potential of film made it an ideal medium for wartime propaganda, so the Chongqing regime tried to encourage film production. Another characteristic of film – its specialized nature – meant that the progressive filmmakers who made the journey from Shanghai to Chongqing found work and a creative outlet in the studios in Guomindang hands, much as they had in right-wing-controlled studios in Shanghai.[22] In 1941, however, the studios in Chongqing effectively ceased production for almost three years as the Guomindang leaders' adherence to the principles of the United Front with the Communist Party faltered and their suspicions of the political loyalties of progressive film artists grew. Many filmmakers joined traveling theater groups, a professional activity less conspicuous and less vulnerable to Guomindang interference.[23] Production in

Chongqing revived in 1943 under the control of the reactionary CC clique, one of the regime's factions associated with Jiang Jieshi's in-laws, with some experienced film artists participating in the revival.[24]

While production was limited and somewhat restricted, the experience in Chongqing and elsewhere in the interior (in filmmaking or play performance) was an important one for many filmmakers. Driven out of the cosmopolitan enclave of Shanghai by Japanese guns, film artists, like other intellectuals, were forced into firsthand exposure to other, perhaps more typical parts of Chinese society and sought to use their art in the service of the whole country in fighting the Japanese. This wartime experience was a major factor in the achievements of the late 1940s. The experience also laid the groundwork for the post-1949 orientation of film art to serve a broader, less educated audience. War was thus a major step in the slow sinification of film.

Progressive filmmakers like Cai Chusheng (1906–68) and Situ Huimin (1910–87), who moved to Hong Kong after the fall of Shanghai, added a Mandarin component to the existing Cantonese film effort there. In 1939 in Hong Kong, Xia Yan wrote his first film script using his own name rather than a pseudonym, as he had been obliged to do during the previous decade. The earlier story of the rise and fall of film enterprises in Shanghai was repeated in the British colony. A Chongqing-sponsored studio lasted through 1938 and 1939 before succumbing to Guomindang objections to the leftist tendencies of its staff. In mid-1940 progressive artists founded their own company, but after one film it collapsed under financial and political pressures.[25] At the end of the following year, all filmmaking in Hong Kong stopped under the Japanese occupation.

During the four years after November 1937 in which the foreign concessions in Shanghai remained an "orphan island" surrounded by Japanese-controlled territory, filmmaking there continued in fits and starts. The precariousness of the "orphan island" was reflected in the uncertainty in film production. Broadly speaking, at the beginning of the period the studios that had escaped war damage were in the hands of conservative financiers, while progressives controlled artistic and literary journals. Given all these constraints, the films produced soon settled into the relatively safe mold of costume dramas (*guzhuang pian*), occasionally not without disguised patriotic suggestions.[26]

Films during the Civil War

Chinese films in the late 1940s reflected nationwide concerns to an extent seldom seen in the artistic innovation of the previous decades. The explanation for this film achievement lies in the impact of the War of Resistance to Japan on audiences, filmmakers, and the political authorities. The relationships between audiences and artists became closer in these years. At the same time, the political control the Guomindang regime tried to exercise over filmmaking could not effectively undermine this stronger connection between audiences and filmmakers. The lesson of the importance of strong audience–artist links, however, was not really learned until thirty years later.

The Spring River Flows East (*Yijiang chunshui xiang dong liu*, Lianhua/Kunlun, 1947 and 1948, 2 parts) was the most significant of the films of the late 1940s, becoming China's equivalent of *Gone with the Wind*, though with a contemporary setting. In two parts, the film tells a melodramatic story of a single family during the War of Resistance to Japan and in the postwar years. Sufen, a textile worker, and Zhang Zhongliang, an idealistic schoolteacher, fall in love and marry in the course of their work in the war effort. They soon have a son. Corruption in the anti-Japanese ranks, however, slowly eats away at the idealism of Zhang, who has left his family for Chongqing. There he becomes the lover of a fashionable hostess. Meanwhile Sufen, her son, and her mother-in-law wait patiently for news of Zhang, never giving up hope despite their reduced circumstances. The story reaches a climax after the war when Sufen discovers that the husband of the woman for whom she has been working as a maid is in fact her own husband. This happens in the midst of an elegant Shanghai soirée, when Sufen drops a tray of drinks and collapses. Zhang Zhongliang spurns Sufen, despite his own mother's pleas to return to his first and real wife. Sufen drowns herself in a river.

As this story outline suggests, the film has some resonance with both traditional literature and modern, middle-brow fiction popular in the 1920s through 1940s. The story of a wife abandoned by an ambitious husband and her journey to find her spouse is an ancient one. The fourteenth-century play *The Lute* (*Pipa ji*) is one instance of its use, of which many viewers of *The Spring River Flows East* would have been unconsciously aware.[27] The alternating focus of the film between the simple life, hope, and poverty of Sufen, her son, and mother-in-law and the urban complexity, dissoluteness, and corruption of Zhang's other world makes use of a favorite device of "mandarin duck and butterfly" fiction. The story itself, and some of the less savory of the characters, verge on the melodramatic, with a tendency to caricature and make almost maudlin the contrast between Sufen and Zhang's lives and worlds.

The power of *The Spring River Flows East* in the late 1940s was its ability to encapsulate in an epic story (the two parts last for over three hours) of one family so much of the feelings and emotions of an entire nation in a way that is occasionally done by "classic" works of art. No single film could present the whole story of the War of Resistance to Japan and its aftermath, but with its concentration on a family, its emphasis on morality or its absence, and its view of individuals in the vastness of the natural and human order, in the postwar context this work struck a deep chord among Chinese audiences.

The achievement of *The Spring River Runs East* and other such films arose out of the the war experience. Filmmakers (or at least those who formed the corps of artistic personnel in the film industry after 1949), who had been a Westernized elite confined to Shanghai, drew closer to the totality of Chinese society in the course of the war and its aftermath. For audiences, the trauma of the War of Resistance to Japan, a massive, nationwide humiliation and eventual triumph, created a common national feeling which a film, perhaps the medium most accessible (in artistic, though not practical terms) to a wide range of Chinese, could help articulate. Indeed, if the dominant form for expressing the national consciousness was the short story in the 1910s, poetry in the 1920s, and essays (*zawen*) in the 1930s, it could be argued that film held this position in the 1940s.[28]

The postwar experience of filmmakers was in some respects similar to their position in the industry before 1937. The specialization of the medium meant that the managers of even the Guomindang-controlled studios had to tolerate progressive filmmakers exercising their talents under their auspices. Jin Shan (1911–82), for example, wrote and directed *Along the Sungari River* (*Songhuajiang shang*), strongly influenced by Soviet film art, for the Changchun studio while it was briefly in Guomindang hands.[29]

Notwithstanding films like *Along the Sungari River*, the Nationalist government made more forceful efforts to intervene in filmmaking in the late 1940s than it had in the 1930s. Guomindang censors were aware that film audiences were growing. Intervention ranged from crude intimidation and beatings in the studios (in the manner of the Blue Shirt gangs before the war) to more orthodox censoring of scripts and completed films. Of the 162 Chinese-made films (including short subjects) submitted for censorship from October 1945 to September 1948, 48 had to be cut.[30] The script inspector often made major changes. Guomindang censors insisted, for example, that the Chinese traitors in the original script of *A Life of Hope* (*Xiwang zai renjian*) be changed to Japanese characters to blunt the direct criticism of the Guomindang in the work.[31]

The last-named film was made in 1949 at the Kunlun studio, center of left-wing filmmakers to a greater extent than the equivalent Diantong company had been in the 1930s. Formed in mid-1946 by what the official Chinese film history calls "relatively enlightened capitalists,"[32] Kunlun took over responsibility for completing the two parts of *The Spring River Flows East* at the former Lianhua premises in Shanghai. The studio capitalists needed artistic talent to produce films, so artists who had been active in the League of Left-Wing Writers Film Group in the previous decade stepped in. They came from the two wartime Guomindang studios, which continued production after 1945, and from theater circles. The close associations and interchange between film and spoken drama, the two most non-Chinese artistic forms, thus continued after the War of Resistance to Japan.

The success of *The Spring River Flows East* and of *Eight Thousand Li of Clouds and Moon* (*Baqianli lu yun he yue*), about a wartime traveling drama troupe, was unprecedented. *Spring River* played for three months in Shanghai to an audience of almost three-quarters of a million people. The capitalist investors, "enlightened" or otherwise, and the artists were clearly delighted. The government was not: Censors applied even more rigorous standards to Kunlun films. But audiences, unlike celluloid, could not be directly controlled. Many viewers saw parallels between the War of Resistance experiences of the intellectual hero of *A Life of Hope*, for example, and the position of intellectuals in the civil war currently being waged, even if the censors had insisted that the bad characters in the film change national identity. The Kunlun filmmakers hid the real script of *Crows and Sparrows* (*Wuya yu maque*), the story of the resistance of the assorted tenants in a Shanghai tenement house to their Nationalist army landlord, in the ceiling of the sound stage where they were filming the work. They showed the censors a false script, but even that caused problems, and the film had to completed after the Communist victory.[33]

In 1948 the forty-one-year-old film veteran Fei Mu directed a feature whose psychological dimension and stylization recalled the finest films of the 1930s, at the same time that it made indirect reference to the dilemmas of the postwar world. *Spring in a Small Town* (*Xiaocheng zhi chun*) told a simple story of a love triangle involving an intellectual war veteran, and did so with an assurance and stylistic innovation that sets it apart from its contemporaries. Fei Mu's use of dissolves within scenes, for example, is probably unique. *Spring in a Small Town* is another example of the pre-1949 Chinese contribution to world cinema history.

In late 1948, as Fei Mu completed this film, most progressive filmmakers had withdrawn from Shanghai to Hong Kong, where they built on the foundation laid in the late 1930s. Once again they made Mandarin and Cantonese features side-by-side. Cantonese equivalents of the postwar triumphs like *Spring River* were attempted. *Tears of the Pearl River* (*Zhujiang lei*), for example, enjoyed considerable success among Cantonese-speaking audiences in China and Southeast Asia (and was dubbed into Mandarin for showing in the north), but had more of a melodramatic, soap opera flavor than its Shanghai, Kunlun models. As was the case in Shanghai, a high proportion of the films produced were little different from the ordinary entertainment movies of the prewar era. In the same way as they had done in Shanghai, left-wing artists used the rarity of their skills to infiltrate a number of Hong Kong enterprises.[34] But by mid-1949 many filmmakers began the trek north to the Communist-held regions as the People's Liberation Army moved south. The first National Congress of Writers and Artists, held in Beijing in July 1949, was attended by a host of progressive film talents from the 1930s and the postwar period.

Change and continuity after 1949

The place of film in Chinese society, at least in theory and only slowly in practice, was very different after the establishment of the Communist government. The continuities from the 1930s, however, should not be overlooked. Similarities and differences that turn on the dividing year of 1949 are apparent in the changing roles and expectations of filmmakers, film art, and audiences.

One of the most obvious links between the period before 1949 and the Chinese film enterprise after that year was the considerable number of filmmakers who continued to practice their art. The men and women who had been instrumental in creating what was soon called the "progressive film tradition" in the 1930s under the influence of the Communist-dominated League of Left-Wing Writers Film Group were the key figures in the artistic achievements of the late 1940s. In the next two decades (and even later), people like the writers and directors Xia Yan, Cai Chusheng, Zhang Junxiang, Zheng Junli, Sun Yu, and Shen Fu; the actors Bai Yang, Tao Jin, Zhao Dan, Shi Hui, Liu Qiong, and Lü Ban; and less well-known cinematographers and other technical personnel played significant roles in the newly nationalized film industry.

Although the people to a considerable extent remained the same—again in large part because of the specialized nature of the medium—their roles were somewhat different after 1949. The progressive tradition was an underground tradition of opposition to studio owners, government authorities, and the social order in general. The leftist filmmakers had to adjust this habitual attitude after 1949, when they could modify their previous caution about film themes, but were faced with new inhibitions. Moreover, before 1949 the progressive artists did not all necessarily subscribe to the authority of the Communist Party, the ranks of which in Shanghai cultural circles were marked by deep factional cleavages. For both film artists and the cultural leadership, previous experience did not necessarily offer direct models for behavior in the new circumstances after 1949.

The habits of film art which filmmakers had established in a strictly commercial environment were also not directly transferable to the new circumstances after 1949. Artists had had to appeal to urban, middle-class audiences whose tastes were shaped by their reading of "mandarin duck and butterfly" fiction and viewing of the Hollywood movies that had dominated the Chinese market. After 1949 Party cultural authorities, in tones of moral puritanism, labeled as petit-bourgeois vulgarity much of what had earlier seemed progressive.

A long-lasting feature of pre-1949 film art was the close ties among filmmaking, the theater, and literature. Scenarists and actors who made films in Shanghai and elsewhere were almost equally at home in spoken drama, the other and most modern of literary forms in China. This tendency was reinforced during the War of Resistance to Japan when theater work, often in traveling troupes, was the only creative outlet available to writers and performers. The emphasis on the literary aspect of film, on the scenarist rather than the director, started early in China and remained strong long after 1949. In part it can be explained by the filmmakers' urge to find a respectability for the modern medium by association with the most honored of cultural activities. The association with literature was also not surprising given the relatively small numbers of activists in the May Fourth literary and artistic endeavors. After 1949, these ties among film, theater, and literature remained firm and could be said to have hindered the emergence of an independent art of film in China.

Before 1949 film enjoyed an ambiguous position in Chinese society and only weak or tentative connections with the potential mass audience so vigorously hoped for by artists and officials in the People's Republic. To be sure, the achievement of the late 1940s represented an unprecedented linking of national feeling and film art. Despite these positive moves in the direction of the sinification of film art, film remained limited in terms of its place in Chinese society. Most popular films, and even those classics of the postwar era like *The Spring River Flows East*, still reflected an urban and somewhat literate view of the world. In 1949, moreover, most of the mere 500 theaters and other places that showed films were in large cities. The new task for both filmmakers and managers was to reach out to the nonurban, less educated population. In doing so, film would at last become a truly mass medium, as audiences rather different from their counterparts in the 1930s and 1940s began to see movies.

The artists who made the films and the people who controlled their production and distribution, however, were socially less different from their pre-1949 counterparts than were these new, increasingly rural, audiences from their urban, middle-class predecessors. The May Fourth intellectuals who had created the progressive film legacy continued to be prominent artists in the new industry. Their colleagues, who in the preceding two decades had articulated Communist Party policies on art and organized film artists in an environment hostile to leftists, remained in positions of cultural leadership long after 1949.

But the environment in which both filmmakers and cultural leaders worked changed considerably with the rise to power of the Communist Party. The leaders called on film artists to reorient themselves to the new expectations placed on culture. In the new decade, cultural authorities and artists worked in a setting very different from the underground and insurgent position they had had in Shanghai in the 1930s and 1940s. The problems both groups confronted in making these transitions were many.

(*here & next page*) The most popular Chinese film of the 1940s, *The Spring River Flows East,* 2 parts, 1947 and 1948.

Socialist China's first feature film, *Bridge*, 1949.

The transition to socialism in Chinese filmmaking was a dual process. The Party cultural leadership made the transition from Yan'an to Shanghai, erecting a system of film production and art designed to serve the policies the leaders had articulated in Yan'an. For their part, filmmakers during the six years to the mid-1950s tried to make the transition in ideological terms from Shanghai to Yan'an. Both artists and cadres found it far from easy to surmount tensions between the new, Yan'an-derived expectations of film as "the most important art" and the old position of the Shanghai-based filmmakers as inheritors and purveyors of an elite May Fourth tradition. Moreover, film artists' differing responses to the new circumstances exacerbated divisions within their ranks. The failure of the Party and cultural authorities at different levels in the new system to spell out and apply the new policies clearly also caused difficulties.

By 1955 the transformation of the system of production and distribution was complete, but filmmakers had proved less thorough in transforming themselves and their relationships with the new regime. Furthermore, by 1955 the audiences that saw the new films were less different from their pre-1949 counterparts than Party leaders and artists had hoped. Film had not yet become a mass medium.

Yan'an to Shanghai

Yan'an as the center for CCP.

Film in Yan'an

Despite the early association of Chinese Communist Party activists with Shanghai filmmaking in the 1930s, the Communist film industry started in a more official sense not in Shanghai, but in Yan'an. Yan'an would seem an unlikely place for the birth of a new film enterprise. Inhabitants of that remote hill-country town may not even have seen a movie unless a Western missionary obliged. Certainly it was a great geographical and cultural distance from the cities where most of China's filmmakers had

25

worked. But in the autumn of 1938 a handful of such filmmakers set out to show and make films in Yan'an. If film seemed a foreign medium in places like the great treaty-port cities of the coast, in the hills of Shaanxi (Shensi) Province it was truly exotic.

The filmmakers who made their way to the Communist headquarters at Yan'an were part of a broader stream. After 1936 and particularly with the start of the War of Resistance to Japan in July 1937, hundreds of young intellectuals made the difficult journey from the cities of the coast and riverine hinterland to join the Communist effort centered on Yan'an. In a sense they brought the twenty-year-old May Fourth tradition to the countryside. Although few of the filmmakers who journeyed to Shaanxi managed to parlay their movie experience into something like marriage to chairman Mao Zedong, as did Jiang Qing (Lan Ping), many former artists put their talents to work in the propaganda teams, drama troupes, and writing groups in Yan'an and the Communist-led anti-Japanese base area. These workers found it as natural in Yan'an as in Shanghai to move between film and other cultural work, particularly drama.

These propaganda activities were limited to the audiences that performers and writers based in Yan'an could reach. Producing film of the Yan'an effort and the Eighth Route Army appealed to the Party leadership as a way to reach the parts of China under Guomindang control, and indeed beyond China, with an immediacy no other medium could match. Zhou Enlai himself asked a famous Shanghai actor-director to bring a movie camera from Hong Kong on his way to the base area. Once the camera arrived in the autumn of 1938, the Yan'an Film Team was formally established as part of the General Political Department of the Eighth Route Army.[1]

Having several members of this first, Party-controlled film effort with no film experience created significant precedents for the post-1949 film studios and management. After 1949 most cadres, both artistic and managerial, were new recruits sometimes given brief specialized training in addition to their backgrounds in cultural work in the military.

A second feature of this film staff after 1949 was the distinction between artistic and management cadres. The former, while in theory granted a degree of autonomy to practice their art, were ultimately subordinate to management at the studio and higher levels. In the case of the Yan'an Film Team, only three of the six original members had had any experience in film work. Yuan Muzhi, the most prominent member, had been a successful actor in Shanghai films in the 1930s and had become a writer-director in the leftist-controlled studios. It was he who brought the team's first camera to Yan'an.[2] Before his departure for Moscow to study the Soviet film industry in 1940, Yuan was in charge of artistic matters for the Film Team. Political and administrative work, however, was in the hands of a Long March veteran. Yuan's dispatch to Moscow indicates that the Party leaders were already concerned with preparing a model for their own film apparatus once they had returned to the cities.

Despite conditions that prevented any film being completed during the Yan'an years, and at the same time as economies were being made in many other areas of Yan'an life, the Film Team continued to expand. It grew to about three dozen persons in 1942. But filmmaking was a machine-intensive art, more prone than others to Guomindang blockade of the base area. Film stock was exhausted by 1943, and thereafter, the Film Team found an alternative role as merely one of many cultural groups in the base area, mounting exhibitions and conducting propaganda work. In August 1945 the Yan'an Film Team was disbanded. Its members made their way to the Northeast, where preliminary work for Communist China's first film studio was beginning.

Meanwhile, in the spring of 1942, at the Yan'an Forum on Literature and Art, Mao Zedong had delivered his pronouncements on the function of art, in which film would play an important part. Mao himself made only passing mention of film (and even these brief references were eliminated from the 1950s versions of the *Talks*), indication both of the indigenous derivation of Mao's literary views and of the concomitant prejudice in his attitude toward May Fourth literature in general.[3]

Mao in 1942 had two central emphases: that literature and art should serve political purposes, and that art should seek to widen its audiences, at the same time raising its own and its audiences' standards. A major theme throughout Mao's remarks was the contrast between these aims for literature and the May Fourth heritage, which most of his audience of artists and intellectuals gathered at the Forum (and indeed in some senses Mao himself) represented. Film was an important part of this urban May Fourth literary heritage.

Three areas in which Mao drew a distinction between the new literary aims and the May Fourth heritage had particular relevance to the future of filmmaking. First, both audiences and artists in the anti-Japanese base areas (and by implication in a future national regime) were very different from those elsewhere:[4]

In the Shanghai period, the audience for revolutionary works of literature and art consisted primarily of students, office workers, and shop assistants. In the general rear [the Guomindang-controlled areas] after the war broke out, this circle expanded a little, but it still consisted primarily of the same people because the government has kept workers, peasants, and soldiers away from literature and art. It is a completely different matter in our base areas. The audience for works of literature and art here consists of workers, peasants, and soldiers, together with their cadres in the Party, the government, and the army.

Mao reminded his listeners, in his speech at the closing session of the May 1942 Forum, of the differences between Shanghai and Yan'an:

Because of their many ideological problems, many of our comrades are also largely unable to distinguish between base areas and nonbase areas, and in consequence make many mistakes. Many comrades have come from Shanghai garrets, and the passage from the garret to base area involves not just two different localities but two different historical eras.

These differences, at least as Mao perceived them, between the base areas and the Guomindang-controlled parts of China contributed to many of the tensions after 1949 between Party and filmmakers and within film ranks.

Mao's emphasis on the need for artists to establish close links with their new mass audiences had particular relevance for film:

Workers in literature and art . . . until now have been heroes without a battlefield, remote and uncomprehending. . . . [They] are unfamiliar with the people they write about and with the people who read their work, or else have become estranged from them. Our workers in literature and art are not familiar with workers, peasants, soldiers, or even their cadres.

Mao's stress on the need to learn in particular the language of the worker/peasant/soldier masses was in inherent contrast to the specialized nature of film production. Yet film was a highly accessible art at the receiving (audience) end. Film was vulnerable to criticism by its audiences of falseness of language when dealing with events and characters more familiar to the new audiences than to older filmmakers.

Mao's brief allusion to the pitfalls of artistry had relevance to film's future, given the art's unfamiliarity to most Chinese. "Insofar as a work is reactionary," Mao noted, "the more artistic it is the more harm it can do to the people and the more it should be rejected."[5] Although Mao in this context immediately went on to condemn art only concerned with political sloganeering and not with artistic form, censors and literary critics later tended to invert the purpose of this sentence. Films (and other works) which were artistically of a bold nature or of more than usual interest often attracted the attention of cultural leaders at the studio level and above. A common presumption was that the more complex a work was in artistic terms, the less it should be trusted politically. Mao's major emphasis on widening audiences reinforced this tendency. Party cadres' distrust of film's artistic and technical complexity and of its specialist producers could undermine film's potential, as Lenin's "most important art," to reach the broadest, most popular audiences.

Beginnings in the Northeast

Filmmakers had the opportunity to apply Mao's 1942 outline of cultural orientation not in Yan'an, but in the Northeast. There in the city of Changchun, capital of the Japanese colony of Manchukuo, was one of the most advanced film facilities in East Asia, the Manchukuo Film Company. After the Japanese surrendered in August 1945, conditions in the city were far from stable, so the decision was made to dismantle one-third of the Northeast Film Company, as the employees had renamed their studio on October 1, 1945, and transfer it from Changchun. On October 1, 1946, the establishment of the first Communist Party film studio was formally proclaimed at Xingshan. Somewhat reminiscent of Yan'an in its remoteness, Xingshan was a mining town in the extreme northeast of Heilongjiang Province, hard by the Russian border.

By October 1946 over forty former members of the Yan'an Film Team had arrived. The staff, under a leadership group drawn from old Yan'an hands like Yuan Muzhi, fresh from Moscow, Tian Fang, Chen Bo'er, and Qian Xiaozhang, were a mixture of those experienced in film production and officials from outside film circles. The mix was to become the standard pattern throughout the new industry. Some personnel were former leaders of the Japanese-run studio. Most of the group from Yan'an had had no exposure to film production and urgently needed familiarizing with their new responsibilities. Army propaganda troupes provided a third group, which underwent training in the studio itself. As much effort at the new studio went into training new cadres as producing film documentation of the southward progress of the People's Liberation Army. By mid-1949 close to a thousand cadres had been trained in four sessions at the studio. They provided the core of managers for the film industry after the Communist takeover.[6]

In this early period in the extreme Northeast, the artists in training at the makeshift studio completed one short experimental fiction film which exemplified the artistic policies Mao had enunciated at Yan'an. The film appeared in February 1948 as one edition of the newsreel "Democratic Northeast." *Leave Him to Fight Old Jiang (Liuxia ta da lao Jiang)* was based on a newspaper report of an actual incident. In a village in the Northeast a young soldier accidentally shoots and kills a young peasant. According to strict military discipline, the soldier is promptly sentenced to be executed. An appeal by the father of the dead youth saves his life. The old peasant, moved by the army's discipline and closeness to the villagers, realizes that the young soldier had not intended harm and should be allowed to remain in the army to fight the common Guomindang enemy led by Jiang Jieshi, as his son might have done. The old man goes so far as to adopt the young soldier. Even a plot summary suggests the simplicity of the piece, a feature reinforced by basic and deliberate film techniques. Its makers regarded the film as no more than a testing of style, equipment, and personnel before production of full-length feature films could be contemplated.[7]

The leadership at the Northeast studio emphasized the need for a new, simpler film style. Given the primitive conditions at the studio, simplicity was natural. It also reflected, however, the concerns of experienced film artists both at the studio and in areas still not under Communist Party control. Some artists at the Northeast studio, having spent years in other pursuits in the base areas, were probably anxious to take up film work again, but found themselves frustrated by the backward conditions. They may have felt that the new films needed defending, by praising simplicity and the new style, before they reached their audiences. Another factor was undoubtedly the cultural cadres' urge to allay the concerns for artistic quality felt by filmmakers in Beijing and Shanghai who would shortly be working under a new regime. Their future participation was essential for the new industry. Cooperation between Party and film concerns that had begun in Yan'an grew in the Northeast, and would be extended to the whole country.

The temporary political standards Party central set for films, in particular those already in distribution, also reflected a concern for cooperation between the Party and other elements at a time when most of the country was not yet in Communist hands. The standards were in line with the Party's New Democracy policy, which allowed for considerable concessions to noncommunist elements in the new political regime. A November 1948 Party central directive took a relatively generous view of what audiences could watch. Films with political content need only not favor imperialism, feudalism, and bureaucratic capitalism. They should not attack the Soviet Union, the Communist Party, or its policy of "people's democracy." Films without much connection with politics, as long as they had artistic value, were acceptable if their message was harmless. There was no insistence that all films immediately be about worker/peasant/soldier subjects (with a concentration on the latter). As for new films, modern events set in the liberated areas should not be neglected, but other Chinese or foreign, modern, or ancient settings could also provide the basis for fiction films.[8] At this stage toleration of films that did not even acknowledge the Yan'an view of art was the norm. Given the level reached by the fledgling industry, policy could not be otherwise and there still be something to fill China's screens.

To Shanghai

By the time the studio had moved back to Changchun, the scope of the new film industry had expanded to include Beijing film units and was on the eve of embracing China's film heartland, Shanghai. The manner in which the new regime incorporated the film enterprise in these two cities reflected and deepened a broad cleavage in filmmaking ranks (and indeed in literature and art circles in general) between "old liberated areas" and "Guomindang-governed areas." Mao Zedong in his 1942 Yan'an *Talks* had distinguished between writers and artists from the two areas.

The takeover in Beijing and Shanghai perpetuated this division, which remained significant throughout the following decade. The Party and managerial cadres in charge of film production often came from Yan'an or the other wartime base areas. Many film artists, on the other hand, could not make similar claims of presumed ideological reform, having spent the war years in Shanghai, in Hong Kong, or in the Guomindang-controlled regions. Those who had spent time in the old liberated "red" areas often encountered resentment or distrust from their less privileged filmmaking colleagues.[9]

Although the employees of the film units taken over in Beijing, including some well-known progressive artists, remained at their posts, the leadership of the expanded film enterprise came south with the army. Among the units taken under direct military control when the People's Liberation Army entered Beijing in January 1949 were branches of Shanghai- and Changchun-based studios, the North China branch of the Central Film Services Agency (Zhongguo dianying fuwu chu), the instrument of censorship of the Guomindang government, and nine cinemas owned by Guomindang officials.

When the Beiping (Beijing) Film Studio was formally established on April 20, the studio leadership was drawn from old Yan'an hands who had some prewar film experience. Tian Fang, formerly Party secretary at the Northeast Studio, became studio head. His deputy, Wang Yang, and other production workers were almost all from Yan'an or the film teams and short-lived studios set up in the interim between the Japanese surrender and the start of the civil war in 1947. The artists at the Beiping studio took over the task of making documentary films from their colleagues at the Northeast studio, who at the same time had moved back to Changchun.[10]

In the same month, April 1949, the new cultural leadership began setting up a national organization for the film industry. Yuan Muzhi had left his post as head of the Northeast studio and moved to Beijing in March to start preparatory work. Yuan had left Yan'an in early 1940 to study Soviet film production for six years. In April 1949 the Propaganda Department, which was the Party organ responsible for culture, formed the Central Film Management Bureau (Zhongyang dianying guanli ju). Yuan served as its first head. After the formal establishment of the People's Republic, the Film Bureau shifted from being under direct Party leadership to become a state organ under the Ministry of Culture. The Film Bureau remained the highest organ specifically responsible for film from 1949 onward.[11]

The Communist takeover of the Guomindang-controlled film enterprises in Shanghai, the center of production since film's beginnings in China, was in the hands of a triumvirate: The military command was in overall control, working with representatives of the two strains, Yan'an and Shanghai, of artistic outlook. Zhong Jingzhi, who had led the remnants of the abortive Yan'an Film Studio and others from the North China base areas to the Northeast in 1947, was joined by the Shanghai playwright Yu Ling, who had been active in leftist film circles before and after the War of Resistance to Japan, and by Xu Tao, a Kunlun studio director.[12]

Although these men took over the direct running of only a portion of the Shanghai film industry in the spring of 1949, most Shanghai filmmakers, including those in the private studios, appear to have welcomed the arrival of the troops and government from the north. Shanghai had a strong tradition of leftist filmmaking which had revived, in the face of Guomindang reaction, after the Japanese defeat. In addition to taking over several film studios which had been under direct Guomindang control, numerous sound stages, and forty cinemas, the military authorities incorporated the general office of the Guomindang's Central Film Management Agency in the city.

The new cultural authorities immediately began to organize the filmmakers in Shanghai. As early as June they established the Shanghai Drama and Film Workers Association (Xiju dianying gongzuozhe xiehui) with almost a thousand members. The combination of drama and film reflected a Shanghai tradition – the absence of boundaries between these two fields. The executive of the new association organized political study for filmmakers and arranged for their members to do propaganda work and perform for the public throughout the city. Progressive film artists started working again, some returning from voluntary exile in Hong Kong. These people filled cadre positions in the new industry.

By November 1949 the Shanghai Film Studio, incorporating the studios directly under state ownership, was formally established. The leadership again combined Yan'an and Shanghai backgrounds. Yu Ling served as studio head, Zhong Jingzhi was his deputy, and the scriptwriter Chen Baichen, formerly of the Guomindang-controlled Central Film Enterprises second studio, acted as head of the artistic committee. China's film industry, like the nation, had entered a new age.

Cleavages among filmmakers

The ranks of Chinese filmmakers, however, were not united. The establishment of the Shanghai Drama and Film Workers Association in June was a necessary preliminary to the National Congress of Writers and Artists, held in Beijing in July 1949. This was the first cultural gathering on a national scale since the promulgation of Mao Zedong's *Talks at the Yan'an Forum on Literature and Art*. Several features of the meeting illustrated the divisions that were to affect filmmaking (and indeed other cultural work) throughout the next decade.

The two streams (communist and other) of literary effort in the war years were paralleled by the division of labor among the speakers at the congress of over eight hundred representatives. First, however, Guo Moruo, the poet and archeologist, reported on the overall struggle for a new Chinese literature since the May Fourth incident. Then the novelist Mao Dun spoke on the previous decade of art and literature in Guomindang-controlled China, and Zhou Yang, a writer and cultural commissar, did the same for the liberated areas.[13]

Specific reports on filmmaking continued this Chongqing–Yan'an division. Yuan Muzhi, late of Yan'an, Moscow, and the Northeast, spoke on Communist-controlled-area film work. Yuan emphasized the relative success there in uniting a somewhat diverse corps of filmmakers from a wide range of backgrounds.[14] By this he implied that similar success was achievable on a larger scale throughout the country. The report on both drama and film work (here again treated in combination) in Guomindang China since 1937 was given by the playwright and scenarist Yang Hansheng.[15] Yang's career after 1937 had been typical of progressive filmmakers who were not in Yan'an or in the Communist-held areas. After the war years in Chongqing, the Guomindang capital, Yang had been active in the Shanghai Kunlun studio before moving to Hong Kong in late 1948 to escape Guomindang pressure. Most of the prominent left-wing film artists seem to have made this round-trip journey between Shanghai and Hong Kong.

The anti-Guomindang credentials of filmmakers like Yang Hansheng were unquestionable, as were their motives in fleeing Shanghai in late 1948. Nevertheless, Party leaders could not but have felt that if they had earlier fled from one government's restrictions on artistic creation, they might also chafe under another regime. Those who had made their way to Yan'an and spent the anti-Japanese and civil war years in the base areas were more familiar to the Party's cadres and hence less suspect than their southern colleagues. The relative degree of trust based on distance from the leadership, a characteristic of Chinese politics from ancient times, rather than proven ideological differences, figured in Party attitudes toward Shanghai artists like Yang Hansheng. The leadership of the Film Workers Association, established at the end of the 1949 Beijing congress, accordingly reflected a balance between the old and newly liberated areas.[16]

Yan'an-versus-the-rest cleavages did not affect filmmakers more than other writers and artists. For all, the distinction mattered more to the Party than to the artists themselves. However, the position of filmmakers, already prone to suspicion by the nature of their foreign, modern medium, was further clouded in the new circumstances. Film, most directly as documentaries, promised to be a useful propaganda tool for the leaders from Yan'an. Film should therefore be in the right hands. It was not surprising, then, that former Yan'an cadres were so prominent in the early years of the Communist film industry. The close modeling of the new industry on the Soviet example, despite the irony of its foreignness, is also not unexpected.

Film was also different from other literary and artistic activities because it was an industry as well as an art. A substantial proportion of film workers in its Shanghai heartland remained, at least for the time being, in the privately owned studios. These enterprises may have been financially weak, but they offered alternative outlets for film artists. The new film system had to take this state–private distinction into consideration.

Shaping the system

One of the first tasks of the new controllers of the industry was the establishment of a national system for the production, censorship, distribution, and projection of films. Central institutions to coordinate these activities were set up in 1949–50, as was a network for distribution. Projection teams would widen distribution by taking films to audiences for whom films had been a rarity. By 1953 a unified national system for film production had been established when the last of the privately owned Shanghai studios was incorporated into the state enterprise. Problems with centralized leadership of the new film system and the way the Party leadership took over the private studios again illustrated the Yan'an versus the rest tension seen in other areas of cultural life.

Centralized control

National direction of the industry came from the Ministry of Culture Film Bureau, which called a large-scale conference in November 1949 to set targets. Representatives of all film units, nationalized and private, discussed their problems for about a month in Beijing. The meeting approved an ambitious plan for 1950, envisaging the production of 26 feature films, 17 documentaries, 1 animated feature, 48 newsreels, 40 dubbed Soviet features, and a similar number of shorter Soviet films.[17]

A system for the licensing of approved films was promulgated in mid-1950. The emphasis in these regulations on the importance of centralized censorship decisions, and on the referral of matters of dispute to the Film Bureau in Beijing, suggests that local cultural authorities tended to abuse their powers of control or to be overcautious. Chinese films for nationwide showing, all imported films, and those for export to Hong Kong, Southeast Asia, and elsewhere, required Film Bureau approval. Every film unit needed licensing. Thus the Film Bureau gathered valuable information, including details of ownership, equipment, and income, on privately owned studios, cinemas, and exporters and importers of films and other materials.[18]

A nearly simultaneous measure was perhaps designed to sweeten the pill of increased centralization. In early 1950 the minister of culture announced the formation of a Film Guidance Committee (Dianying zhidao weiyuanhui). The thirty-two members of the committee included a range of literary and artistic figures, with Yan'an and other backgrounds, most of whom had experience in spoken drama or filmmaking. Among them were such honored May Fourth writers as Cao Yu, Ding Ling, Lao She, Zhao Shuli, Hong Shen, Ai Qing, the historian and journalist Deng Tuo, and even the former Party chairman Li Lisan. Mao Zedong's wife, Jiang Qing, was the twenty-ninth named in the list of members. The committee was charged with raising the ideological and artistic standards of the new films. In conjunction with the Ministry of Culture, the members would consider story outlines and scripts for the three state-owned studios. They would examine completed films and distribution figures, and comment on films made by the private Shanghai studios. In setting up the Film Guidance Committee, the cultural authorities were attempting to involve literary talents in the new film industry. In this way artistic standards, which the November 1949 Film Bureau meeting had also concluded were inadequate, might be strengthened. Having a broader range of voices at the top of the film enterprise with at least nominal influence might also provide reassurance to those filmmakers, particularly in Shanghai, who until then had had little direct experience with the Communist Party.[19]

Distribution and audiences

The distribution network, which was to get duly licensed films to the viewing public, was established in 1950 in the form of regional film management companies (Dianying jingli gongsi) in the Northeast, Beijing and Shanghai, and in the South-Central, Southwest, and Northwest military administrative regions. These companies were to set up networks of distribution stations and projection teams according to local conditions and the size of audiences. Later, in February 1951, a national Film Management Company in Beijing, under the Film Bureau, took over the duties of the Film Bureau's distribution section (*faxing chu*). It was to supply all nationalized cinemas in the country, at a time when most theaters were still in private hands.[20]

The central distribution agency purchased completed films from the studios at a rate based more on the length of the feature than on its artistic quality. This system was used until the 1980s, and its indifference to artistic effort had a profound effect on Chinese filmmaking for over thirty years. However much individual artists might be concerned for the quality of their work, many of their colleagues in the studios and their managers did not share this concern, for the distribution system that they supplied was to a large extent indifferent to quality.

The weakness of central control over local activities was soon evident. A writer in the *Literary Gazette* in February 1952 reported that cinemas in Changsha gave only short showings of Soviet films, while less worthy movies enjoyed long runs.[21] Changsha cinema owners were responding to the greater popularity of non-Soviet movies. In Shanghai, where Western-made films were only just beginning to disappear from the market, the local Film Bureau allegedly sought to delay the viewing by the censors of some films in order first to allow them to earn some money in the marketplace for the cinemas and the local studios that made them.[22] The same East China Film Bureau judged a Soviet feature film of negative merit and refused to give it preferential treatment by charging the lower rental to cinemas which Soviet films usually enjoyed.[23] In the eyes of the Beijing and local Party authorities, this episode was further evidence of the inadequacies of Party leadership in literary and art work in Shanghai. The problem with this Soviet film contributed in a small way to the Yan'an–Shanghai cleavage, which lasted through the 1950s.

Building on the Yan'an and Northeast experience, the major achievement in the early 1950s was the film projection teams (*dianying fangying dui*). While in some cases city audiences may have actually decreased, the projection teams found new audiences in the armed forces, in large industrial enterprises (such as mines), and in the countryside. One hundred such teams, which usually numbered between two and four persons, were at work by the end of 1949. A year later short-term training courses had brought the total to 600, including 100 mobile teams (*liudong dui*), presumably for country audiences, 260 teams serving the armed forces, and the rest attached to government organs, associations, and large enterprises.[24] By 1955, 2,300 projection teams were operating, a total which in theory meant that the ideal of at least one team working in every county had been achieved.[25]

The teams played a significant part in increasing audiences for films and forging links between the foreign medium and Chinese society. Statistics on audience size, although often contradictory, demonstrate the general trend. The total film audience in 1949 numbered 47 million. In 1950, attendance had increased to 146 million. In 1953, a total of 752 million saw films. In 1954, 822 million tickets were distributed.[26]

The composition of these audiences is more difficult to gauge, but again the general trend was toward new types of filmgoers. The editors of *Popular Film* (*Dazhong dianying*), the largest circulation film magazine, estimated that in 1951 as much as one-third of the audience were workers, peasants, and soldiers, the groups in society that Mao and Party policy had singled out as the principal audiences of the new art and literature. By 1954, 70 percent of nonmilitary audiences were allegedly workers and peasants, although in this case, worker was probably defined rather broadly.[27] There were other indications that throughout the 1950s the most enthusiastic filmgoers were drawn from students and relatively well-educated city dwellers, groups that had formed the bulk of film audiences before 1949. Letter writers to *Popular Film*, and the readers of that magazine, were predominantly from these two groups.[28] It took some time for film to reach a mass audience. Some people needed persuasion to go to the movies, because they apparently assumed that the new socialist morality ruled out such essentially frivolous pastimes. Even students at the People's Liberation Army officer training school held this view.[29]

Forging links with new audiences was also not easy. Some audiences, perhaps encouraged by discounted tickets distributed by labor unions, were not used to the new medium and brought old habits to the experience. An exasperated letter writer to *People's Daily* complained of people disrupting film shows by leaping to their feet and enthusiastically crying out "Bravo," actions more appropriate to the opera theater.[30] At this time the appearance on screen of Mao Zedong reportedly had an effect on country viewers as moving as the screen arrival of trains at stations had had on terrified Western audiences of early Pathé films at the beginning of the century.

Nationalization of the Shanghai studios

The locomotive of the Maoist state bore down upon and eventually steamed over the private film studios, as nationalization of the film industry was completed by the mid-1950s. This process was inevitable, given the economic and political pressures on the private studios in Shanghai. Culture, and film as its potentially most effective component, were too important to be left for long in private hands.

Economic pressures were not caused by the new regime. The history of Chinese filmmaking until the 1950s is littered with companies which could not survive without government subsidy in competition with American and other films. After 1949 the nationalized studios and Soviet films competed with the older studios. The state and other institutions provided some economic assistance to the private companies: Kunlun, Wenhua, Datong, and Guotai received loans from the People's Bank of Shanghai and help with supplies of film stock. With this help, the private studios completed 13 films between October 1949 and July 1950.[31]

The energetic work of artists in the private studios helped compensate for the slow production of the nationalized studios, staffed by less experienced artists, technicians, and managers, who were self-consciously mapping out a new film style. But the pressure on the private studios increased with the start of the Korean War, the Three Anti (*san fan*) mass movement against "bourgeois habits" in 1952, and the campaign against bourgeois intellectual attitudes allegedly encouraged by the Kunlun studio film *The Life of Wu Xun* (*Wu Xun zhuan*).

The final moves toward complete nationalization of the film industry came after the campaign against *The Life of Wu Xun* had exposed Shanghai filmmakers to a strong blast of Yan'an-inspired Party condemnation. Participants in discussions on the film called publicly for the closing down or takeover of Kunlun because of its responsibility for the criticized film.[32] In January 1952 eight studios merged into the Shanghai United Film Studio (Shanghai lianhe dianying zhipianchang), which seems to have superseded an earlier state-sponsored combination of private studios. The writer-director Yu Ling, an old Shanghai film hand, who had been active in the initial takeover of film enterprises in the city, left his post as one of the leaders of the state-owned Shanghai Film Studio to become head of this new private combination.[33]

Yu Ling's move from the state studio to the private suggests both that the leadership of the former felt established and that the days of the private studios were numbered. Finally, at the start of China's first Five Year Plan, which envisioned the nationalization of most of the remaining private sector of the urban economy, the last of the private studios were incorporated into the state's Shanghai Film Studio.[34]

From February 1953 onward, all production of "the most important art" was in Party hands. A process which had taken over ten years to complete in the Soviet Union in China took a mere three.[35] This was perhaps further proof of the weakness of film in Chinese society and the vulnerability of the medium to outside pressures. By 1953 the cultural apparatus first constructed in Yan'an was in control of all film production, in Shanghai and elsewhere.

Reshaping the product

A similar transformation took place in the kinds of films Chinese audiences watched in the early 1950s. The cultural authorities called on filmmakers to repudiate the Shanghai heritage, which included the American films so popular with big-city audiences and so influential with film artists over the previous half century. In its stead, the Yan'an-derived view was made official. Three interrelated developments formed this process. First, the new regime gradually eliminated American and other Western movies from the market. Second, the Soviet Union and other socialist bloc countries provided films to fill the gap. Third, artists began to make a new kind of Chinese film, modeled on Soviet styles and inspired by Mao's Yan'an *Talks*.

The decline of Western films

At a time of official "People's Democracy," which allowed for a variety of views, the cultural authorities could not abolish outright the two-thirds to three-quarters of the film market which American films represented. As in the case of the nationalization of the studios, the nationalization of the film market was a gradual, though inevitable, process. Some semblance of initiative from below was maintained. In September 1949, for example, "all circles in Shanghai" urged the elimination of "poisonous" (*youdu*) American and British films.[36]

In 1950 the cultural authorities began to move. In April the Shanghai City People's Government, responding, it alleged, to rising levels of film appreciation on the part of audiences, promulgated temporary regulations on cinema screenings which reduced the number of days each month on which American and other Western films could be shown. Outright banning of films at this stage was rare. Of the 700 American films left in Shanghai after the Communist takeover, the censors deemed only 23 wholly reactionary and confiscated them. This did not mean that the rest were considered harmless; in the spring of 1950 a spate of antisocial activity by young hoodlums was blamed on the bad influence of certain Hollywood films.[37]

The Korean War, which began in June 1950, sealed the fate of these Western movies. In September Shanghai public opinion (*yulunjie*) was reportedly asking for American films to be banned immediately. Officials preferred more indirect methods, arguing that the American film market would disappear as the political consciousness of audiences rose, as the problems of film supply were solved, and as measures on behalf of socialist films, such as lowering ticket prices, took effect.[38] The social stigma associated with going to American movies as the Resist America–Aid Korea movement got underway in October was probably the most important factor in the marked slump in the Western film market. The statistics for Shanghai conflict.[39] Nevertheless, nationwide there was a definite decline, as attendance at Western films fell from an already low level of 32 percent of the national market in the first half of 1950.[40] The editors of *Popular Film* proudly argued that "progressive films" enjoyed over 90 percent of film attendance in 1951, close to a 25 percent increase over the previous year.[41]

But the substantial reduction and eventual elimination of Western and "nonprogressive" Chinese films were not without cost. In some instances the size of film audiences seems actually to have diminished. Some of the Shanghai statistics on the decline of Western films at the same time indicate a heavy decrease in overall audiences in the city. In the first half of November 1950, when in one source American movies accounted for a mere 10 percent of film admissions, total attendance was at about one-quarter of the level it had been when American films were important. While film was finding new audiences in factories and the countryside, in some cases it was apparently losing followers.[42]

The rise of Soviet films

Films from the Soviet Union and other socialist bloc countries were to fill the gaps, in both film supply and audience numbers, caused by the decline of Western and older Chinese films on the one hand and the growth of the national film audience on the other. Special groups, first at the Northeast Studio in Changchun and later in Shanghai at the state-owned studio, set about dubbing Soviet and Eastern European films into Chinese. The 1950 national film plan envisaged the dubbing of 40 Soviet features (26 Chinese films were to be produced). By early 1953 there were one hundred employees at each of the dubbing centers. In the four years to mid-1952, audiences for the more than 180 dubbed films (including shorts) totaled 300 million, a substantial proportion of the total audience.[43]

Transforming Russian films for Chinese viewers, however, was not easy, particularly because the viewers of this new type of foreign film were increasingly different from earlier foreign-film audiences. To appreciate, and even understand, the plot of a foreign movie, filmgoers required a degree of familiarity with foreign ways of life, geography, and so on. Viewers of Hollywood films in Shanghai before 1949 undoubtedly had acquired some knowledge of these things, and were attracted by the very exoticism of the foreign scenes presented in these movies. The new, often less educated, viewers do not seem to have appreciated the exoticism of many of the Russian films. Tianjin film critics, for example, pointedly spoke of local audiences "knowing" (*renshi*), rather than "liking" (*xihuan*) Soviet movies.[44] If this was true in a former treaty port like Tianjin, peasants in Shaanxi who had never seen a film before might have been even less attracted. In Shanghai, one reporter argued, nobody wanted to go to Soviet films, no matter how cheap the tickets.[45]

Notwithstanding reports like that of the broad masses of the Northeast (an "old liberated area," it should be noted) "loving" Soviet films,[46] the management of the film distribution network put much emphasis on explanatory efforts to assist viewers' understanding. One Shanghai audience was reportedly uncertain whether the Soviet film they had just seen had been set in Spain, Iran, or the United States.[47] The China Film Management Company, the national distributor, encouraged efforts to explain the dubbed films to filmgoers, many of whom attended in organized parties from their work units. As with other aspects of distribution, managers of local cinemas, particularly those in private ownership, did not always bother to distribute handouts or otherwise introduce the content and lessons of the unpopular, and therefore unprofitable, Soviet movies.[48] Newspapers performed an explanatory function, but problems remained with the popularity of Soviet and similar films. The minister of culture in his 1953 annual report spoke of dubbing such films "in proportion" to total film output, as if to acknowledge that a diet of too many Soviet films turned audiences away.[49]

In addition to filling empty screens and a lot of empty seats, Soviet films provided a model of socialist cinema for Chinese filmmakers. The Party leadership's perceived need for a new kind of feature film, and the general imitation of Soviet experience in most areas of national life, made the turn to Soviet cinema hardly surprising. Films themselves illustrated the Soviet model, publications disseminated translations of Soviet film theory and practice, and Russian filmmakers provided guidance in person. At the film school established in 1952 in Beijing, Russian directors gave lectures and also participated in joint productions with their Chinese counterparts.[50] A special section of the central Film Bureau handled Soviet experts, who assisted at the Northeast and Beijing studios. Such direct Soviet assistance was not extended to the state-owned Shanghai studio until later, and was always less influential than the Soviet presence in Changchun and Beijing.[51] In 1953 a Chinese study group of twenty film artists and technicians spent a year in Moscow examining the Soviet industry.[52]

There were two ironies about the turn to the Soviet film model: First and most obvious was the condition of the Soviet industry at the time. Under the onslaught of Cultural Commissar Zhdanov, Soviet filmmaking had reached its lowest ebb since at least the 1928 nationalization, if not the October Revolution. In 1948 Soviet filmmakers managed to produce a total of 17 feature films (down from 27 the year before). In 1952 the annual total reached a new low of five fiction films.[53] Realism, socialist or not, might have made others balk at turning to such an enterprise for guidance.

The second irony in the use of the Soviet model was its reinforcement of other changes which contributed to blocking the potential sinification of film. Those newly in charge of the film industry already undervalued indications of the emergence of a national Chinese style of film art in the late 1940s, in large part because these beginnings had taken place in Guomindang-controlled Shanghai and Guangzhou, and in Hong Kong. In elevating Soviet film art, the leadership deliberately presented an alternative to both the Hollywood model and the achievements of the 1940s. Here again, the Yan'an outlook took precedence over the Shanghai heritage.

New-style Chinese films

Artists at the Northeast studio self-consciously outlined the new subject matter and style of socialist China's film art in their first full-length feature. Released in the spring of 1949, *Bridge* (*Qiao*) was a paean to mass mobilization. In the civil war in the Northeast, a railway bridge over the Sungari River must be repaired within a month. The work force at the engineering works in which the film is set has two weeks to fabricate the necessary girders and bolts for the job. Although Guo, the chief engineer, is convinced the time will not be enough, all the progressive employees of the works quickly rally to the task. They even take part in the on-site repair of the bridge, where Guo eventually joins them. They greet the completion of the task with cries of "Long live Chairman Mao!" It was not the last time that a film would end this way.

The striking characteristic of *Bridge* is its plainness. Apart from the simplicity imposed by conditions at the studio in its temporary quarters on the Russian border, the film is very plain in terms of plot and characterization. The story is explained often throughout the film, using such devices as a telephone call or a radio broadcast to reiterate the problem and the story so far. Some critics complained about the broadness of the portrayal of most of the characters. The process of conversion of engineer Guo, for example, is not made clear.[54] Mao's Yan'an *Talks* provided sanction for some of this crudeness. Nevertheless, elements which might appeal to more sophisticated film audiences were included. The film begins with a fast-paced montage of battle scenes, both to establish background and to draw viewers into the less exciting action that follows. Lü Ban, the popular comic actor of the 1930s, played one of the workers' leaders, and Shanghai audiences would have recognized other familiar faces.

Just as the technical skills of engineer Guo in the *Bridge* are combined with the enthusiasm of the workers, so the making of this first new-style feature film was an amalgam of the new ideas on the political function of art and the film experience of artists like Lü Ban and Chen Bo'er, a former actress who was the chief scenarist. Yuan Muzhi, the head of the Northeast Studio, reiterated this theme in July 1949 in his report to the National Congress of Writers and Artists. In a curious echo of the essence–technique (*ti–yong*) dichotomy, much used by modernizing Chinese over the previous hundred years to distinguish between fundamental Chinese ideas and Western techniques, Yuan spoke of combining the ideological strength of the "old liberated" area's film ranks with the artistic and technical achievements of filmmakers from the Guomindang-controlled regions to produce China's new film style.[55]

The subject matter of the feature films from the nationalized studios in the first few years of the new decade certainly satisfied Mao's emphasis on workers, peasants, and soldiers. Most stories were set in the recent past, during the anti-Japanese and civil wars. The Northeast Studio's second feature, *Returning to Our Own Ranks* (*Huidao ziji duiwu lai*), set in enemy-occupied territory in 1947, told a tale of army–civilian relations. It was not well received. Apparently the director had felt bound by Chen Bo'er and his own script. He was quoted as arguing: "I'm not worried about the success or failure of this movie. All I'm frightened of is making a [political] mistake."[56] The fourth Northeast feature, *Daughters of China* (*Zhonghua de nüer*), presented the sacrifice of eight women fighting the Japanese in the Northeast in 1936. A reviewer warned that art should not be compromised when creating heroic characters. The same reviewer, Zhong Dianfei, complained that *Zhao Yiman*, released in 1950, took as its subject women guerrillas in the Northeast. With so few state-produced films, two on the same subject seemed to Zhong a waste.[57]

Not all the state studio's films focused on military exploits. Like *Bridge, Boundless Light* (*Guangming wanzhang*) had a factory setting. Chen Bo'er also wrote this script, after "going down" to live at the Harbin Electric Power Company works in the Northeast for a period. The production team for *White-Coated Fighter* (*Baiyi zhanshi*) had similarly spent time in a hospital.[58]

This fieldwork was in the spirit of Mao's Yan'an *Talks*, which held that artists in this way could lessen their distance from their mass audiences. One problem with producing films on worker/peasant/soldier subjects was that worker/peasant/soldier audiences could be particularly critical of what they saw. Familiarity in any audience anywhere breeds contempt, and some viewers were much more knowledgeable about the subjects of many of the new films than most of the people who made them. This may help explain the more enthusiastic reception given *Spring Rays in Inner Mongolia* (*Neimeng chunguang*), set in a remote area among exotic peoples. Unlike other, rather documentary-style films from the state studios, one reviewer remarked, this film developed its characters and had interesting content.[59] Chinese audiences over the next three decades continued to appreciate films about national minorities, in part because they allowed the exploration of themes, such as love, that were less common in other movies.

Filmmakers who had formerly worked in the private studios often dealt with these new subjects with an assurance and artistic success difficult to find in the work of less experienced personnel. *Shangrao Concentration Camp* (*Shangrao jizhongying*), made at Shanghai under the direction of Sha Meng and Zhang Ke, is a powerful meditation on human relations under pressure. Unusually long, slow takes with a mobile camera in the prison add to the elegiac quality of the work. The artistic expertise of the writers, technicians, and actors shows clearly, in contrast to the not infrequent crudeness of aspects of most products from the three state studios. The depth of talent reflected in *Shangrao Concentration Camp* was not generally available in these studios, particularly in Beijing and the Northeast. Nor were the factory or military settings of their films as familiar as a prison to the Shanghai artists. *Shangrao Concentration*

Camp broke box-office records when it was released in 1951 in Shanghai: 424,000 tickets were sold in seventeen days.[60]

Scripts and guidance

A shortage of suitable scripts caused the gap to widen between the high expectations placed by the Party on the new film industry and the disappointing products that reached China's audiences. Some scenarists continued to write scripts after the 1951 campaign against *The Life of Wu Xun*, but the censors under the Ministry of Culture's Film Bureau more rigorously scrutinized the draft scripts, in large part in response to the Wu Xun warning. From late 1951, film production almost ground to a halt in a slowdown that lasted until early 1954.[61]

Part of the problem was not so much censorship itself as the lack of clarity in both the censorship criteria and the leadership of the film system. In 1951 twelve new works were rejected after they had been filmed. The editors of the *Literary Gazette* in early 1953 complained that "so many leaders and so much examination along the way" severely inhibited production of scripts.[62] Participants at two large-scale national meetings in Beijing in the spring of that year addressed these difficulties. One general problem they singled out for harsh criticism was the tendency of those in charge of scriptwriting, in the Film Bureau's own scriptwriting section (Dianying juben chuangzuo suo), for example, to draw up unrealistic quotas for scripts on particular subjects and then expect creative writers to be able to produce these predetermined screenplays on time. The principles of industrial management could not be applied to this part of the film industry.[63] The minister of culture in his 1953 annual report spoke of the need to avoid making what he called "inappropriate demands" on filmmaking. He considered twelve to fifteen feature films per year, rather than the earlier plan for twenty to twenty-five, more appropriate.[64]

These more sober production targets reflected poor performance. The staff at the Northeast studio had not made a single film in 1952–3 for lack of scripts. From mid-1951 through the end of 1952, the state-owned Shanghai studio completed only two feature films.[65] The State Council in its late 1953 resolutions on "strengthening film work" called on the Chinese Writers Association (Zhongguo zuojia xiehui) to organize its members, especially younger writers, to study scriptwriting.[66] That the State Council, the highest organ of the government, should be discussing film work indicates both the importance attached to film as a tool for national purposes and the nadir to which the industry had sunk.

If a writer could oblige with a script according to the assigned subject matter and other requirements, the work was often marred by formalism (*gongshi hua*) or stereotyping (*gainian hua*), or attained these unwelcome qualities in working its way through the process from screenplay inspection to completed film. Several directors at a 1953 national meeting on feature-film making complained of the tendency, given the Party cultural authorities' emphasis on literature and art reflecting contemporary life, to concentrate on events and plot at the expense of characterization and the development of a theme.[67] Two years later, at a similar meeting, after the industry had managed to produce, by one count, fourteen films in 1954, the same complaints were raised. The formalism and stereotypes in scripts were compounded, speakers argued, by directors and actors having only a general grasp of the subjects and themes of the new films. Moreover, "for a long time there has been a tendency among film workers to ignore artistry and undervalue artistic techniques. Nobody addresses artistic problems. Some even say, 'As long as I can make a living, it's O.K.' "[68]

The problems filmmakers encountered in effecting the artistic policies enunciated in Mao's Yan'an *Talks* were epitomized in one typical movie, the 1952 screen adaptation of Lao She's *Dragon's Beard Ditch* (*Longxu gou*), made at the Beijing Film Studio. The two-part story contrasts the miserable life of the residents of a Beijing slum area with the changes in the district after 1949. As critics pointed out when the film was released, each of the two parts of *Dragon's Beard Ditch* leaves a very different impression on audiences.[69] For all its deprivation and suffering, the first half of the film has a lifelike quality not dissimilar to that of the leftist films of the late 1940s. The makers of the new film clearly drew upon their artistic experience in the postwar Shanghai movies. Depiction of the Yan'an legacy of reform and hope in the second half of *Dragon's Beard Ditch* flattens the depth of the portrait. The new government cadres who take the place of the bad characters who dominated the district before 1949 are a rather dull and predictable lot. How to portray life after 1949, Party cadres and their actions, and conflict in the new age were problems that continued to trouble filmmakers throughout the subsequent three decades.

The Life of Wu Xun

The history of the production and criticism of the best known of modern Chinese films, *The Life of Wu Xun*, offers a case study in the problems of the transition from Shanghai to Yan'an. The film itself contributed to the difficulties the whole film industry encountered in the early 1950s. A project dear to the hearts of a number of prominent figures in the Shanghai film world, *The Life of Wu Xun* had its origins during the War of Resistance to Japan. As political circumstances changed at the end of 1940s the film became a liability, but by this time Kunlun and its artists found it difficult to abandon their investment of effort and money in the movie. Soon after the film's release the criticism began, given impetus in

May 1951 by an anonymous critique from the pen of Mao Zedong (his only lengthy film review). The campaign prompted by *The Life of Wu Xun* targeted "bourgeois" attitudes that were alleged to characterize its makers and others in film circles, particularly in Shanghai. Film production grinding to a halt for several years after 1951 was one result of the Wu Xun episode, the first major campaign of criticism in literature and art after 1949. Another result was the triumph of the Yan'an over the Shanghai heritage.

The making of the film

A historical figure, Wu Xun (1839–96) by the mid twentieth century was something of a folk hero, at least for many reformist intellectuals. Starting life as a poor peasant, Wu Xun hit on the idea of providing education to the poor. He spent many years as a beggar, carefully accumulating enough capital to buy land, become a moneylender, and establish a charity school in his native district in Shandong Province. Wu Xun's efforts at mass education struck a responsive chord for Republican China's social reformers, such as Liang Shuming, Yan Yangchu, and Tao Xingzhi. A revival of interest in his life is indicated by a number of publications from the 1940s. A collection of biographical essays was published in 1948, with a prefatory essay by the late reformist philosopher Liang Qichao, as part of a series of books commemorating Wu. The Shanghai Wu Xun School Foundation assisted publication. On the eve of the War of Resistance to Japan, a more popular pictorial biography of Wu Xun had been published in Chongqing and reprinted there three years later. Another biography, by Fudan University professor Zhang Mosheng, went through two printings, one in 1946, the second as late as October 1949.[70]

Given this level of interest in Wu Xun, it is not surprising that telling his story on screen attracted reformist and even leftist filmmakers. This would bring to wider public attention the exemplary tale of an early effort to educate the poor. Writer-director Wang Weiyi in Chongqing saw the possibilities for a film and showed the newly published pictorial biography to Zhao Dan, a fellow Shanghai film artist. Actor Zhao was convinced that the person who played such a part would become a world-class star. Wang Weiyi began a script, but soon put it aside under pressure from other work.[71] Later the second printing of this same pictorial biography inspired Sun Yu, the forty-four-year-old director of the 1934 *The Highway*, to start an outline for a film biography in the autumn of 1944 in Chongqing. After three years spent on other projects, Sun took up the story again, adding to the source material the biography by Zhang Mosheng.

In the summer of 1948 the Guomindang-controlled China Film Studio, where Sun worked, began filming the script, but because of economic problems gave up the work in November. The leftist Kunlun studio, also in Shanghai, in January 1949 bought the film rights and about one-third of the film in unedited rushes from the faltering studio. Sun Yu appears to have transferred to Kunlun along with his project. The rushes could not be used, as Kunlun made changes in casting and the script.

Soon the context in which the film was being made also changed. After the Communist takeover of Shanghai in the spring of 1949 and the National Congress of Writers and Artists in Beijing in July, which Sun Yu attended, the writer-director had second thoughts. Sun began to feel that "the tenacity of [Wu Xun's] style of struggle" was not positive enough in the new political circumstances.[72] His doubts about the suitability of the script and subject caused Sun to set the project aside for a period.

In November 1949 Kunlun had to continue production because it needed revenue and was in financial difficulty.[73] Sun Yu reworked the script with the help of a committee of Kunlun's writer-directors. Commemoration in December 1949 in the *Guangming Daily*, a non-Party newspaper favored by intellectuals, of the one hundred and tenth anniversary of Wu Xun's birth, probably encouraged the filmmakers to continue the project.[74]

Sun Yu considered the revised script "a critical biography" which now emphasized the limits of Wu Xun's reformism and his failure to liberate the poor. Sun added a character, a present-day teacher, who recalls Wu Xun's life to her young students at the beginning and end of the film. She points out to the children and audience at the end that such educational reformism could not save the poor, a task possible only through revolution. Zhou Da, a former soldier from the ranks of the huge mid-nineteenth-century antidynastic Taiping Rebellion, in the revised script was more critical of his friend Wu, calling him a landlords' lackey. Sun Yu in effect rewrote Wu Xun's story to become a tragedy—a change, Sun later explained, which he felt was "appropriate to 'the needs of the time'."[75]

In the new political times, doubts remained about the appropriateness of a film, however critical, on a Qing landlord and educator. A half dozen representatives of the Shanghai military authorities' Literature and Art Office (a civilian Cultural Bureau had not yet been established) and several notable Shanghai writers voiced such concerns at an informal discussion in January 1950. Xia Yan, the senior person present, argued that Wu Xun was not a good enough exemplar for the times. Yu Ling, in charge of film administration in the city, agreed and suggested that they make a film of the life of a model teacher from the "old liberated" areas in wartime China. Such a film would, of course, have been in the mainstream of products from the state-owned studios and more in keeping with Yan'an cultural concerns. Despite these suggestions, most of the discussants, Sun Yu reported after the release of the film, concluded that the revised *Life of Wu Xun* was worth finishing. Their argument was that, while modern audiences should recognize the historical limitations preventing Wu Xun from liberating the Shandong peasantry, the hero's selfless concern for the cultural and educational reconstruction of the masses made an appropriate historical parallel with the efforts at popular education by the new regime.[76]

The Wu Xun project continued, spurred on by Kunlun's deepening economic crisis and Sun Yu's determination to finish what he had begun in 1944. After location work in Wu Xun's native district in Shandong, it was clear that faulty planning with the revised script had produced a surfeit of material on celluloid. In early August 1950, with over 80 percent of the film completed, the Kunlun management decided to make use of the excess material by turning the film into a two-part epic. As a result, the contrast between Zhou Da and Wu Xun was made more important than originally intended, and rather a lot of time was devoted to the Qing court of the empress dowager Cixi and the statesman Li Hongzhang, who publicly honored Wu Xun's charitable work. These last-named characters appeared in scenes which, by their elaborate settings and costumes, were expensive to film and to discard. The film was released at the end of 1950; it starred Zhao Dan, who ten years earlier in Chongqing had been so taken by the idea of playing Wu Xun.

Having spent two years and rather more than was usual for a single feature on the film, the Kunlun studio made an extra effort in distributing *The Life of Wu Xun*. The response was encouraging. The Shanghai-based major film periodical *Popular Film* listed *The Life of Wu Xun* as one of the ten best films of 1950, although the editors took the precaution of putting it at the bottom of the list.[77] With so few films released in that year, being counted in the ten best may not have been a high distinction, but Kunlun seemed to have produced a more than modest success. The script was published in book form, and the Chongqing pictorial biography was reissued in early 1951.[78]

Wu Xun, Yan'an, and Shanghai

The checkered career of *The Life of Wu Xun* had not finished; it had merely entered a new and more critical phase. The questioning of the film began with an article by Jia Ji, a high-level cadre in the Party's propaganda apparatus, titled "Wu Xun is not *xun* [exemplary] enough." It appeared in the April 1951 issue of the *Literary Gazette*, the journal of the All-China Federation of Literary and Art Circles and chief organ of Party cultural policy. Jia Ji's article reiterated the criticisms about the dubious class background of Wu Xun and his relations with the Qing ruling class, which some Shanghai artists and cultural workers had anticipated at a meeting on the uncompleted film over a year earlier. The editors prefaced this article with a quotation critical of Wu Xun from the late Lu Xun, China's preeminent twentieth-century writer, canonized by Party literary cadres, as if to emphasize the official disapproval of Sun Yu's film.[79] Favorable reviews of the film stopped appearing in the press, and *People's Daily* reprinted the first and subsequent *Literary Gazette* articles to bring them to a wider readership.[80]

The impetus for a full-scale campaign against the film came on May 20, when *People's Daily* carried an editorial called "We should pay attention to discussion of the film *The Life of Wu Xun*." Although anonymous, it was widely known at the time that the editorial was the work of Mao Zedong himself.[81] This editorial and the subsequent campaign were not confined to the film itself. To the critics, the film represented a consensus among intellectuals that Wu Xun was an exemplary historical figure worthy of praise, if not emulation. From this point the criticism went beyond the film to incorporate a rectification campaign in the style of similar wartime efforts in Yan'an among writers, educators, and other intellectuals. Wu Xun's true colors, as negator of the importance of historical succession and class struggle, as a lightning rod of ideological confusion, made him "appropriate to 'the needs of the time' " in a sense that Sun Yu had not recognized when he had used this phrase about his 1949 script rewrite.

While the emphasis in the campaign sparked by *The Life of Wu Xun* was on broader questions of intellectuals' political views, the discussions on the film exemplified the Yan'an-derived standards for new Chinese films. Discussants made implicit contrast between the new style and the film modes of pre-1949 Shanghai, perpetuated in *The Life of Wu Xun*. Simplicity and directness were the characteristics most "appropriate to 'the needs of the times' " and suited Mao's Yan'an *Talks*' emphasis on popularization. The minutes of a discussion on *The Life of Wu Xun* by writers and artists in Guangzhou reflect this concern.[82] The writer-director Wang Weiyi, who years earlier in Chongqing had himself contemplated writing a script based on Wu Xun's life, complained about the lack of clarity in the film. In setting up his school, for example, Wu is helped by both good and evil persons. The ex-Taiping soldier Zhou Da would give audiences the impression, Wang argued, that revolution meant nothing more than killing people. Another participant thought that confusion would arise from presentation of Wu Xun and Zhou Da as both partly right.

Particularly insidious for Wang Weiyi was the use of good film techniques to convey bad content, thereby even more effectively misleading viewers. Here Wang and the other discussants reflected a reading of Mao's *Talks*, where he warned that "the more artistic [a reactionary work] is, the more harm it can do to people and the more it should be rejected."[83] In its crudest interpretation, Mao's *Talks* argued that art by the masses eschewed the effete complexity of bourgeois art. It followed that art for the masses (particularly for workers, peasants, and soldiers) should be simple and direct to ensure the widest possible comprehension. As the artistic medium inherently most able to reach the broadest audience, film, in this view, should not promote the ambiguities detected in Kunlun's *The Life of Wu Xun*.

A second feature of the campaign against *The Life of Wu Xun* was its emphasis on the film as the work of artists who represented the Shanghai legacy of leftist filmmaking in the 1930s and 1940s. The critics, many of whom were themselves products of the Shanghai literary scene, now demanded a reform of that legacy. At the Guangzhou meeting in late May 1951, the novelist Ouyang Shan, who in the 1930s had been associated with the League of Left-Wing Writers, argued that the release of the film suggested that writers and artists had not sufficiently reformed themselves over the previous two years, a problem complicated by "the heritage of so-called progressive bourgeois artistic activity."[84]

Xia Yan, playwright and nominal director of the Shanghai Culture Bureau (a position he held from January 1950 until 1953, when the last of the private film studios was nationalized) epitomized the progressive tradition. In the 1930s he had led the Film Group of the League of Left-Wing Writers in Shanghai. Xia's self-criticism on the Wu Xun affair, which he made in August 1951, showed that the problems of adjustment to the new cultural policies, to what could be called the Yan'an heritage, were persistent in Shanghai. When participating in the early 1950 discussion on the Wu Xun script, Xia now argued, he had not used a proper Marxist viewpoint to analyze Wu Xun's historical significance. In late 1951 Xia perceived that there was still a gap between the art workers of Shanghai and their worker/peasant/soldier audiences. Drawing a parallel with the joint Communist–Guomindang united front during the War of Resistance to Japan, when this worker/peasant/soldier Yan'an line was first promulgated, Xia emphasized that "the cultural and literary-artistic battleground in China today is still a united front." Much remained to be done in cultural leadership to realize the full potential of film, Xia wrote, citing quotations from Stalin on film as a propaganda weapon and from the 1928 Soviet film congress which completed the full nationalization of the Soviet film industry.[85]

The criticism of Shanghai artistic circles was put more bluntly by Zhang Yu, himself a member of the Shanghai branch of the Writers Association, in a critique of Xia Yan's self-criticism. *The Life of Wu Xun* was made in Shanghai, Zhang observed, was first shown in Shanghai, was praised first by Shanghai critics, and as Xia himself had noted in his confession, Shanghai's criticism of the film, three months after Mao's anonymous *People's Daily* editorial, was far from thoroughgoing. In publishing Zhang Yu's attack in December 1951, the *Literary Gazette* editors noted that Shanghai writers and artists had still not followed the example of their Beijing colleagues and launched a rectification and study movement.[86] Meanwhile the editors of the Shanghai-based *Popular Film* had admitted a lack of responsibility in praising *The Life of Wu Xun*. The magazine, at the time the film periodical in widest circulation, suspended publication. When it resumed operation in May 1952, it had moved its offices to Beijing.[87]

In the second half of 1951 the criticism of Shanghai literary circles and the concomitant emphasis on the Yan'an-derived cultural policies broadened to include other targets. Critics turned some of their attention to two other films made by private Shanghai studios. The Wenhua studio's *Platoon Commander Guan* (*Guan lianzhang*), despite a soldier-hero subject which bore a superficial resemblance to the films of the nationalized studios, allegedly presented Guan as a rather coarse young man, lacking in culture. His giving his life to save several hundred children apparently could not outweigh this impression of roughness. Here the Shanghai heritage of critical realism met the Yan'an expectation (itself with much older Chinese origins) of exemplary heroes, now called "socialist realism."[88] *A Married Couple* (*Women fufu zhi jian*), based on a best-selling Shanghai novel, told a comic story of the tribulations of a Party cadre who returns to the city with a countrified wife. In a sense this Kunlun production was a parable of the Communist Party's own return to an urban context after years in Yan'an. The film, directed by Zheng Junli in the spirit of the late 1940s social comedies, was said to cater to the vulgar, petit-bourgeois tastes of unreformed Shanghai audiences.[89]

As the campaign begun by *The Life of Wu Xun* proceeded, there were other indications of Shanghai's unfavored position. Twelve Chinese filmmakers were presented with Stalin Prizes for their work on two Sino–Soviet coproduced documentaries that had been completed somewhat earlier, soon after the establishment of the People's Republic. The presentation of the prizes was an indirect comment on the Wu Xun affair, for most of the winners had backgrounds in Yan'an, in film enterprises in the "old liberated" areas, or in the state-owned studios in the Northeast and Beijing.[90] In July 1951 an investigation team made up of representatives of the Ministry of Culture's Film Bureau, the Film Guidance Committee (including Jiang Qing), and *People's Daily*, reported on their fieldwork on Wu Xun's life, which they had conducted in his native Shandong district.[91] Zhou Yang, the senior Party spokesperson on cultural matters, shortly thereafter presented the authoritative view of Wu Xun, which stressed the historical limitations of his reformism.[92] The next May, in commemoration of the tenth anniversary of Mao's Yan'an *Talks*, which Zhou Yang was vigorously promulgating, Xia Yan wrote what amounted to a second self-criticism. Given the anniversary, his timing was better than his August 1951 confession. The cultural leadership in Shanghai, Xia conceded, had lacked discipline, particularly in relation to private cultural enterprises. Now, three years after 1949, there was still an audience for petit-bourgeois (*xiao shimin*) art, while commercialism and petit-bourgeois attitudes characterized people in literary and art circles.[93] In short, the reformist outlook, which had made Wu Xun a sympathetic historical figure for many intellectuals, had not changed much in the minds of film artists, local cultural leaders, and some viewers, even if historical circumstances during the previous three years had been revolutionized.

Artists and cadres

The Wu Xun campaign did not represent simply a problem of relations between the new cultural regime and Shanghai artists. The fate of Kunlun's attempted blockbuster was symptomatic of a broader problem, that of relations between the Communist Party and the artists it sought to use in its cultural effort. Putting these relations on a proper footing required adjustment on all sides: The Party's cultural leaders found that in the new circumstances, management styles developed in the relatively small world of Yan'an needed modification. For their part, filmmakers, and artists in general, were far from united. Accordingly, the adjustment to the Party's expectations was at best uneven.

These problems of relations between artist and cadre did not suddenly appear in Shanghai: They had not been absent in Yan'an, and the staff of the first Party-controlled studio in the Northeast had confronted these issues. In a March 1950 report on the Northeast studio, Chen Bo'er, its artistic director and Party secretary, and a former actress, had outlined these early difficulties. The expectations and requirements of Party central were clear, Chen acknowledged, unlike the means of actually putting these policies into effect at the studio. Artists took second place, as they had done in the Yan'an Film Team—being excluded, for example, from important political meetings. Writers and actors heard of major policy changes sometimes three or four months after administrative cadres had been informed. The latter's frequent lack of agreement at the studio level on censorship matters confused scriptwriters, directors, and others who found their work rejected, often after they had expended considerable time and money on a project. The not unexpected response of artists to this confusion was a self-imposed caution. Writers and directors, fearing mistakes, put great emphasis on the content of their films at the expense of form. Making films that were full of politics and had considerable educational significance seemed to be a way of avoiding mistakes. If this was the case before the Wu Xun campaign, is was even more true for several years after 1951.

Another difficulty at the Northeast studio to which Chen Bo'er alluded were divisions and disagreements among artists themselves. If a scriptwriter and director, for example, could not cooperate and share their views on the project at hand, few films would prove successful. Differing levels of caution and confusion among artists undoubtedly exacerbated the divisions within their ranks.[94]

Chen Bo'er's report on the Northeast experience was to serve as a guide, not to say warning, to the rest of the film industry, which encountered similar problems of adjustment to the worker/peasant/soldier ideal. For the rest of the industry too, the adjustment was difficult on both sides, for artists and for cadres. At the Guangzhou discussion on *The Life of Wu Xun* referred to above, the novelist Ouyang Shan argued that the shortcomings of the film were symptomatic of a lack of agreement (in China and elsewhere, he noted in an indirect reference to the Soviet Union) among the cultural leadership on the question of art serving politics.[95] Xia Yan, the former artist who was now an official, ascribed some of his problems in Shanghai as being the result of cadres like himself spending too much time talking and rushing about in "a tangle of routinism," and not enough time thinking. He concluded in August 1951: "We have not clearly decided on the new tasks for today's literary and art work."[96]

The problems of adjustment for artists were examined by Jia Ji, the Propaganda Department cadre and sometime scriptwriter, who had initiated the public criticism of *The Life of Wu Xun*. With their greater experience, Shanghai film artists felt superior to their colleagues from the "old liberated" areas. The Shanghai artists' alleged desire to "serve" the four classes (which included patriotic bourgeois elements) of the current New Democratic period of government amounted, in Jia Ji's view, to an attack on the principle of art primarily serving workers, peasants, and soldiers. Jia claimed that some filmmakers even argued that, with the progress of dialectical materialism, the ten-year-old Yan'an *Talks* were now out of date.[97] Members of the Guangzhou People's Theater Troupe were not alone in feeling that Soviet film art did not measure up to American standards.[98] Whatever the rationale, adding a little "politics" onto films that continued to cater to petit-bourgeois tastes, Jia Ji observed, was an inadequate solution.[99]

Divisions within the creative ranks served as warning against a simplistic differentiation of Party versus artists and complicated the process of adjustment in cultural circles. With 1,700 employees at the Shanghai studios, about 1,000 in the Northeast, and perhaps a similar number in Beijing, divisions were not unexpected.[100] Three major types of cleavage among film artists can be discerned: geographical, generational, and those based on degree of involvement in recent productions.

The geographical distinction between filmmakers who had spent the War of Resistance to Japan and the civil war years in the "old liberated" areas (Yan'an and the Northeast) and the rest was one largely imposed on artists from outside in the Party's differentiated treatment of the two kinds of artists. It remained an important factor into the 1950s. Management cadres tended to feel more comfortable with artists with whom they shared a Yan'an background. Likewise such artists, although a small proportion of the filmmaking ranks, were most familiar with Party expectations and ways of working within them.[101] The singular failure of the film representatives at the First National Congress of Writers and Artists in the summer of 1949 in Beijing to appoint executive officers for the newly established Film Workers Association indicated the importance of this division in the ranks. At the Second Congress in October 1953, no report on filmmaking appears to have been made.[102]

The generational cleavage in filmmaking ranks was also closely bound with the Yan'an–Shanghai distinction. Most filmmakers were relatively young: Even at the 1949 Congress, the median age of all delegates (in film, the fine arts, literature, and so on) was between thirty-one and thirty-five years old.[103] Older artists were therefore those who had helped create the Shanghai leftist film heritage. They were expected to undertake ideological remolding, but they also had skills essential to the growth of the industry. The youngsters were assigned to assist in the remolding of their seniors, a process likened to escorting criminals by Wang Rong, a young member of the Shanghai Film Bureau's scriptwriting section who was later accused (in 1955) of supporting the discredited writer Hu Feng.[104] For Wang Rong, this prejudice against older artists was further evidence of cadres' "sectarianism," a charge more common during the Hundred Flowers period a year later. On the other hand, older directors tended to prefer to work with their peers, causing frustrations among young artists anxious to learn their craft.

The latter complaint was related to the third major cleavage among film artists, between those who were actually involved in production of the limited number of films made in the six years after 1949 and those, often younger and inexperienced, who were not. The establishment of Film Actors Troupes for stage performances by underemployed actors at all three studios in 1953 was a symptom of this problem at a time when film production had almost ground to a halt.[105] During the post–Wu Xun Shanghai film workers' rectification–study campaign, some artists, who felt they had usable skills, were reportedly frustrated by the lack of public recognition. Given the low level of film activity in mid-1952, they detected little opportunity to earn the recognition they jealously saw other, often older, colleagues enjoying.[106] Even as film production regained momentum and surpassed its former levels in the course of the 1950s, the underemployment of filmmakers, particularly actors, remained a source of division.

The transition to socialism in Chinese filmmaking, nominally completed in the six years to the mid-1950s, was a dual process. On the one hand, the transition was from Yan'an to Shanghai as the Party leadership, and the cultural cadre which it had formed in Yan'an, took over the three major centers of film production. In applying the managerial and artistic standards that had been broadly defined during the War of Resistance to Japan, the transition was less obviously a movement from Shanghai to Yan'an. The Party's cultural purposes superseded, and largely dismissed, the heritage of filmmaking epitomized by the Shanghai achievement of the late 1940s. Although by 1955 film's transition seemed complete, events would show that the tensions between the Yan'an and Shanghai inheritances were not easily overcome.

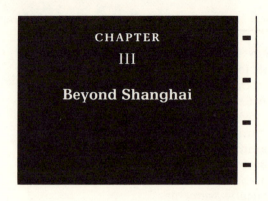

CHAPTER

III

Beyond Shanghai

Yan'an had triumphed over Shanghai by the late 1950s. Building on the basis of the first half of the decade, the promulgators of the Yan'an cultural outlook in the nine years after 1956 consolidated their preeminence over the emerging mass, national culture in which film was a major component. Shanghai, however, was not vanquished. Events during these years modified the Yan'an culture in ways that represented concessions to the Shanghai heritage. Secure in the superiority of the Yan'an view, the cultural authorities increasingly acknowledged both the May Fourth literary tradition and the more ancient popular cultural traditions.

These modifications of Yan'an dogma came in two stages: first in the Hundred Flowers discourse on national problems during the relative political relaxation of 1956–7, and later, after a Yan'an-style rectification campaign against "rightists" and the subsequent abortive mass mobilization of the Great Leap Forward, for a brief period in the early 1960s. In effect, by this latter period a tentative balance had been achieved between the views of culture molded in Yan'an and Shanghai.

Two themes pervaded these nine years: the developing tripartite relationship among Party, artists, and audience, and moves toward the sinification of film.

Cadre and artist achieved an unstable balance between the political concerns of the cultural authorities and the concerns of filmmakers. Even the more interventionist wing in the Party could see the unproductive results of heightened intervention in the aftermath of the Anti-Rightist campaign and the Great Leap Forward. This encouraged in the early 1960s a pulling back from intervention in culture as well as in other areas of Chinese life. Second, artists showed a greater willingness to work together within the new cultural boundaries and an ability to stretch them. With an increased tempo of production and more experienced younger artists, the divisions among filmmakers revealed during the Hundred Flowers seem to have become less obtrusive. The more flexible cultural policies allowed considerable range, which some filmmakers were bold enough to explore.

Last, the films of the early 1960s evinced increased awareness by both groups of the tastes and expectations of a third group, the film audiences, and a greater willingness to cater to these tastes. The new cultural slogan of combining "revolutionary realism and revolutionary romanticism" indicated more awareness of audiences. Filmmakers' efforts at more varied subject matters and styles were another indication.

These nine years saw moves toward a sinification of film. If Shanghai, the heartland of Chinese filmmaking until the mid-1950s, represented the most cosmopolitan center in China, then the establishment of film studios in inland cities and the extension of audiences to include a greater proportion of country folk suggested that film was putting down stronger and deeper roots in Chinese society. The abandonment of foreign-derived "socialist realism" in favor of greater ambiguity also enabled film artists to make more use of content and styles drawn from China's literary and artistic heritage. In consequence, the importance of Shanghai and what it represented in Chinese filmmaking declined, and the film industry took on a more national character.

Mass culture and the expansion of the film industry

Film was a major part and indeed shaper of a new, mass national culture that emerged by the early 1960s. This culture was the work of a range of actors, not simply the product of the cultural demands of national authorities. To say otherwise would presume an omnicompetence to which even the most ambitious Party leaders could not aspire. Nor did the new culture represent a break with the mass culture that had grown up since the late nineteenth century.[1] In reality, the mass culture can be better understood as popular culture overlaid by elite concerns. Party authorities, modern May Fourth intellectuals, and film artists, among others, sought both before and after 1949 to modify, incorporate, and nationalize popular culture. Two characteristics of the twentieth-century mass culture are noteworthy: its homogenized, nationwide character, and its supraclass relevance. The mass culture deemphasized regional and class variation. Although art, literature, and the media after 1949 extolled what were called proletarian class values, the new culture gathered all into its somewhat stifling and cool embrace.

Film, as a medium and an art, was an ideal means for the elite to disseminate the mass culture. As a medium, it has a more immediate appeal than the printed page or radio. As an art, it is less open to local abuse by distributors than stage art is by local drama and opera troupes, painting exhibitions by local art societies, or radio by local station managers.[2] One film from a studio in Beijing or Changchun in several hundred copies can be seen in the same version by herders in the far northwest in Xinjiang, peasants in Sichuan, students and clerks in Shanghai, and fisherfolk in Hainan in the south. A local distribution manager may choose to show a film in a short run, in out-of-the-way cinemas, or to restrict ticket distribution, but tampering with the image on the screen is a difficult technical feat. Nationally distributed newspapers can reach the same audience in an undifferentiated version, but exhortations, both aural and visual, from a film are usually more appealing. Moreover, a reader can put aside a newspaper. It is less easy to leave a picture theater.

As a major component of the mass national culture, film spoke in a nationwide language, and, increasingly after 1956, in a superficially national style. Characters in almost all films spoke *putonghua* (ordinary speech; i.e., Mandarin), be they Tibetan serfs, Mongolian soldiers, or Guangdong peasants. Film was a powerful medium for language standardization, so producers made only rare concessions to the huge language subgroups, such as the Cantonese spoken in Guangdong. Occasionally they dubbed feature films into Cantonese for showing in the south, or into Mongolian or Uighur for northern screenings. Almost all features, however, were filmed in "standard" Chinese. Moreover, the accents of film characters tended to be standardized into a watered-down version of the Beijing accent. Producers made little recognition of regional or class accents in *putonghua*, forgoing an opportunity to enrich the texture of the spoken dialogue.[3]

In the nine years after 1956, cadres and artists also made moves toward a national Chinese film style. Party leaders promulgated changes in cultural policy which reflected their increasing disillusionment with the efficacy of foreign (Soviet) models for Chinese practice. Socialist realism, which had been derived from the Soviet Union, gave way to "revolutionary realism and revolutionary romanticism." Responding to this policy transformation, filmmakers, along with other artists and writers, sought inspiration from two national legacies: popular art and literature, and the generation-old May Fourth literary heritage. Audiences welcomed these additions to the mass culture which film represented. Modern May Fourth literature appealed to the urban, relatively educated audiences who were the successors to the typical pre-1949 viewers. These urban filmgoers joined newer audiences in other areas in appreciating film artists' use of stories, genres, and styles derived from popular culture.

With these changes, film was expanding beyond the realms represented by both Yan'an and Shanghai. Expansion occurred in three major areas: production facilities, audiences that were served by wider distribution networks, and a growing corps of experienced artists and technicians.

New studios

The establishment of new film studios in Guangzhou, Chengdu, Xi'an, Changsha, Nanning, Urumchi, and Huhehot, places at a great distance geographically and culturally from cosmopolitan Shanghai, where film was strongest, represented a step toward the sinification of film. The more exaggerated efforts in this direction, such as plans for a film studio in every provincial and autonomous region capital, were a Great Leap phenomenon that mostly came to naught. Decentralization of film production was pursued in Shanghai, where the Shanghai Film Studio was subdivided into four separate components.

The Pearl River Film Studio was set up on a then suburban–rural site southwest of Guangzhou city. Groundbreaking took place in 1957, production of newsreels and documentaries started in 1958, and the first feature films were released in 1960. Most of the creative staff – directors, scenarists, actors – and technical personnel, who in the early days numbered only between 20 and 30 people, transferred to Guangzhou in 1958 from the Beijing Film Studio, the Shanghai studios (particularly the newly established Jiangnan studio), and from literature and art propaganda departments in the People's Liberation Army. Here was an echo of the origins of the older state-owned studios, with their mix of artists from the "old liberated" areas, from Shanghai, and from the military. The prominence of the military as a source of personnel indicates both the army's significance in efforts after 1949 to create a new mass culture, and the importance attached by the Communist Party to film art as an instrument in those efforts.[4]

The establishment of a film studio in Guangzhou was not a full gesture toward the regionalization of Chinese film: Nonmusical feature films in Cantonese were never produced at the Pearl River Film Studio through to the 1980s. Chinese feature films, with the exception of regional opera, were always in standard Chinese. The huge Cantonese language subgroup was treated like the smaller language groups, with limited dubbing (mostly of an ad hoc nature–on tapes, for example) for generally rural audiences. Beijing regarded film as an effective tool for language standardization and an element in the socialist mass culture, even if Guangdong audiences were likely to try to see a Cantonese dubbed feature several times and watch a *putonghua* movie only once.[5]

The Xi'an Film Studio represented a more conscious effort at the decentralization of film production, as part of the industrialization of interior cities like Xi'an undertaken in the late 1950s. The planners envisioned cooperation between the Xi'an unit and smaller studios in the Northwest. After almost four years of preliminary work, the studio was completed in the spring of 1960. Responsible cadres came from three main sources: the older studios in the coastal cities, art workers from Shaanxi Province who underwent training at the older studios, and, after production began, graduates from specialist schools.[6]

The Emei Film Studio in Chengdu in the western province of Sichuan likewise was dependent upon assistance from the older studios when work began there in 1958. The PLA's August First Studio, already six years old and beginning to add feature films to its military-educational documentary output in Beijing, provided help. So did the Changchun studio in the Northeast, and the Tianma studio in Shanghai.[7]

Four smaller studios were established in the late 1950s in more distant regional centers, but each found it difficult to survive because of the high costs of a medium like film at a time of national economic disaster. Both the Xiaoxiang studio at Changsha in Hunan Province and the Guangxi studio in Nanning were set up in 1958 amid high hopes, but were forced to halt production because state subsidies were unavailable after 1962 following economic retrenchment.[8] The latter studio's swan song was assisting in the Changchun studio's production of *Third Sister Liu* (*Liu Sanjie*), a musical drama based on Guangxi provincial folktales. The Tianshan studio in the far northwest in Urumchi, capital of the Xinjiang Uighur Autonomous Region, staffed after 1956 by cadres sent to Beijing for training and by artists and specialists from the older studios, grew from a 60- to a 320-person operation before economic problems forced a cutback. It became a dubbing facility for films in minority languages. A similar fate overtook the Inner Mongolia studio in Huhehot in 1962.[9] As "national minorities" (*shaoshu minzu*), Mongols, Uighurs, Kazaks, and other peoples in the north and northwest could see films dubbed into their own languages. Cantonese speakers, in contrast, were regarded as ethnic (Han) Chinese and did not enjoy a similar privilege. Cantonese is considered a "dialect" of Chinese, although it amounts in reality to a distinct spoken language.

This flurry of activity in new geographical areas for film production was paralleled by changes in the heartland of Chinese cinema. In 1957 workers in feature film production at the Shanghai Film Studio divided into three separate studios. The workers assigned to the new Haiyan and Jiangnan studios remained at the original address at Longhua in the southwest suburbs, while the new Tianma studio relocated its staff on premises which had been a film studio before 1949.[10] Animated film production was also moved to a separate studio at this time.

The cultural authorities' reasons for this division of filmmaking in Shanghai in some respects resembled their considerations in establishing the new studios in the interior cities. They saw overcentralization of production in all these instances as an impediment to administrative efficiency and artistic productivity. In the Shanghai case political motives were also important, as will become clear.

Further administrative decentralization was effected when in 1958 a Shanghai Film Bureau (*dianying ju*) was strengthened to fill the intermediate level between the central Film Bureau of the Ministry of Culture and the four new studios (along with cinemas throughout the city). The officials of the local bureau performed the functions which had been handled previously by their colleagues in the Beijing bureau and the upper echelons of the Shanghai Film Corporation, the management body of the former Shanghai Film Studio.[11] With these changes in Shanghai and elsewhere, the central position of Shanghai in the Chinese film industry became less dominant. Filmmaking took on a more national character.

New audiences

During the nine years after 1956, film audiences continued to grow in number, and apparently in sophistication, through greater exposure to increasingly more complex films. Higher levels of production of Chinese (as opposed to foreign, dubbed) features and the growth of facilities for showing movies allowed the expansion of audiences. As audiences grew, so connections between film artists and filmgoers gained strength. Where the connections did not grow stronger was in large part the outcome of intercession by the third party in this tripartite relationship, the cultural authorities, ever anxious to ensure an orthodoxy largely defined by the Party.

Statistics for the size of film audiences, though often unreliable or incomplete, indicate substantial growth in the 1950s. In 1949 more than 47 million attendances were recorded. Admissions in 1956, the last of several post–Wu Xun years of limited production by Chinese studios, were almost 600 million, a twelvefold increase over the 1949 baseline.[12] One figure for 1957, 2.05 billion, indicates an almost fourfold increase in the space of a year, accounted for in part by the release of films completed at the very end of 1956.[13] In 1958, according to a *People's Daily* estimate, over 2.8 billion tickets were distributed.[14] A figure of 4.15 billion attendances in 1959 indicates the success of the Great Leap Forward mobilization in filling theater seats (or threshing ground spaces) between bouts of amateur steel furnace construction and the other economic foolishness that characterized the Leap.[15] After this movement national statistics are difficult to find, but scattered figures and claims about popular access to film viewing show that these numbers from the late 1950s were generally sustained until the mid-1960s, even if the Great Leap growth of 1958–9 did not continue.[16]

Expansion of distribution activities made much of these increases in audience possible. Projection units, either fixed cinemas or mobile and semimobile projection teams, grew in number before the mid-1960s. Here again there was a big leap in the statistics for 1958–9. There had been almost 700 projection units, mostly cinemas and converted halls, throughout China in 1949. Six years later, at least one projection team was operating in every county, although with a team total of 2,300, some counties enjoyed the services of two or more teams in 1955. Projection units by 1958 had increased to roughly 10,000. By 1960, 14,565 projection teams were working throughout the nation, 87 percent of which were apparently in the countryside or in mining areas.[17]

Despite these impressive and rapid advances in distribution, it took time for filmgoing to become less typically an activity for urban, relatively educated people. In 1957 a rural Chinese attended on average only 1.5 film screenings per year.[18] Change in this respect was uneven, for some country people saw more films: In 1958 each inhabitant in rural Jiangsu Province, in the highly developed lower Yangzi plain, attended six film shows, three times the national average. By 1962 the national average had grown to three film screenings per year.[19] On the other hand, officers and other ranks in the People's Liberation Army averaged four shows each month in 1959.[20] City dwellers continued to dominate filmgoing ranks. The 118,000 voting papers submitted in the first Hundred Flowers film popularity poll conducted by *Popular Film* in 1962 came mostly from city students, workers, and office workers (*jigou ganbu*, literally "organization cadres"). Next came soldiers, with countrypeople (*nongmin*) last.[21]

Complaints of incomprehension, frequently heard before 1956, were not as common by the early 1960s, even if problems remained for uneducated audiences. A letter from a projection team member in Shandong Province's Heze County noted persistent difficulties. Some names of films were too long, "making it hard for peasants to say them in one breath." The outer appearance of film characters could differentiate their age more clearly. Stronger lighting and louder sound tracks could spare projection teams, usually outsiders in the villages, from being accused by angry viewers of trying to save fuel by projecting films dimly and without sufficient amplification. Finally, Ms. Ru Ru suggested in her letter, film credits should combine art with popular styles. That way peasants with some literacy could read the slow-moving titles, while their illiterate neighbors would at least have something to engage their attention.[22] Whatever the problems, films found increasingly broad audiences in the ten years before the Cultural Revolution.

New filmmakers

By the late 1950s a new corps of filmmakers, trained in the forms and styles of Chinese socialist film, was gaining experience. One 1956 estimate put the number of film personnel (including technical and service employees) at approximately 10,000, most of whom were newcomers to the industry after 1949. Several hundred scriptwriters, editors, directors, and composers, in addition to a similar number of technical specialists, had begun work by 1956. While at this time the vast majority of working directors and scenarists had had film experience since at least 1949, a new generation of film artists was beginning their careers.[23]

Many of these new filmmakers were enlisted by the studios and learned their craft on the spot, but the most important group underwent special training programs. In 1952 a Film School (Dianying xuexiao), attached to the Beijing Film Studio, opened its doors. In the autumn of 1955, students with some experience who had been nominated by the three feature film studios started two-year classes in directing, acting, cinematography, and production management, with Soviet teachers. Most returned to their studios, although some remained to serve as instructors at the Beijing Film Academy (Dianying xueyuan), which opened in June 1956. To the original directing, acting, and cinematography departments were added an art department in 1959, and engineering and scripting (*wenxue*) departments in 1960. Diplomas required four or five years of study, as in universities. By 1960, 586 students had been accepted. Short-term training classes were also conducted. Between 1952 and 1966, close to 2,000 students attended the central film school.[24]

New styles and subjects

In the years after 1956, cultural leaders and film artists began to experiment with styles and subjects. A more indigenous type of feature film began to emerge as strict "socialist realism" gave way to greater variety. These changes reflected simultaneous broader adjustments in other areas of national life. Chinese were questioning their dependence on Soviet models and attempting to evolve local solutions to a range of problems.

The cultural bureaucrats coined a major new slogan, "the combination of revolutionary realism and revolutionary romanticism" (*geming xianshizhuyi yu geming langmanzhuyi xiangjiehe*), which allowed more opportunity than before for artists to use the screen to present the breadth of the nation's artistic and literary heritage. Filmmakers explored a wider range of styles and subject matter, were able to acknowledge the May Fourth heritage, and made some films that brought Chinese popular culture, notably musical drama, directly to wider audiences.

New formulas

Cultural policymakers in the early 1950s had adopted the concept of "socialist realism" in its Soviet, Zhdanovian guise, with no great enthusiasm. In effect, they paid little more than lip service to the concept by making reference to socialist realism when some allusion to theory seemed appropriate.[25] Nevertheless, in a system of centralized cultural pronouncement and management, even lip service could amount to a powerful endorsement. The appearance in 1958 of a new artistic rubric, "the combination of revolutionary realism and revolutionary romanticism," reflected an urge on the part of cultural bureaucrats and artists to find a more indigenous aesthetic formula, one that might better serve the concern for mass audiences that Mao had endorsed in his 1942 Yan'an *Talks*. The new formula, moreover, could accommodate a range of aesthetic styles, from the "romanticism" of the native forms, which Mao strongly favored in Yan'an, to the "realism" of modern literature, grounded in the May Fourth movement. The way the new formula was presented to cultural circles emphasized its Chinese foundation rather than a Soviet pedigree. Zhou Yang, arbiter of literary policy in the 1950s and chief proponent of the Maoist Yan'an line, used the formula in a June 1958 article on Chinese folk songs and new-style poetry. A few months later, a report by Zhou Yang appeared in the *Literary Gazette* under the title "Establish China's own Marxist literary and artistic theory and criticism."[26]

The new literary formula offered Chinese filmmakers a way to overcome, or at least lessen, the difficulties inherent in a foreign-born medium. Some perhaps were less concerned than the Party thought they should be with China's own artistic tradition. In an article on film's achievements written in mid-1958, Wang Lanxi, the long-serving head of the Film Bureau of the Ministry of Culture, complained of "dogmatism" among some film artists, who continued to treat foreign models and styles seriously while showing little interest in Chinese styles.[27] At about the same time Xia Yan, discussing the Great Leap Forward in filmmaking, contrasted the eager adoption of "foreign styles" with the same artists' problems in accepting and implementing the Party's political and artistic orientations.[28] Superficially, these two complaints seem merely a continuation of the criticism, cited in the Wu Xun campaign, of cosmopolitan, petit-bourgeois tendencies among film artists. Wang Lanxi and Xia Yan, however, with these same words were authoritatively suggesting dissatisfaction with the foreignness which the Stalinist aesthetic, epitomized in socialist realism, helped perpetuate in Chinese film. Writing in 1960, Xia noted that some artists still displayed "foreignness" (*yangqi*) and were divorced from the mass of the people. He praised those films made since 1959 which affected a national (*minzuhua*) and populist (*qunzhonghua*) style.[29]

The new emphasis on national styles promised audiences a wider range of subjects. Film audiences, like readers of fiction, had long chafed under a regime of revolutionary war and land reform stories. Although filmmakers had attempted, notably in the Hundred Flowers period in 1956–7, to expand the range of films, sustained change came only after the 1958 introduction of the new artistic slogan and the comparative liberalization of the early 1960s. The director Xie Jin, maker of *Girl Basketball Player No. 5* (*Nülan wuhao*, 1957) and *The Red Detachment of Women* (*Hongse niangzijun*, 1961), summed up the new climate in an August 1961 article.[30] Xie took pains to quote Xia Yan on the masses' expectations of art being many and variegated. A range of subjects and styles should serve these demands, Xie Jin argued. The messages an audience received from a film need not, Xie suggested, be reducible to one or two pat phrases. Such an authoritative view, published in *People's Daily*, meant audiences could expect greater variety in forthcoming films.

One major trend between 1958 and 1964 was the rediscovery of the Chinese past. "Socialist realism" had effectively denied that a prerevolutionary past existed: China's audiences, filmmakers, and (after 1958) cultural bureaucrats, knew better. The revolutionary realism and romanticism slogan provided a sanction for film artists to seek material and inspiration from history. They began to make films of the regional opera repertoires, of May Fourth fiction, and of historical persons and events.

The historical drama *Lin Zexu* (1959) was an example of the new films set in the prerevolutionary past. With the exception of the 1955 *Song Jingshi*—a film about the Nian peasant rebel leader in the late Qing dynasty (scripted by Jia Ji, a Wu Xun critic, and directed by Sun Yu), which took at least three years in actual production—*Lin Zexu* was the first film set in the nineteenth century since the ill-fated *Life of Wu Xun*. Imperial Commissioner Lin Zexu, a high-ranking officer of the Qing bureaucracy, would seem an even less likely candidate for cinematic apotheosis than the founder of schools for the poor. The film, however, took care to emphasize the popular support Lin enjoyed in his efforts in Guangdong against Western opium smuggling, and popular efforts, led by fisherfolk, to resist these foreign incursions. Melodramatic exaggeration of the good or evil on each side in the Opium Wars avoided the pitfalls of the Wu Xun project.

Naval Battle of 1894 (*Jiawu fengyun*, 1962) was also set in Qing times and told of the struggle of a righteous official (a motif with a long pedigree in Chinese literature and historiography) against bureaucratic and dynastic corruption. As in the Lin Zexu film, the hero was linked with popular nationalism to make his central role compatible with official views of history.

The abandoning of the emphasis on socialist realism, with its solemnity and high purpose, contributed to the broadening of subject matter and styles to include comedy. Comedy provided an opportunity for filmmakers to deal with contemporary, everyday subjects by lending stories a momentum which noncomic works derived from the dramatic tension in their significant political and social subject matter. In the absence of scowling Guomindang generals and cunning landlords, comedy was a vehicle for the presentation of events in ordinary citizens' lives. Films set among minority peoples provided another vehicle for the deemphasis on class conflict.

Typical of the new comedies was *What's Eating You?* (*Manyi bu manyi*, 1963), in which a young waiter in a restaurant in Suzhou, near Shanghai, becomes reconciled to his job and convinced of the value of his work. The film draws on popular culture in the service of a current political campaign. The screenplay was based on a contemporary southern farce (*huaji*) from the Suzhou–Zhejiang region, equivalent to northern comedians' dialogue (*xiangsheng*: "crosstalk"). Variety (*quyi*) performers play major roles in the film. Indeed, *What's Eating You?* preserves something of the flavor of a popular performance. Twice, a recital by teahouse singers (to be sure in somewhat "sanitized" surroundings and flanked by matched electric fans) is featured, and several of the restaurant customers speak in local accents, with one couple using pure Shanghai dialect. It was almost only in such comedies (and films of local opera) that any departure was made from the standard *putonghua* used in all feature films, no matter where their stories were set.

In *What's Eating You?* the teahouse musicians perform a song that encapsulates the inspiration of the film and the conversion of Waiter No. 5. The song tells of the sufferings and altruism of the young soldier Lei Feng, who died in the service of his fellow citizens. In 1963 a mass campaign to "learn from Lei Feng" was directed at young people throughout China. In the restaurant itself there is a large wall hanging with a portrait of the late soldier and Mao Zedong's calligraphic exhortation to study his example. After a series of comic embarrassments, Waiter No. 5 finds himself mistaken for a colleague who is a model worker, and is called upon to give a speech at a factory meeting about being an exemplary worker. The factory employees greet Waiter No. 5's spontaneous and extemporaneous account of his learning to "serve the people" with obvious enthusiasm. One implication is that a more usual, ritualistic speech (which the real model worker might have given) would be less effective. The film audience has no chance to test this hypothesis, for as soon as the real model worker arrives and starts his speech, the scene ends. The film concludes with Waiter No. 5 working merrily among happy customers whom he had formerly offended with his rude service.

Big Li, Little Li, and Old Li (*Da Li, xiao Li he lao Li*, 1962) also uses comedy and farce to show up the shortcomings of an ordinary worker, in this case in a meat-packing plant during a campaign to promote physical fitness. The film, however, lacks the local color that gives *What's Eating You?* its special interest. Director Xie Jin compensates for this with more rounded characters and a greater consistency of tone. Much of the film takes place among the inhabitants of a workers' apartment building, so there are echoes of several pre-1949 films, such as *Crows and Sparrows*, with similar settings.

The emergence of "middle characters" (*zhongjian renwu*), which was part of the shift away from simple "socialist realism," made possible comedy and other films on everyday life. By the early 1960s writers were producing stories, plays, and film scripts that featured characters who were neither resolute standard-bearers for a socialist millennium nor die-hard opponents of the new order, but somewhere in the middle. Characters like Waiter No. 5, Big Li, and Old Li have a potential for good, but are wrongheaded, muddled, or misled by others. The drama lies in the process by which the middle characters, usually with the help of enthusiastic socialists, make good. Such characters clearly lend themselves to comic treatment more readily than their flag-waving comrades.[31]

The trend in the late 1950s toward a sinification of film subjects and styles included adaptations of the May Fourth literary heritage. Given May Fourth writers' determined modernism and their self-conscious rejection of traditional elite literature, adaptation of such fiction does not seem to fit readily into the emphasis on the rise of national, Chinese elements. The writers' use of the vernacular (*baihua*) made May Fourth fiction heir to the long history of vernacular fiction traditionally condemned (though often privately enjoyed) by Confucian literati. The use of narrative techniques and other devices derived from Western literature, however, made May Fourth literature a somewhat elitist and acquired taste. Xia Yan noted in 1959, on the fortieth anniversary of the May Fourth demonstrations, what he called the "nihilism" toward the national heritage (*minzu chuantong*) shown by the May Fourth generation, himself presumably included.[32]

But May Fourth writing was more securely part of Chinese literary history by its fortieth anniversary in 1959. The same may not have been true in 1942, when Mao Zedong in his Yan'an *Talks* took a rather negative view of even the May Fourth literary types who had made the trek to Yan'an. By the late 1950s, after a steady diet of Soviet-inspired realism, even May Fourth writings must have seemed more Chinese than previously thought. Adaptation to the mass medium of film was a means to further popularize this literature by bringing it to a much wider audience than the educated urban elite that had hitherto appreciated it. The older generation of filmmakers, heirs to and even part of the May Fourth legacy, welcomed the task.

The effort at screen adaptations, however, was limited, despite the more open cultural policies after 1956. Although May Fourth literature abounded with "middle characters," its degree of romanticism was often considered excessive. In the case of *Early Spring in February* (*Zaochun eryue* [literally, *Early Spring in the Second Lunar Month*], 1963), a story chosen in part because of its martyred author's "revolutionary" credentials, allegations of ambiguity and worse were leveled at the resulting film. Less controversial was the treatment of May Fourth intellectuals in a 1957 novel, Yang Mo's *Song of Youth* (*Qingchun zhi ge*, filmed in 1959). In the film, more than in the novel, revolutionary resolution triumphs without the equivocation implied in *Early Spring in February*.

The difficulties of adapting May Fourth fiction were apparent in Xia Yan's screen version of *The New Year's Sacrifice* (*Zhufu*, 1956), by Lu

Xun, the greatest May Fourth writer. A more popular May Fourth novelist, Ba Jin, had presented a sentimental picture of a generation's anguish in the midst of the decaying familial system in his 1933 novel *Family* (*Jia*). The 1956 film version was a faithful re-creation of the fictional Gao household, with a slow tracking camera subtly underlining the claustrophobic atmosphere. A concession to the 1950s is a rather positive portrayal of the youngest Gao son, seen in a final, standard revolutionary shot on his way to a new liberated life downriver, beyond the Yangzi gorges.[33]

The other type of adaptation, which received more attention in these nine years, was screen versions of opera. In their efforts to adapt the popular heritage of musical drama, filmmakers encountered direct conflicts between the fixed conventions of these national forms and the fluid potential of the foreign-derived film medium. They had found no satisfactory solutions before severely modernized musical drama replaced the historical repertoire in the mid-1960s.

Although films of musical drama were not a new form, filmmakers had paid relatively little attention to them before the late 1950s changes in artistic policies. Some of the earliest motion pictures made in China had been scenes from Beijing and other opera styles. In the 1930s and 1940s, catering to an urban audience disinterested in such "antique" forms or able to attend live opera performances, film artists had concentrated on other types of feature film drawn from modern, nonmusical drama (*huaju*).[34] This emphasis sat well with the modern, Westernized backgrounds of the filmmakers. The persistent view of film as a foreign medium had made movies seem more appropriate for presenting modern drama rather than folk opera to mass audiences.

Some filmmakers took a new interest in the artistic challenge of adapting folk opera as part of the shift in the second half of the 1950s toward Chinese forms in economic, social, and cultural life. For artists and audiences, such movies added to the variety of films. For Party cultural leaders, adaptations provided an opportunity to bring to a national audience the corpus of reformed or modified popular operas in a standardized form not open to local abuse by live performers. Moreover, some critics argued that traditional opera and modern cinema shared some common features, notably freedom of transition in time and space.[35]

Filmmakers, however, found it difficult to strike a balance between audience expectations, nurtured by live performances, and the characteristics of film. The Changchun studio's adaptation of the Henan provincial opera (*yuju*) *Hua Mulan* (1956) tried to combine traditional stage techniques with what one disgruntled reviewer labeled "some expert's so-called modern methods of artistic portrayal." Apparently audiences laughed at the film because, although real settings and props were used (including a weaving loom), one character rode a horse in normal stage style – that is, minus horse. All that this reviewer could find acceptable were the performances of the featured actors, a customary central concern of the aficionado of such a conventionalized art. The reviewer ended rhetorically: "Chinese artistic forms, such as painting and opera, have a special nature which we are all used to and which are fixed. Do they need to be improved upon?"[36]

In taking up the alternative approach to filming opera, making a stage documentary (*wutai jilupian*), filmmakers also confronted the difficult task of preserving the strengths and peculiarities of an opera performance while shaping a film. A stage documentary did not mean simply setting up a camera as if in the front of the stage in a theater. As a 1958 reviewer noted, at a live performance the audience does not fix the entire stage in an unblinking gaze throughout a performance.[37] Participants at a 1962 roundtable discussion on opera films, convened by the national Opera Association and the Film Workers Association, reportedly took a middle view. Several speakers argued that the emphasis on realism which film implied and the centrality of artifice in opera could be complementary, particularly as film need not be bound by reality and could add to the richness of opera's artistry.[38]

Opera audiences were harder to please than other filmgoers, for they had established their notions of good opera directly in relation to the genre. With audience expectations less fixed, other types of feature films were easier to make. But reformed versions of a portion of the repertoire of Beijing, Shaoxing (south of Shanghai), Guangdong, and other regional operas were considered part of the mass national culture promulgated after 1949, and film was the most effective way of taking standardized versions of this popular art to mass audiences.[39]

The persistence of these local styles, and their promulgation on a national scale through films, are rare examples of regionalism in the new mass culture. Almost in these films alone did characters use language other than the standard *putonghua*.[40]

These developments in Chinese cinema – the expansion of the film enterprise beyond Shanghai, and of film subjects and styles beyond the ascribed narrowness of the Yan'an-defined view of art – pointed toward an increased sinification of both the art and the industry. The changes contributed to film's function as an instrument for the popularization of a new mass culture. A homogenized and standardized art of film presented to nationwide audiences regularized views of the past, of the present, and of older indigenous art. At the same time, the instrumental view of film – an attitude not confined to Party cultural authorities, but shared to some extent by artists – and the notion of film as a foreign art inhibited the emergence of distinctly Chinese styles of cinema. The sinification of film which the new studios and new types of films evinced had its limits. These limits were defined not simply by Party fiat, but by the changing discourse among cultural authorities, filmmakers, and audiences.

The politics of filmmaking

While audiences were enjoying opportunities to see a greater variety of films after 1956, the other two groups in the Chinese film enterprise, the Party and the filmmakers, proceeded to adjust their relationship, sometimes in startling and destructive fashion. The leadership encouraged candid criticism of its regime during the Hundred Flowers period (1956–7), but then banished many writers and artists from creative activity during the Anti-Rightist reaction (1957–8). The subsequent Great Leap Forward (1958–60) made unrealistic demands on film production as on other spheres of public life.

Increased intervention by the Party in the work of filmmakers during the post–Hundred Flowers backlash against "rightists" and in the enthusiasm of the Great Leap apparently cowed film artists into adjusting themselves to the might of the authorities. Closer analysis suggests, however, that adjustment during these two episodes was mutual, though accompanied by a great deal of destruction. Filmmakers, to be sure, remained in a subordinate position in relation to those in charge of cultural policy, but this arose in part also from their other difficulties in establishing links with their audiences. Political interventionism in the late 1950s paradoxically showed Party leaders how much they depended on filmmakers in their efforts to create a socialist mass culture. The comparative calm of the early 1960s in the film world reflected this mutual awareness of interdependence.

The Hundred Flowers discourse

In 1956 Mao Zedong used an ancient, conventional phrase–"Let a hundred flowers bloom, let a hundred schools of thought contend"–to encapsulate an unconventional period in which he encouraged debate and criticism of his own regime. Mao was attracted to toy with liberalization by the examples of de-Stalinization in the Soviet Union and the consequences of rigidity displayed in Hungary in that year. After initial hesitation, many scholars, writers, and filmmakers answered Mao's call with often bitter denunciations of aspects of life since the founding of the People's Republic. In mid-1957 the authorities responded in some alarm with an "anti-rightist" backlash, and the flowers withered.

In the film industry, the Hundred Flowers revealed problems that had not been so thoroughly addressed before. The leadership of the industry was roundly condemned by some, and cultural policy discussed more

vigorously than at any time since Mao's Yan'an *Talks*. Time allowed few
filmed essays in new directions. The Hundred Flowers discourse and the
subsequent pulling back also revealed divisions in the film industry. The
older cleavages between Shanghai and Yan'an, which usually meant
older film artists vis-à-vis the Party, were now complicated by other fis-
sures within filmmaking ranks.

Critics of the cultural leadership frequently used heavy sarcasm or two
"codewords" prominent in all types of Hundred Flowers critique: dogmatism (*jiaotiaozhuyi*) and sectarianism (*zongpaizhuyi*). The former was
manifested, the critics argued, in unrealistic demands being made on
filmmakers by the Party leadership since 1949. Xia Yan, the most successful leftist scenarist of the 1930s and 1940s, and now in charge of cultural
work in Shanghai, himself noted how artists were expected to do a bit of
everything: making films in the form of "commemorative steles" for the
heroes of the past, while at the same time tying their work to current
political movements and campaigns.[41]

Excessive interference in artists' work, both from the studio-level management and from outside the studios, from the Film Bureau of the state
Ministry of Culture and from the Party's Propaganda Department, was the
prime expression of "dogmatism." At each level in the film production
apparatus, from the center out to the studios, there was a parallel structure of Party and non-Party or managerial leadership. In reality, however,
as the Hundred Flowers critics confirmed, at all levels the voice of the
Party—in a section of a studio, at the studio level, in the local cultural
offices, up to the central Film Bureau—could override other voices. A film
script or completed film required approval at each level in this hierarchy,
with central approval usually being pro forma.

The Hundred Flowers critics complained that unnecessary delays
were caused by having to get scripts approved at higher levels. Some
critics even went so far as to assert publicly that concern by such bodies
as the Film Guidance Committee to "strengthen Party leadership" had
been as much to blame as script shortages for the post—Wu Xun slowdown.[42] Further interference came at later stages in production. One celebrated critique, "Gongs and drums at the movies"—soon the target of a
strong official backlash—cited the case of prolonged discussion at high
levels over just when and in what exact manner the unfortunate heroine
of *The New Year's Sacrifice*, scripted by Xia Yan from the Lu Xun short
story, should drop a sacrificial fish. Similar careful, high-level censorial
attention was paid to the behavior of dogs, to whether characters should
wear black-framed spectacles (a mark of an intellectual), and to how an
actor should express thanks or even knock on a door.[43]

The Film Bureau and other cultural leaders acknowledged this problem of "dogmatism," although they had been doing so (less emphatically)
for several years. The most acerbic Hundred Flowers critics, however,

were not satisfied by general statements that Party inexperience in how to manage a socialist cultural enterprise lay at the root of the problems. The division of the huge Shanghai Film Studio in April 1957 into three feature film units was apparently motivated by an urge to placate the critics by decentralizing some levels of leadership in Shanghai filmmaking. The move did not persuade one commentator: "They are changing the soup, but not the main courses," he complained.[44]

Many filmmakers greeted with skepticism promises by cultural leaders to take more account of the special peculiarities of the art, for example by allowing scenarists to choose their own subjects, and directors the scripts with which they felt most comfortable. Promises to give more autonomy to the studios and to the artistic personnel there aroused a similar response. Shi Hui, a prominent actor since the 1930s, welcomed the establishment in Shanghai and Changchun of "creative groups" (*chuangzuo zu*) to take charge of the process of production of individual films, but wondered if the groups' independence might be undermined by bureaucratic intervention from unsympathetic managers.[45] Other artists reportedly felt thwarted when lay (*waihang*) managers directed expert (*neihang*) filmmakers.[46] Lü Ban, an actor since the 1930s in Shanghai and a director at the Changchun studio, was blunter, allegedly seeing little chance for a hundred flowers to bloom: "There is no spring at Changchun; all seasons are winter."[47]

A major reason for the chilly atmosphere in the film industry was the other central subject of Hundred Flowers discussion in 1956–7, the persistent tendency of Communist Party cadres to distrust and discriminate against non-Party personnel, which was called "sectarianism." Film artists who had been active before 1949 were a particular object of discrimination. Although now outnumbered by newer recruits, the more experienced artists continued to be a vital element in the industry. The Party cultural apparatus, however, still tended to look upon the former denizens of the Shanghai film world as tainted by unorthodoxy and cosmopolitanism.

The authorities probably had good grounds for presuming that the makers of petit-bourgeois fantasies in the 1940s had not been uniformly transformed in the space of a few years into committed socialist artists. The Hundred Flowers discussion of "sectarianism" suggests that many in the cultural leadership went further, still holding a view of art and artists molded in the mountain fastness of Yan'an. Film, the art perhaps most alien and distant from the Yan'an ethos, was therefore most liable to intervention. Their awareness of the importance of film as the most accessible component in the new mass culture reinforced this concern. The Film Bureau's response to its task was, in the words of one director critic, to "overload the bold, and scare the timid."[48]

Anxious to improve relations between Party and filmmakers, the leaders of the Film Bureau acknowledged their "sectarianism" in a May 1957 reassessment of awards given just a month earlier to the best films and film artists of the period 1949–56. *Crows and Sparrows*, made by a group of prominent leftist artists at the Kunlun studios in Shanghai before the fall of the Guomindang and released after 1949, was added to the awards list. Inclusion of *Crows and Sparrows* among the prizewinners was a recognition of the contributions made by non-Party artists. The bureaucrats also apologized for slighting the work of older actors who had been active before 1949, but had had little opportunity to practice their craft since then.[49] As one frustrated thespian remarked in another context, they had acted in the teeth of Japanese attack, but since 1949 had been idle.[50]

The establishment of a formal, nominally independent, organization of filmmakers, the Film Workers Association (Zhongguo dianying gongzuozhe lianyihui), during the six weeks in the spring of 1957 when the Hundred Flowers discourse was at its height, was a similar gesture toward granting artists a measure of autonomy. The association's list of aims made no mention of "socialist realism," referring instead to "new films of a socialist national nature" (*shehuizhuyi de minzu xin dianying*). The body's executive even included such experienced artists as Sun Yu, writer-director of *The Life of Wu Xun*.[51]

The relatively open discourse in 1956–7 (and the subsequent Anti-Rightist accusations) revealed that, quite apart from the "sectarianism" of the cultural leadership, filmmaking ranks were themselves divided and faction-ridden. The Party's encouragement of the expression of grievances made these conflicts more public. A young reporter, in a controversial article in the *Literary Gazette*, described the plight of younger actors at the Changchun studio. The reporter was bold enough to offer details of the failure to pay attention to the actors' problems, during visits to the studio, on the part of Lu Dingyi, head of the Propaganda Department, Chen Huangmei, a deputy head of the Film Bureau, and other high-level bureaucrats.[52] These younger, resentful, and "mixed up" actors were later said to have been encouraged to "oppose Party leadership" by an older, established "rightist" actor.[53] Competition among younger artists for jobs on screen or in production caused disaffection and provided malcontents with fertile ground for causing trouble. Zhang Ying, who had played Dong Cunrui's platoon leader in that soldier's 1955 film biography, reportedly felt that winning the part in that film gave him sufficient "capital" (*ziben*) to criticize the leadership.[54]

Older filmmakers were also dissatisfied, and sometimes displayed a sense of superiority toward less experienced or, in their view, less sensitive artists. Lü Ban, leader of a comedy-making group at Changchun, reportedly scoffed at those he saw as too willing to accept the comfort of Party-subsidized conformity: "Just copy Yan Xiucun and Han Lan'gen [two of Lü's 1930s acting colleagues, who returned to the screen in Hundred Flowers comedies] and you've got it made."[55] Several artists who had been active before 1949 allegedly sought more power for experienced directors like themselves and their friends. They also were said to have fanned the flames of discontent in Shanghai, where ex-Yan'anite cultural leaders were in charge of older artists who had spent the War of Resistance to Japan in Guomindang- or Japanese-controlled areas.[56] Attempted reform in the system of filmmakers' salaries, apparently designed to give more to those directly responsible for a film's success, with less regard for seniority, was in part a response to divisions within film artists' ranks.[57]

This factionalism among filmmakers, like the weakness of connections between filmmakers and their expanding audiences, made it easier for the third party in this tripartite relationship, the cultural authorities, to use "divide and rule" tactics to preserve its preeminent position, as became clear in the second half of 1957 during the Anti-Rightist backlash.

In addition to the charges leveled at the leadership of the film industry, a secondary area of Hundred Flowers discourse was cultural policy as applied to film art, and the films which had been produced under this policy. Most of the criticisms singled out not "socialist realism," which had never been emphatically endorsed, but the orientation to serve workers, peasants, and soldiers (*gongnongbing*).

Zhong Dianfei, a thirty-seven-year-old literary editor soon to be condemned as a "rightist," approached the problem with a directness not seen since Mao had presented the *gongnongbing* artistic orientation as Party policy in his 1942 Yan'an *Talks*. Zhong was emboldened in his critique by weeks of candid discussion of the problems of film published in the non-Party Shanghai newspaper *Wenhui Daily* (*Wenhui bao*) at the end of 1956. Zhong in effect summarized and sharpened the earlier criticisms. Since the abolition of popular Hollywood films at the start of the decade, concern about the box office performance of films had been officially condemned. In his celebrated and anonymous critique, published in early December 1956 in the *Literary Gazette*, Zhong argued that the abysmal box office records of many recent films was a warning of problems with the sacrosanct *gongnongbing* policy.[58] More than 70 percent of the films made since 1953 (referring to the year in which the last of the private Shanghai studios had been nationalized) did not recoup their costs, with some earning a mere 10 percent of the funds expended in making them. Box office returns like this indicated that the connection between audiences and art, a major concern of Mao in his Yan'an *Talks*, was in danger of being severed.

Zhong laid the blame for the imminent break on a tendency to treat the *gongnongbing* orientation of art and literature in an abstract and ossified way. If the orientation deserved more than lip service, cadres and artists needed to give more careful consideration to how it might best be put into effect. In partial response, on the eve of the Hundred Flowers six weeks, Xia Yan warned against confusing problems of leadership with the correctness of the *gongnongbing* orientation itself. Xia implied, on the other hand, that the cultural leadership should not try to dismiss legitimate questioning of their actions by wrapping themselves in a cloak of *gongnongbing* righteousness.[59]

The results on China's screens of the Hundred Flowers loosening of censorial standards and greater openness (*fang*, as opposed to *shou*, reigning in) were more limited and less bold than the written and reported criticisms. Film's potential to reach a wide audience made it more subject to Party sensitivities than long articles in newspapers or the *Literary Gazette*. The resources committed to a film also encouraged caution at all levels. Making a feature film also needed more time than proved available.

Nevertheless, the new elements in many 1956–7 films should not be underestimated. Filmmakers attempted comedy for the first time in many years, and their choice of subject matter became broader than it had been since at least 1949. The best known of the new comedies was *Before the New Director Arrives* (*Xin juzhang daolai zhi qian*, 1956), based on a 1954 play of the same name. The film satirizes the false expectations of both cadres and workers in a government bureau. A new director will shortly take over. The present deputy uses the occasion to redecorate the offices ostentatiously, diverting manpower and other resources to the task. The new director turns up unannounced and observes all the fuss for a while before revealing his identity, to the horror of his deputy and the delight of the young workers who had questioned the propriety of the preparations. The comparatively fast pacing of the film preserves the spirit of the comedy while making sure that the satirical points are made. The exemplary character of the new director is also made clear, but indirectly through his modest, premature arrival, unlike the direct presentation of the heroes of *gongnongbing* dramas.[60]

In addition to changes in style, the 1957 Hundred Flowers films also departed from the narrow concentration on unremittingly hearty worker/peasant/soldier heroes in the films of the previous half decade. *Loyal Partners* (*Qing chang yi shen*), made at the Shanghai studio before its division into three, was typical of the new films, having intellectuals as its heroes. Hong Leiguang, the director of a microbiology research institute, invites an old friend, Huang Weiwen, to join him in researching a new antibiotic. Unfortunately, Huang's attitude to research is very cautious, causing delays in the project and anguish to his friend. Huang is forced to make bolder efforts, however, in order to save Hong's life when the latter becomes infected by the bacteria they are using in the experiments. Prompted by his affection for Hong and with the encouragement of their younger colleagues, Huang produces a new vaccine, and all ends well.

While this bare plot outline suggests that the themes of service and sacrifice in *Loyal Partners* were little different from those of earlier films, the characters who articulated these themes were certainly novel. Dr. Huang was played by Xiang Kun, who until then had specialized in portraying maniacal Guomindang generals and other unsavory types. These heroes, whose weapons are microscopes not machine guns, and whose homes and workplaces are astonishingly luxurious, were new to Chinese films made since 1949. Perhaps to indicate to ordinary audiences how they should respond to them, Shi Hui played the part of Old Zhou (he does not have the benefit of a personal name in the script). An introduction to the movie in *Popular Film* noted that Old Zhou, the caretaker at the research institute, "respects and loves the younger and higher-ranking scientists."[61] A viewer need not be an antiintellectual left extremist to detect both a patronizing element associated with Old Zhou's character and an extraordinary nostalgia for middle-class luxury throughout the film.

The Anti-Rightist reaction

The Party leadership delineated the limits of discourse in the summer of 1957 in an Anti-Rightist reaction. The outspoken Hundred Flowers critics were labeled "rightists." They stopped writing, and were frequently subject to internal exile for indeterminate periods. Some committed suicide. After the Hundred Flowers thaw, this early and unexpected winter caused much suffering. Nonetheless, the bleakness of the Anti-Rightist backlash should not obscure the realization on the part of some Party authorities that such destruction would inhibit the emergence of the mass national culture, of which film was an important part. A degree of compromise was essential between concerns for orthodoxy, filmmakers' morale and commitment, and audiences' demands for a more satisfying art and literature. Once again Yan'an orthodoxy had to adjust itself to other legitimacies.

Several artists involved with *Loyal Partners* were singled out for condemnation as "rightists" when the Party put an end to the Hundred Flowers discourse after June 1957. Xiang Kun and Shi Hui were so labeled. The film was said to make a case for friendship above class feeling by having Huang really apply himself to the research project only after his friend (who also happens to be his brother-in-law) must be cured. Such bourgeois sentimentalism (*wenqingmomo*) and the absence of a portrayal of the Party's leadership role in scientific endeavors provided cause for the film to be banned.[62] Shi Hui was also accused of using his considerable prestige in Shanghai to influence younger filmmakers to support the now inflammatory aspirations for artistic autonomy expressed in the previous months. Chinese cinema lost one of its most accomplished actors when Shi Hui drowned himself shortly afterward.[63] The Party leadership was clearly sensitive to charges that they were singling out older artists for criticism, and so prominent artists like the director Cai Chusheng and the actress Shu Xiuwen were reported criticizing "rightists" who had been their close colleagues in the 1940s.[64] Divide and rule was an effective weapon in the fractious filmmaking ranks.

The strongest attacks of the Anti-Rightist campaign in the second half of 1957 were directed at the comedies that had come out of the Changchun Film Studio under the direction of another pre-1949 artist, Lü Ban. When his *Before the New Director Arrives* was released in 1956, Lü had taken great pains to express publicly a foreboding that satirical comedy might be in for trouble, seemingly with the intention of disarming the Party critics.[65] A year later the critics responded, accusing Lü Ban and his colleagues of using satire to attack the Party and undermine socialist morality. Lü, a Communist Party member, was said to have added his own notions that "the old society had not died, but continued to thrive in the new" to the film's script. Emphasizing Lü's meddling with the script helped explain why the 1954 play, from which the film was drawn, could have won national drama awards in that year. The 1957 censors cited slapstick and other farcical elements in this and two other Changchun comedies, *The Man Unconcerned with Details* (*Buju xiaojie de ren*) and the prophetically titled *Unfinished Comedy* (*Wei wancheng de xiju*), as evidence of taking satirical license too far. One of the characters in the last-named film, for example, is described as "an authority in literary criticism," and has a name homophonous with "A Bludgeon" (*yi bangzi*). *Unfinished Comedy*, perhaps the most accomplished film made in the 17 years between 1949 and the Cultural Revolution, was never released and Lü Ban never made another film.[66]

The Anti-Rightist response to the Hundred Flowers critics of the Party and its policies, as with literary campaigns before and after it, was first to mobilize artists and others against relatively minor targets in order to establish the criteria for attack before moving on to larger fry. One of the first victims was Zhong Dianfei, a young film work specialist in the Propaganda Department, whose "gongs and drums in the film world" article in late 1956 had epitomized much of the critique of the film enterprise. Roundtable discussions by film artists and others in August 1957 condemned Zhong and offered alternative explanations for some of his complaints. The officially endorsed explanation for the shortcomings in the *gongnongbing* orientation, of which Zhong had written, amounted to an evasion. A joint article by Jia Ji, one of the early Wu Xun critics, Huang Gang, and Cheng Jihua, the historian of Chinese film, argued that the *gongnongbing* films were a temporary phenomenon, being merely a useful label for movies which in the early 1950s were of a new style.[67] Zhong was even accused of being busy on a film script about the life of the eleventh-century statesman Wang Anshi, a charge which might have appealed to the orthodox, Song dynasty Confucianists whom Wang's reforms had antagonized. "We need not determine if a work of art is socialist or bourgeois. As long as the masses welcome it, it's good," was a disquieting statement ascribed to Zhong after his condemnation.[68] Later the Anti-Rightist backlash extended to more prominent targets, such as Shi Hui and Guo Wei, a Changchun director responsible for the seemingly orthodox 1955 soldier-hero biography *Dong Cunrui*.[69]

A notable feature of the Anti-Rightist campaign was the amount of emphasis on the faults of Shanghai filmmakers. Here was a reminder of the tensions between Shanghai and the rest which had been strong in the first half of the decade. The *Wenhui Daily*, which during the Hundred Flowers had printed some of the most outspoken criticisms of films, was a Shanghai newspaper not under direct Party control. Several Shanghai "rightist" film artists had their membership of the nominally independent, and definitely legal, political party, the China Democratic League, used against them by the 1957 counterattackers. The "rightists" so accused included Wu Yin, who had played the hero's mother in the 1947 blockbuster *The Spring River Flows East*.[70]

Whereas even at Lü Ban's Changchun studio the rectification campaign to isolate and condemn "rightists" did not last long, in Shanghai rectification continued, in four official stages, for almost a year, until May 1958. Those who had said in 1957 that "*gongnongbing* subjects are as dull as ditch-water (*ganbaba*)" were now reported acknowledging their errors. They included the writer-director of *The Life of Wu Xun*, Sun Yu, who argued that in making his latest film, *Braving Wind and Waves* (*Chengfeng polang*, 1957), his intentions had been honorable but, "lacking warm feelings toward the working class," old, petit-bourgeois tendencies had reappeared in his thinking.[71] That Shanghai took so long to put the Hundred Flowers and Anti-Rightist campaign officially behind it suggests that divisions there, both among filmmakers and between artists and cadres, were difficult to surmount.

While the suffering and cultural loss caused by the Anti-Rightist movement should not be underestimated, several episodes provide a caution against presenting a completely bleak picture. In a 1958 New Year statement the actor Zhao Dan (who had played Wu Xun) called 1957 "an abnormal (*bu pingchang*) year," noting that it had brought twin victories not only against "rightists," but also against "leftist dogmatism." This was a reminder that, in the heat of the Hundred Flowers moment, the Party had acknowledged errors in its own leadership.[72] A new style of film review in which the cultural bureaucrat and former director Zhang

Junxiang noted several equally valid views of the techniques of a new movie, appeared in mid-1958.[73] In startling contrast, *People's Daily* in December 1958 published a lengthy article under the headline "Resolutely wrench out the white flags on the screens: A critique of mistaken ideological tendencies in 1957 films."

Chen Huangmei, head of the Ministry of Culture's Film Bureau and a target of Hundred Flowers criticism by disgruntled Changchun actors, in the article made a detailed and bitter analysis of the whole filmmaking enterprise, which he characterized as dominated by unrepentant bourgeois artists.[74] Because eighteen months had already passed since the Anti-Rightist campaign had begun, Chen's acerbic tone seemed out of place in the mounting rhetorical fervor of Great Leap Forward enthusiasm. Three months later, the unusual joint publication of an open letter from the Shanghai-based secretary of the Film Workers Association and what amounted to an apology by Chen showed that wilder interventionist urges on the part of the cultural authorities could encounter some limits.[75] If compromise is too strong a characterization, something close to it was advisable if the Party was to have access to the special skills highly trained and experienced filmmakers possessed.

The Great Leap Forward

Compromise was essential for film to contribute appropriately to the next upsurge in political activism. In 1958 Mao Zedong and Party central launched a Great Leap Forward in Chinese economic life. The nation was to make a Chinese, mass mobilization "leap," if not lunge, to modernization. Film was an obvious tool to encourage mobilization, but it was also something of a foreign art and one whose specialization did not sit well with the Great Leap acclaim for native and technical amateurism. The results of the Great Leap Forward in the film industry were a further illustration of the limits of interventionism, and as such helped prepare the ground for the brief period of relative openness in the early 1960s.

The film leadership, in a surge of Great Leap enthusiasm, mapped out plans for more films and studios, and for greater mutual involvement between "the masses" and film artists. Earlier planned quotas for film production were put aside. The Shanghai studios would produce in 1958 the number of features which their earlier ten-year plan had envisioned would be achieved only in 1967.[76] Reducing the costs of production from a 1957 average for a black and white feature of 210,000 *yuan* (approximately 75,000 1957 U.S. dollars) was another concern of planners.[77] In addition to the recently established studios in Guangzhou, Chengdu, Xi'an, Xinjiang, and Inner Mongolia, one Film Bureau plan foresaw each province having its own film studio, and within ten years, each county a cinema, and each village (*xiang*) a film projection team. Ten new studios would open in the first half of 1959, and the rest would begin production in the second half of 1960.[78] Even the Shenyang Railway Bureau began work on its own film studio.[79] Farther north, the country's first county film studio (*xian dianying chang*) was founded in Jilin Province with 500 *yuan* of capital and a few days' study at the Changchun studio by its solitary employee.[80]

The "mass line" in filmmaking involved encouraging amateur efforts and sending artists to the grass roots to "learn from the masses," as Mao had set out in his Yan'an *Talks*. The dispatch of filmmakers to the countryside for manual labor had in fact begun in late 1957 and was not unrelated to the Anti-Rightist cleanup in the studios. Some of the writers and directors responsible for criticized films from the Hundred Flowers period were among the first to be "sent down."[81] Great Leap concern to diminish specialists' alienation from the rest of society simply added to this flow. "We have no need for the thinking of those timid experts who don't trust their own strength," one commentator sneered.[82] Wang Lanxi, in his last days as head of the Ministry of Culture's Film Bureau, ascribed excessive emphasis until then on industry (*yewu*), art (*yishu*), and technology (*jishu*) to "right-tending conservative thinking" (*youqing baoshou sixiang*), which should give way to more respect for the political uses of film art.[83] Wang was present at an expanded meeting of the Film Workers Association in February 1958 when members passed a motion affirming that literature and art should continue to serve workers, peasants, and soldiers, and have "a hundred flowers, a hundred schools" as their guiding principles. "Our films must have a correct political tendency, because politics is the commander and the soul."[84] Film art took second place. The administrative staff at the People's Liberation Army's August First studio in Beijing resolved to play their part in 1958 by raising a thousand kilos of fish.[85]

The results of the Great Leap in filmmaking were as disappointing as in other areas of Chinese life. A great quantity of films emerged from the studios, but they generally fell short on quality. The 180 films produced in the two years 1958–9 were more than the total number made in the eight years after 1949.[86] The three Shanghai feature studios, which in the calm before the Great Leap had planned to make 20 features in 1958, ended the year with 50, to their dubious credit.[87] Although Xia Yan, in a February 1960 article on continuing the Great Leap in film, claimed that throughout the nation there were now 33 film studios (*dianying zhipianchang*, the standard term for feature film studios), many of these appear to have been little more than bureaus for the processing and distribution of newsreel films.[88] The flurry of training and technical assistance given by the older studio centers in Changchun, Beijing, and Shanghai to provincial and other studios sometimes had limited results. The Nantong Film Studio in Jiangsu Province consisted in reality of one man, a bicycle, an enamel washbasin, and an antique still camera rescued from a pawnbroker.[89]

Many of the Great Leap films were set in the workplaces of workers, peasants, and soldiers and were in a new style, the so-called documentary-style feature [art] film (*jiluxing yishupian*). They were made at almost half the cost of the average 1957 feature.[90] The Great Leap slogan of "more, faster, better, more economical" also encouraged film-makers to produce a feature film in two to three months, instead of the usual year.[91] Typical of the "documentary-style feature films" was *For Sixty-one Class Brothers* (*Weile liushiyige jieji xiongdi*), made as late as March 1960. Adapted in 22 hours by a group of writers from a real-life report published in *China Youth News* (*Zhongguo qingnian bao*) about rushing emergency medicine to a Great Leap work site, the film itself took a mere sixteen days to complete at the Beijing Film Studio.[92] Representa-tive names of such Great Leap films are reminiscent of the titles from the newly nationalized studios in the early 1950s: *Steel Man and Iron Horse* (*Gangren tiema*), *Loving the Factory as One's Home* (*Ai chang ru jia*), *The Big Wave* (*Julang*), and *A Revolution in Twenty Days* (*Ershitian ge ge ming*).[93]

But the emphasis on *gongnongbing* subject matter did not mean that these films represented a revival of "socialist realism." Filmmakers could portray these subjects using the newly coined aesthetic of "combining revolutionary realism and revolutionary romanticism." The Great Leap Forward and this slogan were both explorations of a more indigenous approach to economics and art. *Huang Baomei*, named after the model worker in a Shanghai cotton mill whose biography it tells, illustrates the combination of worker subject matter with "revolutionary romanticism." When the heroine, played by Ms. Huang herself, achieves full automation in her spinning section, she and her comrades are presented on the screen transformed into the fairy maidens (*xiannü*) of folktales, in a gesture reportedly first suggested by the mill's Party committee and man-ager.[94]

Problems with the quality of much of the Great Leap effort, and general economic collapse, caused a pulling back by the beginning of 1960 in film production as in other areas. As early as November 1958 the heads of the feature film studios then in production (Beijing, Changchun, the three Shanghai studios, August First, Guangzhou, and Xi'an), at a meet-ing in Beijing stressed the "three goods" (*san hao*) in feature films: con-tent, style, and sound and lighting.[95] When their successors, the "four goods" (*si hao*)—story, acting, filming, and music—were introduced in 1961, the veteran director Cai Chusheng contrasted them with the "four faults" (*si bing*) of the films of the Great Leap Forward.[96]

Some cultural leaders were less eager than others to abandon the Great Leap's films. A highly defensive review of *For Sixty-one Class Broth-*

ers in the authoritative *Literary Gazette* noted that, "whatever our enemies or modern revisionism may say, we shall always determinedly love (*ku'ai*) this kind of work." For this reviewer, the current skepticism about "documentary-style feature films" was politically unsound.[97] Crudely equating a person's political stand with his or her disagreement with one's own assessment of a work of art was not new, or likely to disappear in China.

Indications that most cultural authorities and filmmakers felt that the Great Leap was over, however, came at the start of the new decade. Five national Film Work Conferences (including one on feature films) in Beijing in January–February 1960 began the process of putting the industry on a sounder footing. At the end of the same year a national meeting on film distribution also put concern for quality first.[98]

The Hundred Flowers discourse, Anti-Rightist reaction, and Great Leap Foward enthusiasm all placed considerable strains on relations between cadres and artists, and within these two groups. Filmmaking survived in better condition than after the earlier Wu Xun episode, for a variety of reasons. Cultural authorities saw the damage that would be done to the mass culture if their demands on filmmakers remained unrealistic. Filmmakers who survived prison or banishment were increasingly united by a sense of professionalism and less divided by old, pre-1949 factionalism. Both groups were becoming increasingly aware of responsibilities to their audience, "the masses," as film viewers.

The early 1960s

As Great Leap enthusiasm waned with the growing realization of the economic disaster it had helped create, Party cultural authorities also began to intervene less directly in filmmakers' work. Once again changes in the film industry reflected broader developments in the rest of society. Following the economic disaster of the Great Leap, the number of feature films produced annually returned to levels typical of the mid-1950s. Advocates of the Great Leap style of mass mobilization, such as Mao Zedong, gave way to a Party leadership, under Liu Shaoqi and Deng Xiaoping, which advocated less interventionist means to reach the same goals. The consequent moderation of Party expectations of filmmakers was evident in several areas. In cultural and literary policy, the narrow interpretation of "serving workers, peasants, and soldiers," seen in the early 1950s and again during the Great Leap, gave way to views of the function of art which were broader than this strictly Yan'anite definition. Perhaps as important, several key addresses by the Party leadership set out its policy with a clarity and unanimity often lacking in the past. In filmmaking activities, there were moves, which had been mentioned during the Hundred Flowers but never fully effected, toward a rehabilitation of the May

Fourth Shanghai artistic heritage and the people who represented that tradition. Audience tastes and needs were also given more attention than had usually been the case in the previous decade.

Premier Zhou Enlai displayed the new, moderate tone of cultural policy in a June 1961 speech to a joint meeting of participants in a forum on literary and art work and in a meeting on film scriptwriting.[99] A year earlier, when the Great Leap was being abandoned, "cultural commissar" Zhou Yang at the Third Congress of Writers and Artists had shown only limited inclination to be evenhanded.[100] Zhou Enlai in 1961 promised less of the arbitrary criticism and pressure to produce that had been characteristic of recent years. Speaking of artists, he remarked: "It is unavoidable for people to err a little in thought, speech or action. It does not matter, as long as free criticism is allowed." Indirectly alluding to Mao, and probably also to Zhou Yang, the premier noted:

If only one person were allowed to speak and all others forbidden, would that not mean "What one man says goes"? How did this . . . come about? It has something to do with the leadership. So we must create a democratic atmosphere.

Zhou placed responsibility on cadres in literature and art to change their "style of work." "In a word, we must allow others to have their own opinions."[101] The tone of the speech was more important than its substance.

Although Zhou Enlai warned that force of habit took time to overcome, there were other signs of an easing of Party demands on filmmakers. The *gongnongbing* emphasis of Mao's Yan'an *Talks* was subtly modified by Chen Huangmei himself on the eighteenth anniversary of their delivery. Chen argued that mass art satisfied "the needs of other classes" as well as those of workers, peasants, and soldiers.[102] On the twentieth anniversary of the *Talks* in 1962, Chen, as head of the Ministry of Culture's Film Bureau, made only passing reference to *gongnongbing*,, and praised the effectiveness of Italian neorealist films.[103] For his part, Yuan Wenshu, secretary of the Film Workers Association, on the same occasion made no mention at all of the *gongnongbing* orientation, which had been central to cultural policy through most of the 1950s.[104]

During the three to four years of relative relaxation in the early 1960s, the Shanghai legacy in Chinese film made something of a comeback. Since its subordination in the early 1950s to the more Yan'an-derived orientation in cultural affairs, the May Fourth "progressive" tradition associated with the pre-1949 film world in Shanghai had been resuscitated briefly only during the Hundred Flowers. In 1956–7 some older filmmakers had boldly referred to the pre-1949 experience as showing what could be achieved if the current problems of leadership were overcome. At that time audiences were able to see Chinese films made before 1949 for the first time in half a decade. Like a barometer of the changing cultural climate, these films reappeared in the early 1960s. In Beijing the Film

Archive (Dianying ziliaoguan), which had been established in 1956, began work on cataloging and preserving films made since the 1920s.[105]

The commemoration of the thirtieth anniversary of the League of Left-Wing Writers, which might have been played down for fear of reviving old factional bitterness among artists and cadres active in the 1930s, was a fairly expansive occasion in 1960.[106] Apparently a degree of unanimity or at least mutual toleration had evolved between such cadres as Zhou Yang and older writers and artists, who had once been his critics and even his victims. Even as potentially divisive an effort as writing a film biography of Lu Xun, the May Fourth literary hero and iconoclast, was completed by a group of Shanghai scenarists.[107] A two-volume history of Chinese films by Cheng Jihua appeared in early 1963, and it cast a glowing light on the pre-1949 Shanghai achievements. The rehabilitation of the Shanghai legacy was given symbolic acknowledgment when the editorial office of *Popular Film* returned to the city. It had been closed down in Shanghai nine years earlier during the *Life of Wu Xun* campaign and transferred to Beijing.[108] In 1963 Li Lisan, a former Communist Party chairman disgraced after the 1930 failure of the urban putschism favored by the Shanghai-based Central Committee, published a film review in several newspapers. The film, *Fire on the Plain* (*Liao yuan*, 1962), was about a young revolutionary mobilizing workers at the Anyuan mines in western Jiangxi Province. Mao Zedong, Liu Shaoqi, and others had been active there in the 1920s. A film-inspired reminiscence by Li Lisan could not be a better indication of a measure of compromise between the Yan'an and Shanghai legacies represented by these men.[109]

An article in *Film Art* (*Dianying yishu*) in mid-1962 indicated the extent to which interventionism had been modified. Qu Baiyin's "Monologue on the problem of innovation in films" was reminiscent of the candor of Zhong Dianfei's Hundred Flowers "gongs and drums" article. If anything, Qu went further than Zhong. "Film is the youngest art, but it has already reached the stage of being stuffed with antique sayings." These oblique references to Mao and the cultural policies inspired by his Yan'an *Talks* were a striking feature of the stylishly written piece. Qu pointed to three "gods," those of theme, structure, and struggle, which dominated screen writing.

These various gods each demonstrated his divine power, and littered the universe with magic and mystic words about what ought to be done and what ought not to be done. Attacked by the various gods in unison, artists found all their movements hampered, and so had to find a way out, while protecting their heads with their hands. And the antique sayings [*chenyan*] constituted their only refuge.

Insistence on clarity of themes, Qu argued, should not "preclude all works of a far-reaching and profound significance." He questioned why films made for the broadest mass audiences had to be so predictable:

Such a magic power of the god of structure has an unexpected effect, which is that the blind can understand [the films] by listening and the deaf by looking, but those who are neither blind nor deaf find them totally uninteresting.

Qu urged that films not just deal with conflict between classes, but also with problems in socialist society, with the internal conflict in heroes' minds, and with other themes, such as love.

These words were as bold as any reported from the Hundred Flowers critique of the film industry. Moreover, they were closely associated with the Shanghai May Fourth film legacy. Elsewhere in his "monologue," Qu reflected his cosmopolitan outlook by contrasting current innovation in world filmmaking with the "antique sayings" of China's film efforts. He singled out Chinese filmmaking of the 1930s and 1940s as an exemplary time of innovation.[110] The extent of the cultural thaw of the early 1960s can be gauged by this article, for Qu, a film scenarist, also served as deputy head of the Shanghai Film Bureau.

The adjustment between cultural authorities and filmmakers (who were occasionally combined in one figure, as in Qu Baiyin's case) extended to other areas. In these years real discussion and exchange of views became possible regarding controversial films. A report on a meeting to assess *A Revolutionary Family* (*Geming jiating*, 1960), directed by Zhang Shuihua from a script by Xia Yan, is remarkable for its even-handed acknowledgment that some participants felt that the film had shortcomings, while others held an opposite view.[111] In his capacity at the Shanghai Film Bureau, Qu Baiyin helped draw up new regulations for censorship in late 1961. Filmmakers should be given the benefit of the doubt: "[In] all cases where it is difficult to determine whether a problem is a political, ideological, or artistic problem, it shall be dealt with as an artistic problem for the time being."[112]

In the studios, artists were encouraged to work collectively with a measure of greater autonomy. Qu Baiyin's censorship regulations suggested that "explanatory remarks added to a script by the film director shall not be subject to censorship," that "rehearsals shall not be visited by censors," that "no outsider shall be invited" to see the rushes of films in production, and that the studio head "shall notify the director of his intention to see sample rushes."[113] Creative groups (*chuangzuo zu*) continued to be active at the Changchun studio, combining directors, scenarists, cinematographers, and other specialists, who formed groups among colleagues sharing similar interests. Responsibility for most matters rested with the groups. Whereas the studio-level leadership once had been directly in command of separate groups, each working on one of the ten to twenty films in production at any one time, the five creative groups at Changchun provided a middle level of leadership in the studio. The Party secretaries who served as group leaders were apparently not just political watchdogs, for they were said to have "specialist film duties."[114] Such production collectives contributed toward an easing of generational tensions between older artists and a newly trained cohort, which began to find an outlet for its talents in the early 1960s. Some "rightists" returned to the studios in 1962 after four years in the political and artistic wilderness. Among them was Xiang Kun, who had played a microbiologist in the 1957 *Loyal Partners*. He returned to portraying a Guomindang general in a Beijing studio production.[115]

Both the cultural leadership and the filmmakers showed a greater awareness of audiences in the early 1960s. The general relaxation in Chinese political life was paralleled in a wider range of film subjects and a more ready recognition that films not only educated, but also entertained.[116] Viewers participated with apparent eagerness in the first of two national readership polls conducted by *Popular Film* to select the favorite movies of 1961 and 1962. The choices included some of the new comic and musical films which changes in artistic policy had produced.[117] The polls provided filmmakers with valuable information on their audiences' tastes and sophistication. These linkages in the 1960s between artists and audiences, which might help balance the relationship between Party and artists, were soon cut short; but they were reestablished at the end of the following decade.

The "ease of mind" which Zhou Enlai hoped to foster among both artists and cadres did not last long. Like the filmmaking ranks, the Party and cultural leadership was not a monolithic entity, manageable by a united executive at the top. Intra-Party divisions resurfaced. In late 1962 *Popular Film* could publish a relatively factual report on the death of Marilyn Monroe.[118] But a year later the magazine reproduced photographs of the National Day parade in Beijing in which a phalanx of marchers carried a huge slogan, "Literature and art serves peasants, workers, and soldiers," in front of a massive statue of Mao Zedong.[119] Although film had come a long way in the previous fourteen years from the narrow confines of Shanghai to finding a national mass audience, the parade float in 1963 indicated that some people wanted to return to the narrowness of Yan'an.

During the nine years between 1956 and 1964, film took its place as a major component in the new mass culture of China. The slowdown that had followed the Wu Xun episode was not repeated, despite the successive waves of interventionism in the second half of the 1950s. The mass culture, which feature films took to the furthest corners of China, was a national, homogenized, somewhat artificial culture. The artificiality came from its resolute antiregionalism and its hybrid origins as an amalgam of popular culture, the cosmopolitan, Shanghai-centered May Fourth heritage, and the paternalistic concerns outlined in Yan'an. This amalgam in turn reflected a mutual recognition by popular audiences, specialist filmmakers, and Party cultural leaders.

These three groups were far from static, and they continued to evolve and interact during their years of experience on the cultural battlefield. Audiences grew larger, and were less confined to urban, comparatively literate viewers. Differentiation of audiences became a tacit assumption: Some films would appeal to some viewers, but not to all. The ranks of experienced filmmakers also broadened in these years, diluting the significance of pre-1949 divisions with an influx of younger talent whose aspirations indicated increasing professionalism. Party authorities remained as disunited as ever. But the early 1960s moderating response to the interventionist excesses of the late 1950s was not shared by all factions of the leadership. An insurgent group dissatisfied with the Yan'an–Shanghai compromise of these years was determined to reform the mass national culture that had grown out of this compromise. Their "cultural revolution" brought more destruction than the Wu Xun, Anti-Rightist, and Great Leap episodes combined.

The first color feature, the opera film *Liang Shanbo and Zhu Yingtai*, 1954.

The revolutionary hero of *Guerrillas on the Plain*, 1955.

A May Fourth adaptation, *Family*, 1956.

Lü Ban's controversial comedy, *Before the New Director Arrives,* 1956.

Zhao Dan (left) plays a sixteenth-century pharmacologist in *Li Shizhen,* 1956.

Liu Qiong as the coach in *Girl Basketball Player No. 5*, 1957.

Zhao Dan as "Opium Commissioner" Lin in *Lin Zexu*, 1959.

The student revolutionary heroine of *Song of Youth,* 1959.

Enthusiastic youths in *The Young People of Our Village* (Part I), 1959.

An ancient folktale as a modern musical, *Third Sister Liu*, 1960.

Peasant revolutionaries in *Red Guards of Lake Hong*, 1961.

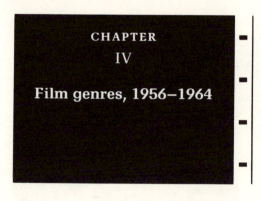

CHAPTER
IV

Film genres, 1956–1964

In the early 1960s, although the political fortunes of filmmaking continued to evolve at a number of levels, both outside and within the studios, feature films reached a degree of maturity that matched the growth of the industry as a whole. Several types of film illustrated this stylistic maturation. The genres analyzed here are not an exhaustive list of film types, but the films have been chosen for their significance. Analysis suggests that the styles were not simply the result of Party insistence on an uncomplicated and ideal film art in the new mass culture; rather, the films show, either directly or by contrary example, that some features were the outcomes of a three-way interaction among cultural authorities, film artists, and their audiences.

Certain stylistic features are shared by almost all films from this period. Movies presented "typical" characters and events, be they from the sixteenth, nineteenth, or twentieth centuries. This concern with types invested heroes and their problems with a direct and supposedly unambiguous relevance to the concerns and people of the present. While all art does this, in contemporary China the "typical" in art was a major theoretical concern of critics and practicing artists.[1]

A second shared stylistic feature of the films of this period owed much to this first feature. Filmmakers presented typical heroes, heroines, and their environments with a striking degree of glossiness and glamour. This avoidance of naturalism or critical realism sat comfortably with the concern for portraying types rather than highly differentiated individuals. The traditional Chinese aesthetic concern for beauty (*mei*), which to modern Western eyes not infrequently seems sentimental, also contributed to the apparent gloss in this modern medium.[2]

A third feature of Chinese filmmaking was the emphasis placed by both artists and bureaucrats on the writer of a film and the script, in contrast to the importance accorded directors. The scenarist was always given prominence over the director in film credits and also in reviews. Part of the reason for this was probably the censorship system. Unwanted elements could be weeded out from a written script before money was expended on rendering it into the much more diverse and potentially ambivalent combination of sight and sound on a screen. This emphasis on the written word, however, had been strong in Chinese filmmaking since the 1930s. It reflected the customary attitude of educated Chinese in granting more respect to the written word and its offspring, calligraphy and painting, than to stage art, for example. Film artists consciously approached their art in similar manner, as indeed did their intellectual companions, the Party cadres who acted as censors.

This respect for the written word helps account for a fourth feature of these films, the extended use of dialogue and stage-derived presentation. Whereas in contemporary Western films short, static scenes with a lot of dialogue are used to link extended periods of action, in Chinese movies from the 1950s and 1960s short action scenes link long sessions of talk in which the story and the characters develop. Directors tended to record these important, dialogue-filled scenes with relatively static cameras, underlining the theatrical quality of these tableaus. Given the strong backgrounds in modern drama of many of the older directors who were active in this period, this theatricality is not unexpected.

These and other features of this relatively mature period of Chinese film style were not simply the results of the paramount importance of the Party and its cultural requirements. On the contrary, these characteristics represent a combination of influences, particularly a shared consensus by Party cadres and artists, as members of the intellectual caste in Chinese society, of what their audiences could see and understand. Cadres and artists had more in common than the political upheavals in filmmaking might suggest; the distance between these two groups and most audiences was certainly wider.

The following six categories of films are arranged in descending order of their significance in the perceptions of Chinese audiences. This significance usually corresponded to the numbers of films in each category which were made in any year, with some exceptions. The first genre, minorities films, for example, had a visibility to Chinese filmgoers far out of proportion to the actual number of such films.[3]

Minorities films: Serfs and smiles

The People's Republic of China includes fifty-five minority peoples in addition to the predominant ethnic group, the Han Chinese. These minorities include Mongols, Tibetans, and Uighurs in the north and northwest, the Miao, Yi, Zhuang, and Bai minorities in the southwest, and Koreans and Manchus in the northeast. Also included in this listing are Muslims, whose religious practices set them apart from other Chinese. Although the minorities amount to a mere 6 percent of the total population, they occupy nearly 60 percent of the land area of the People's Republic, mostly in the strategic border regions.

Minority peoples have had a much larger presence on Chinese screens since 1949 than their numbers would suggest. The central government put great emphasis on the qualified assimilation and proper treatment of the minorities. Films that purported to show the way of life of these minority peoples, and their enthusiasm for socialism, contributed to the policy of national integration.

From the point of view of film audiences and filmmakers, the importance of minority films was related more to the search for the exotic which Chinese had associated with cinema since the first teahouse screening in 1896. Filmmakers could use a minority culture setting to produce films that entertained as much as they instructed. The areas offered the exoticism of a foreign setting, by the mid-1950s less often seen in Chinese theaters. As the equivalent of a foreign movie, artists could use a minorities film to essay subject matter, notably love stories, more infrequently given prominence in "regular" feature films. In this respect the northwest minorities, the Mongols, Kazaks, and Uighurs, might be called "hard" minorities. Films set in Xinjiang and Inner Mongolia more often emphasize class conflict and foreign espionage than do stories from the southwest. The latter was a "soft" area, where perhaps the subtropical climate made love stories more to be expected.

Apart from love, even a subject like social oppression could be illustrated more forcefully in a film set among non-Han peoples. *Serfs* (*Nongnu*, August First studio, 1963) is not a typical minorities film in terms of its depiction of oppression, but the strength of this portrayal may have been possible only in an exotic setting among a non-Han ethnic group. Han Chinese suffer the abuse of landlords and foreigners in a somewhat ritualized manner. *Serfs* presents the suffering of Tibetan peasants with more subtlety and hence with greater impact. The propensity of minorities films to explore normally avoided subjects gives *Serfs* this quality.

The film tells the story of the liberation of Tibet's serfs through the life of one of them, Jampa. Left an orphan after a serf owner has killed first his father and then his mother, Jampa grows up with his grandmother. He too suffers the oppression that has been the lot of his parents. He is made to act as a horse for the serf owner's son, a boy of his own age. Tibetan religious leaders also oppress the serfs, although Jampa's grandmother tries to inculcate religious belief in her grandson. As an adult, Jampa is allowed to become a lama as an act of benevolence by the living Buddha Thubtan, after the serf had transgressed his owner's rules. Scenes in the temple present claustrophobic images of striking artifice, in contrast to the natural simplicity of the landscape beyond the doors. It is not until a third of the way through the film that the first non-Tibetans appear, when People's Liberation Army doctors and nurses treat Jampa after he has been forced to carry Namchal, the serf owner's son, part of the way to the army camp. When he had set out, Jampa had knelt as a human footstool for Namchal to mount his horse. In a parallel scene, when Jampa leaves the field hospital, an officer leads him to a horse. Instinctively Jampa gets down on all fours to let the officer mount. The soldier helps him up, and presents the horse to Jampa to ride back.

The last big event in the film is the revolt of the serf owners and religious leaders in 1959. Jampa is forced to flee with his owner. Nearing the border, Jampa again acts as a beast of burden, carrying Namchal, who holds a gun to the serf's temples. Jampa flings Namchal down. As the two men struggle, Jampa's life is saved by a pursuing PLA soldier, the same Chinese who had given Jampa his first pair of shoes at the field hospital. In rescuing the serf, the soldier gives his life. Jampa returns to expose the treachery of the old religious and social order by bringing out a cache of arms hidden in the statue, which as an artisan lama he had helped create.

The strength of *Serfs'* portrayal of oppression derives from the work of three persons: the scenarist, the director, and the cinematographer. In writing the script, Huang Zongjiang deliberately chose to keep dialogue to a minimum, being aware of criticism, both foreign and Chinese, that overdependence on dialogue was a weakness of many Chinese films. Having a story with an exotic setting of non-Chinese speakers, who for the purposes of audience comprehension would have to speak Chinese, gave Huang a further reason for his decision to minimize the spoken word.[4] The casting of *Serfs* also encouraged the filmmakers to rely more than usual upon visual images. All the Tibetan roles in the film (over 90 percent of the parts) are played by Tibetans.[5] Images are particularly important in scenes featuring the hero, Jampa, who becomes dumb while a young man, in part as an act of defiance. Wangdui, who plays the part of the adult serf, was himself a former slave.

The authentic feeling brought to the acting by the Tibetan players is reinforced by the almost palpable textures of the black and white photography of Wei Linyue. Dark shadows, in or beside temples and serf owners' houses, are juxtaposed with the scorching brightness of nature, reinforcing a sense of the unnaturalness of the landowners' and lama leaders' oppression of the serfs.

The contribution of director Li Jun is seen from the opening sequence. The camera pans leftward along a seemingly endless range of the Himalayas. Mountain tops dissolve into temple roofs as the camera continues leftward to lamas on the roofs blowing long trumpets. The leftward motion proceeds down the length of the trumpets and out to the mountain ranges again, all the while accompanied by the boom of the instruments. Thus in a simple sequence the world of Jampa and other serfs is introduced, apparently cut off in its own sphere by the Himalayas. In the next scene, still backed by the trumpet sound, serfs appear carrying grain to the serf owner's granary, covered by a leftward tracking shot that helps link it to the preceding sequence.

Even in this first reel there are many examples of the masterful use of images. Jampa's mother, going to redeem her husband from the serf owner, hands her mother-in-law the baby without a word, not knowing if her husband is still alive or what her own fate will be. In one long take, the camera tracks and pivots between the two as the older woman takes the child from her daughter-in-law, and then watches through the door as she leaves. Shortly thereafter Jampa's mother is thrown into a dungeon. The darkness makes the process indistinct. The camera joins the eye of a fellow prisoner in tracking along her body from her shackled feet to her face: She is dead.

Simple devices are used effectively to emphasize the serfs' suffering. Jampa's growing up is suggested by a brief shot of the boy spinning a prayer wheel as he walks along. As in the case of his mother's death, suffering is shown indirectly and thus with less than usual rhetorical or theatrical flourish. A shot of horses approaching the camera gradually reveals that the fourth horse is in fact a man carrying the serf owner's son, Namchal. Li Jun avoids the haste that so often undermines the impact of images in many Chinese features. After Jampa has been savagely dragged by his owner's steward riding the horse lent to Jampa by the PLA, the background music stops and the camera stays fixed for a full four seconds (a long time for one silent shot) on the shoes, which have been torn from Jampa's feet. So underlined, the image is not wasted. Preserving the central tone of the film, fighting in the 1959 serf owners' uprising is not pictured but merely heard, as a blind artisan lama wanders through the dark temple seeking Jampa to explain what is going on.

The climactic sequence, when Jampa throws the fleeing serf owner from his back and the young Han soldier is killed, in setting, camera work, and editing sustains the skill of the rest of the film. The setting is a bare, steep slope of sand, allowing great scope to cameraman Wei Linyue, who works sometimes in exaggerated, low-angle long-shot. Nothing detracts from the struggle; the tension is strengthened by tight editing, in contrast to the more fluid camera work throughout many of the preceding scenes. At last Namchal is shot by the PLA man, who himself falls mortally wounded. No words are needed as the dying soldier draws from his chest a white Tibetan *hada* (scarf) and hands it to Jampa. The soldier dies. In a last act of respect, Jampa stretches the *hada*, red with Chinese blood, in Tibetan style down the length of the body as his tears flow. No more powerful image of Han–minorities brotherhood can be found in Chinese film from this period.

Serfs ends with the convalescent Jampa uttering his first words in years, when he sits up (in the living Buddha's former bedroom) and says: "I'll talk. I have so much to say." He turns to the portrait, newly hung on the wall: "Chairman Mao."[6] A cut to melting snow and mountains makes for an ending with a Chinese movie cliché. It recalls, however, the very first shots of the Himalayas. Now they no longer seal off a closed kingdom: Like the serfs' chains, they have been cut.[7]

In contrast to *Serfs*, many other minorities films from the pre–Cultural Revolution period blur the theme of class struggle by tending to glamorize the exotic. The southwest minorities in particular often appear in these films as "happy, smiling natives," more prone to drop axe and bow and burst into song than to take up arms against oppressors. Although film artists pay careful attention to the authenticity of costuming and customs, this type of presentation has pitfalls. A sort of "If it's three feathers, they must be Apache" syndrome arises as grinning Yi, Miao, Zhuang, Dai, Bai, and Dong dance across the screen. While filmed in a spirit of intercultural tolerance, the results paradoxically tend toward a homogenization of minorities culture into two main branches, southwest and northwest. Film as a powerful integrating element in the new mass culture seems often not to allow much differentiation among non-Han ethnic groups.

It is perhaps unfair to criticize the film *Ashma* (*Ashima*, Haiyan studio, 1964) for glamorizing its subject, for the film is a musical version of an ancient Yunnan legend. Nevertheless, *Ashma* illustrates some of the pitfalls of "soft" minorities films. Ashma, a young woman of the Bai minority, catches the eye of a chieftain's son. The girl resists his advances, saying she belongs to Ahei, but she is lured to the chieftain's home. Ahei, a brave young goatherd, uses his magic mountain-boring arrows in an effort to rescue Ashma from her captors. The lovers almost manage to escape before Ashma is drowned in a gigantic flood, and turns to stone. This is the legendary origin of the Stone Forest (*shilin*) in present-day Yunnan Province. The film's weakness lies in its departure from the source material. The legend is dressed up and presented with Western-style music, in a spirit not dissimilar from Rogers and Hammerstein.[8]

Minorities films did not, however, eschew relevance to current political campaigns. *Five Golden Flowers* (*Wuduo jinhua*, Changchun studio, 1959) combines singing and dancing with the Great Leap Forward emphasis on communes and production. Apeng, a Bai youth, made a date a year ago to meet at the Butterfly Spring a girl who called herself Golden Flower. When she fails to turn up Apeng sets out to find her, but he does not know her real name nor where she lives. After a few songs, a lot of scenery, and many smiles, Apeng finds his Golden Flower. During the search he discovers, and momentarily confuses (before smiling explanations), four other young women who are also called Golden Flower. One works at a local foundry, one drives a tractor, one is a stockyard worker, and the fourth is an "exemplary fertilizer and manure collector." At a colorful wedding feast Apeng finally finds his own Golden Flower, who is deputy leader of the commune. Retiring, for a song, to the Butterfly Spring, the couple are joined by the other Golden Flowers and their lovers for a last chorus. Periodically throughout the film the balance between comic confusion and aesthetic excess tilts in favor of the latter, and flowers and smiling Bai faces fill the screen as the music swells.

Settings in the southwest do not always mean love stories and songs. *Menglongsha Village* (*Menglongsha*, August First studio, 1960), the story of the efforts of a PLA work team in a Dai (Thai) village, is closer to the minorities films set in Xinjiang, for it involves foreign spies and class conflict. But even in Menglongsha, a tropical climate seems to soften the lines of class oppression. For example, after three days up to his neck in a chieftain's water dungeon, a Dai youth is released merely a little blue and enraged for the experience. The emphasis on suffering in *Serfs* is not applied to this Yunnan story.

The minorities films set in the northwest put more stress on class struggle and foreign intrigue. *Visitor on Ice Mountain* (*Bingshan shang de laike*, Changchun studio, 1963) is an impressive work, with its story of spying combined with lost love. Amir, a Uighur recruit to the PLA, thinks that the new bride of a local man is his childhood sweetheart Gulandam. When she fails to respond to his singing their favorite song of long ago, Amir begins to suspect that this woman is not the real Gulandam. She has in fact been sent across the border, the film now reveals, by a bandit leader to cause trouble on the Pamir mountain frontier. Although largely preserving the tone of intrigue and menace suitable for a spy film, the filmmakers cannot resist a song or two, as if minorities are somehow more wont to burst into a chorus than their Han brothers.[9]

Exoticism and class conflict are not incompatible. *Red Flower of Tianshan* (*Tianshan de honghua*, Xi'an and Beijing studios, 1964) also mixes an emphasis on revolutionary politics with fascination with the unfamiliar customs of a minority people, in this case Kazaks. Aikuli, a Communist Party member, is elected as brigade leader, much to the chagrin of the brigade veterinarian, the son of a former clan leader. He uses Aikuli's husband's disquiet with his wife's activism to make trouble. By subverting the success of the lambing season through leaving the door of the lambing shed open to the snow and wind, the vet attempts to discredit Aikuli. She and the Kazak masses thwart his evil designs. The locals' propensity for song and dance, however, is not ignored: This is, after all, a minorities story. Thus Aikuli and her friends join in a chorus to celebrate her selection as brigade leader and at various points later in the story.

Songs, of course, are fairly frequent features of pre–Cultural Revolution films set in the majority Han society, but the songs usually serve as background or interruption to scenes of the heroes pursuing their work. . In minorities films, however, the heroes actually dance and sing the songs, often in their native languages. The implication is that these somewhat undifferentiated peoples, as less sophisticated Chinese, are more prone to the pleasures of music than their Han brothers and sisters. Whether this was more than a fascination with the exotic is a moot point.

In a cultural enterprise and "foreign" medium in which a lot of lip service was paid to national style (*minzu fengge*), minorities films offered another attraction almost in contradiction to their exotic appeal. Filming Dai youths dancing in costume was an easier, more immediate way for artists and their managers to fulfill a supposed "national style" quota than trying to find a way of filming with national style a drama set perhaps among Tianjin city laborers or Henan peasants. Unlike steel mills and wheat fields, minorities areas offered instant "national style." The temptation to film such exotica was stronger for artists and the film leadership than the urge to explore, with the time, resources, and encouragement that the filmmaking enterprise rarely had in abundance, the possible filmic rendition of a Chinese style. Film remained, after six decades, a "foreign" medium. Paradoxically, one of the most effective ways to make films with "Chinese" style was to go to the most "foreign" cultural areas in the nation.

The results on screen were a rather homogenized presentation of the non-Han peoples. The mass national culture of which film after 1949 was a major shaper tended to simplify and deemphasize cultural differentiation throughout China. Minorities' differences from the Han majority could not be ignored, on film or anywhere else. Instead, a standardization of minorities was effected by which fifty-five separate ethnicities became classified into broader groups, including a northwestern collectivity in a harsh environment, a southwestern grouping living in a tropical garden, and Tibetans, who were perhaps distinctive and numerous enough to be treated separately.

The revolution: Proletarian nobility

Films about the revolution which ended with the Communist Party victory in 1949 share with minorities films a tendency to glamorize their subject matter. The revolution films from the 1956–64 period find their glamour less in exotic settings (although prerevolutionary Shanghai to many viewers in the 1960s must have seemed exotic) than in their central characters. These heroes share a righteous conviction that their cause will triumph, a belief that allows gestures of revolutionary nobility. Rhetorical flourishes from an otherwise stationary camera emphasize the heroism. What is lost in terms of subtlety and ambiguity is often compensated for by direct emotional power, particularly as Party martyrs march bravely to their deaths.

One of the most popular of revolution films from the early 1960s, however, has a setting similar to the minorities films. *The Red Detachment of Women* (*Hongse niangzijun*, Tianma studio, 1961) takes place in the tropical lushness of Hainan Island on the southern coast of Guangdong.[10] Compounding the exotic, the film follows the exploits of an all-female military unit in their battle against the local landowner. The heroine is Wu Qionghua, a defiant peasant who escapes from service in the landlord's mansion and makes her way to the Communist base area, where she joins the women's corps. There she matures into a disciplined fighter who subordinates her urge for personal vengeance against the landlord to the wider purposes of the revolution. She eventually does have the pleasure of shooting the landlord.

Qionghua shares the heroic center of the film with one of the male commanders of the women's detachment. Hong Changqing is Party secretary to the detachment—which means, of course, that a male is the ultimate authority in the women's troupe. Hong is instrumental in enabling Qionghua to make her initial escape from the landlord. Later, as he educates Qionghua in the revolution's tasks, there is a possibility of romantic interest between the two. This is immediately abandoned as a further assault on the forces of the landlord, Nan Batian (literally "tyrant of the South") takes place. In the course of the fighting, Hong Changqing is taken captive. He refuses to sign a confession and is executed by being burned at the stake. Wu Qionghua and the other women ultimately triumph, and at the end march on out of view, determined to perpetuate Hong's memory by succeeding in revolution.

Given the tropical setting, the filmmakers under director Xie Jin appear to have found it difficult to resist pictorial glossiness. In these film tropics the sun always seems to shine brightly, and it never rains. The base camp is a jolly place where women live in picturesque bamboo cabins. Their uniforms, and they all have them, seem immaculate most of the time. Details of subsistence in a revolutionary base area are given short shrift, unlike the pretensions to conspicuous consumption of Nan Batian as frontier landlord.

The explanation for this feature lies in part in Xie Jin's insistence, made clear in an article he wrote before the filming started, that the story has much of the quality of a legend (*chuanqi*) about it. Xie cited Hong Changqing's forays in the guise of a rich overseas Chinese into Nan Batian's lair as an illustration of the similarities the script shared with episodes from such ancient popular novels as *The Romance of the Three Kingdoms* and *Outlaws of the Marshes* (also known in English as *All Men Are Brothers*). In the same article director Xie hoped the color of the film would not be flashy (*tiao*), and that the element of romanticism would emphasize the characters' positive spirit.[11] After the release of the film, Xie noted that some viewers felt the presentation of revolutionary hardship was not strong enough. He responded that presenting the optimism of the revolutionary spirit was of more concern to the filmmakers.[12]

But the strengths of *The Red Detachment of Women* should not be overlooked. Xie Jin is a director noted for producing strong portrayals of women. He chose an unknown drama student to play Wu Qionghua, with impressive results. The young peasant woman gives way to the mature fighter. As Nan Batian, Chen Qiang makes the most of the negative role and is permitted by Xie to add some theatrical touches.[13] The martyrdom of Party secretary Hong is effectively handled. A zoom shot (one of only four in the film) to his blazing eyes underlines the nobility of the hero in his defiance. This type of shot in similar circumstances soon became a directorial cliché, but Xie Jin's use of the zoom has power because it contrasts with the largely stationary camera work of the rest of the film.

Xie Jin's *Stage Sisters* (*Wutai jiemei*, Tianma studio, 1965) is a more effective display of his talents. The story of two Shaoxing opera performers from their beginnings in a traveling troupe in the Zhejiang countryside to ultimate bitter rivalry in Shanghai in the 1940s might also have been exploited for its glamorous possibilities. Xie Jin's art had advanced considerably in the four years since *The Red Detachment of Women*. He allows the theatrical setting to speak for itself, while directing his camera in a relentless exposure of the decline of the relationship between the two women. Much of the work is reminiscent of *film noir*. The final confrontation takes place in court, when Zhu Chunhua exposes the Guomindang plans to ban a "subversive" Shaoxing opera performance, and a remorseful Xing Yuehong confesses that she was forced by her gangster lover to admit to the attempted blinding of her former stage partner. The emotional power of this confrontation overrides the optimistic, post-1949 ending, in which Zhu Chunhua returns with a new troupe to the country scenes of her early career.[14]

Most revolution film heroes are presented with more flourish. *Song of Youth* (*Qingchun zhi ge*, Beijing studio, 1959) is a more typical example of revolutionary heroics. Adapted with great care and at great length from her own novel by Yang Mo, the film is a florid eulogy to student revolutionaries of the 1930s.[15] The story follows the career of a young woman, Lin Daoqing, from near suicide through a failed marriage, efforts in the Beijing anti-Japanese student protest movement, and eventual triumph in the December 9, 1935, protest marches. Surviving December Niners (including some older filmmakers and Party cadres) might cherish such a self-portrait, but it is an idealization of the revolution. The December 9 demonstrations themselves did not directly stop Japanese encroachment into China proper.

Real revolution is seldom like what is shown in this film. At one point spring buds burst into time-lapsed bloom as Lin Daoqing reads some Soviet books, occasionally staring into the future with noble gaze. There seems to be a fine distinction between a critical presentation of the revolutionary limitations of these petit-bourgeois students and delight in the material details of their lives – for example, one scene is set at a ballroom dance complete with Coca-Cola neon light. In contrast, the most powerful scene is also the plainest. In prison Lin Daoqing listens to a statement of revolutionary purpose from her cellmate before the woman goes to her execution. Qin Yi delivers her lines with the usual nobility, but also with an emotional directness much appreciated by Chinese audiences.[16]

Not all films set in the revolution elaborate on reality. *Red Crag* (*Liehuo zhong yongsheng*, Beijing studio, 1965) shows what could be done in a revolution film with restrained heroics and less falseness. Black and white photography helps ensure restraint and suits the subject matter, a prison in Chongqing in the last days of the Guomindang regime there. The entire film has the feel of a 1940s Shanghai production to it, unlike most post-1949 revolution features. Similarities with the atmosphere, directing, and general style of *Shangrao Concentration Camp*, a 1951 production of the Shanghai Film Studio, are strong.[17] Shui Hua [Zhang Shuihua], the director of *Red Crag*, had served his artistic apprenticeship in progressive film circles in Shanghai before 1949. His cinematographer, Zhu Jinming, had in fact worked in the same capacity on *Shangrao Concentration Camp*, and contributes much to the impact of both films. The 1965 film features fine performances from an ensemble of actresses, headed by Yu Lan, as prisoners and from Zhao Dan, another figure closely associated with the pre-1949 film achievement. Zhao tempers the nobility of his characterization with some earthy touches, which add humanity to the hero. Xiang Kun, who was condemned as a "rightist" in 1957, acts as a Guomindang prison chief in both films. He is consistently filmed in the 1965 work at or under a window, as if to suggest that he too is a prisoner. *Red Crag*, like *Stage Sisters*, is a remarkable work from a year in which, for filmmaking, the Cultural Revolution had already begun.

The more typical revolution films made during the nine years before 1965, however, anticipate the aesthetic excess of the Cultural Revolution. Their emphasis on a stereotyped and often inauthentic heroism was a major element in the socialist mass culture in which film played a central part.

But it would be misleading to imagine that this polished unidimensionality was a new element. Chinese art and literature has always tended to standardize historical figures, particularly in opera, the core of Chinese performing traditions. After 1949, the revolution as a part of history became subject to this same process of standardization and cliché application. The treatment of these years in the film version of *The Song of Youth*, as indeed in the novel, owes as much to this cultural tendency as to a Soviet-inspired concern for the "typical" in socialist culture.[18]

Films like these were an important means of presenting a new pantheon of heroes who underwent, at the hands of filmmakers and cultural authorities, the rendering into idealization to which more ancient cultural heroes had been subjected over a much longer period. The result was a deeper place in the collective psyche. Not surprisingly, one of Jiang Qing's "model performances" (*yangbanxi*) during the Cultural Revolution was *The Red Detachment of Women* in a ballet version.[19] In the ballet the women's uniforms are even cleaner and the sun even brighter than in the 1961 feature film. But the similarity of cultural inspiration for these shared features should not be overlooked in a rush to approve the film and condemn the excesses of the ballet.

Contemporary subjects: Cheerful types

Films made between 1956 and 1964 dealing with contemporary Chinese life shared some of the characteristics of the other genres. Being about present-day ordinary subjects, however, meant that audiences noticed the tendency toward polish and falseness more than with less familiar subject matter. Minority peoples in subtropical Yunnan may in fact live like that, a Hebei Province viewer in the chilly north might feel, while convinced of the inauthenticity of a film set in a northern commune. Nevertheless, the two kinds of movies had much in common.

Film studios produced features on contemporary subjects to assist with current political, social, and economic campaigns. For education as much as entertainment, these films presented model characters in model situations. The "typical" nature of the characters and stories was designed so that the message conveyed by the actions on the screen could be applied by viewers directly to their own lives. The glossiness arose from filmmakers' and cultural leaders' concern to make the persons in the films and their actions attractive ideals.

Hard work is the delight of *The Young People of Our Village* (*Women cunli de nianqing ren*, Changchun studio, 1959). Exemplars of Great Leap enthusiasm in a North China mountain village, a group of young men, together with two young women, set out to construct an irrigation canal, which conventional wisdom said would take two to three years to complete. A subplot, involving two of the youths falling in love with one of the young women, adds interest to the story. It is the unhappy lot of one of the two men, the team leader, to speak on behalf of his friend to their shared object of affection. Eventually both men find love, and the canal is cut through the mountains.

This is hard work, and the director Sun Li presents the efforts of the construction team with the clear aim of eulogizing the heroes. They constantly climb around the mountains, the young men often in a state of partial undress, thrusting dynamite into rock bores and drilling holes into stone. It all gives the hard work an unreal, superhuman quality. Even the sweat on their bodies seems to glisten too brightly. Indeed, the love subplot helps prevent the film from becoming something of a parody of itself. Thrusting young torsos can become more wearisome for viewers than the work evidently is for the characters on the screen.

Youthful idealism is a common subject in these films. Healthy young bodies are also a feature of *Girl Basketball Player No. 5* (*Nülan wuhao*, Tianma studio, 1957), although they are more to be expected in a sports story. Scenarist and director Xie Jin uses the common device of contrast between the present day and life before 1949. Lin Xiaoji of the title finds that her mother, Lin Ji, is reluctant to allow her to pursue her sports career. It transpires that Lin Ji had once been engaged to her daughter's coach. When he was a player in a professional basketball team in the 1930s, coach Tian had been dismissed for refusing to lose deliberately a game with a foreign team. Lin Ji's father managed the team, and refused to allow her to marry the unemployed player. Eventually Lin Ji recognizes the different position of sportspeople in the new China and supports her daughter's ambitions. Lin Xiaoji herself learns that success depends on the sort of sacrifice coach Tian had made so many years before.

Although the flashback contrast with the sporting life before 1949 underlines the attractiveness of the present-day experience of young athletes, Xie Jin cannot resist further emphasizing the brightness of the present. On the screen the Shanghai women's basketball team enjoys comparatively luxurious accommodations: Even a locker room is furnished with armchairs and carpet. The women are an exceedingly happy lot, particularly as a group. This unremitting cheerfulness pervades the film and may help account for its considerable popularity among some Chinese viewers.[20]

Another much-loved film showed what could be done with a contemporary subject in terms of combining education and entertainment. *Li Shuangshuang* (Haiyan studio, 1962) presents a model commune member, with some faults, and her husband, who is annoyed by his wife's activism until he recognizes his own faults and attempts a reconciliation with his wife. The strengths of *Li Shuangshuang* derive from its script and from the skilled ensemble playing of Zhang Ruifang in the title role and Zhong Xinghuo as her husband, Sun Xiwang.

These two peasants, particularly Sun, are typical of the "middle characters" who emerged in fiction in the early 1960s. They are neither faultless nor irredeemable, but simply confused and uncertain. Li Shuangshuang first criticizes her husband, driving him out of their house, then misses him and brings him back. But she cannot contain further criticism and thereby loses him again, before they reach a final and lasting accord.

Although Li actively encourages several of the village women in reporting the menfolk's corruption, the process in which she must try to reconcile her affection for her husband with communal morality is one which more straightforward film heroines do not encounter. Likewise Sun Xiwang, while drawn into a little sideline moneymaking at the collective's expense, is essentially a good character who merely needs to be shown the error of his ways and encouraged to reform.

The comic potential in the domestic clash between Li and Sun is given considerable life and depth by scenarist Li Zhun, adapting his own short story. The dialogue between these two characters is exceptionally witty, in turn biting, teasing, and remorseful. Zhang Ruifang and Zhong Xinghuo use this material for all it is worth to give outstanding performances, drawing on audiences' enthusiasm for comic crosstalk (*xiangsheng*) to engage viewers.[21] These two roles are an acting tour de force.

Nevertheless, even in *Li Shuangshuang* the director and his team cannot resist the urge to varnish their subject. The village and the Li-Sun home are extraordinarily clean, spacious, and well-lit. Even the heroine and hero affect a smooth patina, which reminded some country viewers of urbanites portraying peasants. This shine, in which the film resembles more ordinary works, may in fact help account for its considerable popularity.[22]

The delight of some audiences in *Li Shuangshuang* perhaps derived more from admiration for a skilled theatrical performance than from any concern for authenticity of setting or presentation. The theatricality and skill of Chinese opera performance developed under similar audience expectations of artifice. In this case a film, the most modern medium, on a contemporary subject may have unconsciously tapped a strong cultural continuity.

Most other films on contemporary life did not appeal to audiences as much as some other styles of films. The enhancement of the "typical" perhaps could not be as effective when the types on the screen could be so readily contrasted with the reality outside the cinema. Exoticism, be it among other cultures or in an earlier age, has always attracted filmgoers in China, and elsewhere.

Musical films: Nationalized style

Musical films, which included adaptations of traditional opera, dance dramas, and musicals (*geju*), displayed the glossiness characteristic of other types of movies. This feature was more to be expected in a genre that eschewed naturalism and whose exoticism recommended itself to opera audiences in both theaters and cinemas. Filmmakers could embellish the fantastic aspect of opera by making snake spirits, fairy maidens, and gods of war actually seem to fly through the air. Musical drama, a modern form which combined dialogue and songs, usually dealt with more mundane stories and characters, but false sparkle also pervaded these films.

Handsome young scholars and beautiful maidens contend with evil, often supernatural, forces in most opera films. The opera version of the eighteenth-century novel *The Dream of the Red Chamber* (*Honglou meng*, coproduction of Haiyan and Hong Kong Jinsheng studios, 1962), however, presented no such personified divine intervention. Although Shaoxing opera was an old form, which originated in the region south of Shanghai, this adaptation of the novel was a new work in the genre, written after 1949. The libretto and the film preserve an unusually restrained tone, hewing close to the foreboding and ultimately tragic atmosphere of the novel. The filmmakers do not detract, with an intrusive camera, from the audience's enjoyment of the arias and the familiar love story of Lin Daiyu and Jia Baoyu. Director Cen Fan does not light his sets as brightly as those of many other opera films, nor ensure that his players' costumes and finery sparkle as much as is usual in such films. He adds subtle reference to the wealth and decline of the great families in the novel, for example, at the start of one scene by panning over rows of treasure chests before joining the principals. The integrity of this film version of the opera stands in sharp contrast to the version produced by another Hong Kong studio to compete with it. The glitter of that film does not match the tragedy of the story.

One notable feature of the opera films from these years is that the language used in many of them was not standard Chinese (*putonghua*). The dialogue and songs of Shaoxing and Cantonese operas are delivered in their conventional, local languages, in a rare concession to regionalism in Chinese films after 1949. Filmmakers tended to film more of Shaoxing opera than the other genres, perhaps because the relative intimacy of the stories, even when they included supernatural creatures, lent themselves to the intimacy of film treatment. Beijing opera, with its more martial and overtly political themes, was perhaps more difficult to transfer to celluloid. Female actors traditionally played all the roles in Shaoxing opera and spoke in an operatic version of the local dialect, while the songs, like all filmed opera arias, were subtitled. Thus many filmgoers were more likely to understand the songs than the dialogue. Fidelity to an established theatrical form meant that exceptions had to be made to the language rule in films.

The ostensible regionalism of *Third Sister Liu* (*Liu Sanjie*, Changchun studio, 1960), the most popular of the musical films, though not an opera, was a superficial concession to the origin of the story.[23] Third Sister Liu is a figure in the folktales of the Zhuang minority in Guangxi Province. This bold young woman, who seems to have lived during Tang times (A.D. 618–907), defends her fellow villagers against rapacious local landlords by articulating their folk wisdom in witty songs. The local literati are roundly humiliated by this bright and clever peasant girl. Faced with retaliation, Third Sister Liu and her lover leave on his boat, filling the mountains with her song.[24]

Like minorities films, particularly those set in the southwest, *Third Sister Liu* presents a somewhat generalized image of Guangxi Zhuang culture. The film tends to obliterate, with its pictorial lushness, the regional aspects of the story and the characters. Even the spectacular setting of the karst mountains of Guilin, with all the beauty of water, sky, and mountains which this offers, makes for a national, rather than a specific, atmosphere. This setting, enhanced by the painterly qualities of the cinematography, takes on a symbolic role as a quintessentially Chinese environment, representative of the entire culture. Some critics in fact complained of the film's presentation of somewhat radical peasants, objecting that the folktale had been "modernized" at the expense of its original local qualities.[25] This pictorial homogenization of a regional folktale was a feature which *Third Sister Liu* shared with most other musical films.[26]

Musical films had much in common with the minorities genre, and indeed they were often set among non-Han peoples. Both types of movie illustrated the role of film in propagating a standardized mass culture. Despite concessions to regionalism, notably in local opera styles, the films presented a nationalized version of localism, taking the local features and putting them on a higher and national plane. This "elevation" of regional popular culture was in the spirit of the Yan'an *Talks'* emphasis on elevating and polishing folk art and literature. In the process of joining the mass national culture, however, much of the musical drama and folktale treasury was polished to a sparkle and divorced from its local roots. The contradiction was perhaps unavoidable.

May Fourth adaptations: Remembrance of times past

Many of the most prominent filmmakers in the 1950s had been members of the later May Fourth generation of artists and naturally tried their hands at adapting works by May Fourth writers. Xia Yan, active in drama circles in Shanghai in the 1930s, was one such figure. More broadly, filmmakers of even a younger generation were inheritors of the tradition established under May Fourth influence in the decade before the War of Resistance to Japan. At Yan'an during the war, Mao Zedong had indicated that the Communist cause had little to do with the petit-bourgeois concerns of May Fourth writers, and called on those present to seek a wider audience to popularize their art. The rigidity of the Yan'an outlook regarding May Fourth writing gave way in the early 1960s to a more generous recognition of the pre-Yan'an, progressive literary legacy. With its potential to reach the widest audiences, film adaptation of May Fourth literature was to be expected.

Despite its pioneering use of the vernacular language and its pretensions toward popular appeal, May Fourth literature was an acquired, largely middle-class, taste. Adaptation to film after 1949 required concessions to the taste and expectations of a mass audience. In the process, complex narrative modes, for example, were abandoned for the sake of a more readily comprehensible exposition reminiscent of traditional storytelling. In the changed political circumstances also, some May Fourth ambivalence had to be stiffened and made less ambiguous for mass consumption on screen.

But the May Fourth heroes and heroines in such adaptations, who seemed somewhat prettified, resembled their counterparts in other film genres. This tendency may have derived from the adaptors' urge to make the original stories more widely appealing, and to emphasize positive denouements. With these upbeat endings, the desire to be critical of their heroes by pointing out their petty foibles could backfire. The twin aims to popularize and enlighten ironically could give an adaptation a degree of ambiguity, which disturbed some critics.

Adaptation could undermine the original spirit of a work. Xia Yan himself wrote the first post-1949 May Fourth adaptation, *The New Year's Sacrifice* (*Zhufu*, Beijing studio, 1956), based on a story by Lu Xun, the preeminent twentieth-century Chinese writer. The changes made in the film version are a good indication of the concerns for mass culture of filmmakers and cultural administrators. Lu Xun's narrator starts the story close to its end, when he encounters Xiang Lin's wife and finds he cannot answer her question, "After a person dies, does he turn into a ghost?" Narrator and reader then proceed to discover what has brought Xiang Lin's wife to ask this question. The distancing effect of an inadequate narrator, a favorite Lu Xun device, makes the story of Xiang Lin's wife more poignant and an indirect, though powerful, indictment of the society in which she lived and suffered.

In bringing this story to a mass audience, Xia Yan gives it a beginning and an end. The film follows the life of Xiang Lin's wife chronologically from her first marriage and widowhood, through kidnapping and second marriage, loss of her child and second husband, to eventual insanity and social ostracism. With these changes in narrative technique, the tone of the film version differs radically from the Lu Xun original. Straightforward exposition of the woman's tragedy by an implicitly sympathetic camera replaces Lu Xun's use of irony in showing the indifference of the townspeople, narrator included, to the fate of Xiang Lin's wife.[27] An off-screen voice announces at the start: "For young people today, this is a story of long, long ago. About forty years ago, around the time of the 1911 revolution, in a remote village in Zhejiang. . . ." The same voice returns at the end of the film, as the heroine collapses in the snow: "Xiang Lin's wife, a lively, optimistic woman, after suffering countless difficulties and hardships, fell down and died. This happened more than forty years ago. Yes, this is a thing of the past. What we should celebrate is that times like these finally passed on. They are over and will not return."[28]

Xia Yan also added elements not in Lu Xun's original story in order to make the message of the film clear to all viewers. Xiang Lin's wife is presented resisting her fate, chopping madly, for example, at the temple doorstep, to which she had subscribed in the hope of assuaging the spirits of her dead relatives. A landlord's steward sets out to collect a debt from the heroine's second husband, in a scene not mentioned in Lu Xun. Concern to show viewers landlords' oppression of their tenants reflects a post-1949 view of the past, of which Lu Xun felt his readers did not need reminding.[29]

Leaving aside the problems of adaptation, *The New Year's Sacrifice* shows painstaking care on the part of the director Sang Hu, who had been prominent in Shanghai film circles before 1949, and his team of artists. The film does not lack depth, only most of Lu Xun's particular subtleties. The initial presentation of the Lu family, for example, when Xiang Lin's wife first joins them as a servant, is remarkably well planned. Shots of the plaque above the Lu mansion gate are followed by closeups of New Year slogans freshly written by the master of the house. He is teaching his young grandson calligraphy. Most viewers may not see anything special in this montage of written images, but an educated Chinese audience would detect the emphasis on the literary culture of a rich landlord like Lu, and the preservation of this literate monopoly by his successors. The simplification and popularization that film adaptation of May Fourth writing seemed to require did not preclude a film from appealing on a number of levels.

The subjects of many May Fourth stories did not lend themselves to film adaptation. In 1958 Xia Yan also scripted *The Lin Family Shop* (*Linjia puzi*, Beijing studio, 1959) from a 1932 story by Mao Dun, who in the 1950s became minister of culture. Although this is the finest May Fourth adaptation, Xia's difficulties were compounded by the subject matter, for the central character in Mao Dun's story is a small-time merchant. Xia Yan's problem was to rewrite for 1950s screens (and commemoration of the tenth anniversary of the founding of the People's Republic) a 1930s lament for the patriotic bourgeoisie suffering the economic hardship of foreign competition. The adaptor and Shui Hua, the director, are at great pains to deter audiences from sympathizing with shopkeeper Lin, or indeed with almost anyone in the film. Through camera angles and sound effects, Lin's desk and his clattering abacus are made to dominate many scenes in the shop. An off-screen narrator, as in *The New Year's Sacrifice*, summarizes the film at the end, assuring viewers that Lin's plight is rendered insignificant in the broader context of mass impoverishment. Xia Yan in fact added scenes in which Lin mistreats his subordinates and poorer customers.[30]

The seeming blandness of *The Lin Family Shop* derives in part from the filmmakers' caution with an unorthodox "hero," and in part from respect for a classic of May Fourth fiction. The details of the original are all presented, including a shot of Ms. Lin's cat after its young mistress has flung it off her bed. The closeup, on a large screen in bright color, looks positively cute. Respect for a classic is indicated also in the titles sequence at the start. The credits appear in a book, with Mao Dun's title on its cover, turned by an unseen hand. Film touches, however, are not absent. The turning of the book pages fades into the turning of an oar in a Zhejiang canal. Images of a canalside town follow, then the camera returns to water level. Suddenly a basket of slops splashes into the canal, and as the ripples spread out, the date (1931) appears on the screen.[31] Here again, the adaptation, like any work of art, could appeal at different levels to different viewers, while making sure that its message served the cultural requirements of the late 1950s.

The problems of May Fourth adaptation are most clearly shown in *Early Spring in February* (*Zaochun eryue*, Beijing studio, 1963), scripted and directed by Xie Tieli, who had served as assistant director of *The Lin Family Shop*. The original 1929 novella *February* (*Eryue*) had been criticized for its excesses by Lu Xun himself, even if the martyrdom in 1931 of Rou Shi, its Communist author, may have given the work apparent revolutionary credentials for film adaptation. The story centers on the experiences of a would-be revolutionary, Xiao Jianqiu, who retires from political activism to take up a teaching position in a small Zhejiang town. There he is torn between the attractions of Tao Lan, the young sister of a colleague, and sympathy for widow Wen, whose husband Xiao once knew. After the widow's younger child dies, Xiao out of pity makes a painful decision to save the widow by marrying her. Xiao's pain is obvious, and the widow Wen hangs herself. The story ends with Xiao deciding to leave the school and Tao Lan in order to return to the revolutionary mainstream.

The filmmakers attempted to improve on the ambiguous morality of the original novella. Xiao appears on the screen with more positive traits, such as his commitment to his students' progress. Tao Lan's romanticism, egoism, and ambition to travel abroad are softened in the film version. The two young people even occasionally leaf through copies of *New Youth* (*Xin qingnian*), a radical journal of the 1920s. They also, however, indulge in tempestuous Western piano music (filmed at exaggerated angles) and self-conscious flirting. Xie Tieli's ending emphasizes the noble resolve of Xiao to rejoin the revolution. In the last shot Tao Lan is left rushing over a high, arched bridge, the other side of which cannot be seen, as if she too seeks to become a political activist by catching up with the departed Xiao.

The result of this effort to make these two characters more positive or more acceptable, as critics in 1964 charged, is an inconsistency of tone. This is particularly true in the case of Tao Lan, whose gradual education as a May Fourth radical is unconvincing. Whereas the makers of *The Lin Family Shop* tried to avoid extending sympathy to their central character, Xie Tieli presents an essentially sympathetic picture of two characters whose actions sometimes seem pointless or difficult to defend. A viewer may even want to snigger when "Miss Tao," as she is called in English in the novella and film, stormily plays the piano on hearing of the death of widow Wen. At the beginning of the Cultural Revolution the film came under fire for its "bourgeois humanitarianism."[32] But these critics were not popular, for the book of the film, with all its sentimentality and romanticism, was one of the best-selling volumes among the sort of urban, educated book buyers who before 1949 had formed the May Fourth writers' audience.[33]

Xie Tieli's assured direction of *Early Spring in February* should not be undervalued. The first sequence is an indication of the quality that follows. During the titles, the portrait of the martyred author, Rou Shi, on a paneled wall gives way to moving scenery in the portrait's frame. It is a window, but whether on a boat or train is unclear. Once the titles are over, the camera tracks rightward along the paneled wall of what appears to be a baggage room, and pans and tracks through the frame of a doorway into a crowded boat cabin and across the faces of some passengers to another window, where the Zhejiang scenery is again seen going steadily by. A young passenger has his head turned away from the camera, looking out at this scenery through the window. He turns back into the cabin and toward the camera. It is Xiao Jianqiu on his way to his teaching post. Such careful consistency of direction throughout the film is not matched by the inconsistency of its story and characters.

The adaptors of these May Fourth films found such ambiguity difficult to avoid.[34] One factor was their respect for the original work as a piece of literature by then considered a classic, particularly in view of the failure of most post-1949 writing.[35] Adaptors went to great lengths to preserve the events and characters of the original and something of its tone. On the other hand, the scriptwriters and directors were obliged to make changes in the originals in order to satisfy the more emphatic political expectations of art after 1949 and to ensure the accessibility and appeal of the films to an audience far more heterogeneous than the original works had ever enjoyed. Given this simultaneous respect for the original and the urge to change it, ambivalence in the completed films is not surprising.

History films: Past nobility

During the period 1956–64, nonoperatic film treatments of the more distant past before the revolution concentrated on patriotic figures. Commissioner Lin Zexu, who attempted to block opium imports into southern
China in the late 1830s, was clearly a member of the dynastic ruling
class, but his efforts to defend China against foreign encroachment were
laudable. The same is true of Deng Shichang, a Beiyang naval captain, in
his heroic resistance to Japanese attack and imperial corruption in the
1890s. Going much further back, Li Shizhen, the sixteenth-century pharmacologist who made the greatest contribution to the development of
traditional medicine, could also be presented as a patriot in his insistence on strengthening this Chinese science. The film reincarnations of
these three men placed them firmly in a popular context. The masses –
Guangdong river people, Shandong fisherfolk, and Zhejiang peasants –
enjoy close ties with the three historical figures. The masses support
their patriotic actions and are in turn of major concern to the heroes.

The nobility invested in the film representation of these historical
personages calls to mind the portrayal of the heroes of the revolution
film genre. Given the class origins and official positions of these historical protagonists, the films' ahistorical emphasis on the heroes' connections with ordinary citizens can seem forced and even carry overtones of
paternalism.

Deng Shichang, the hero of *Naval Battle of 1894* (*Jiawu fengyun*,
Changchun studio, 1962) alternates between bureaucratic conflict in the
Qing court and outdoor action leading his men, and their families,
against the Japanese and traitors. Director Lin Nong makes a deliberate
contrast between Deng's two worlds by filming the scenes in which the
captain battles with Li Hongzhang and his supporters with a formality
absent from the relative naturalism of scenes with his crew and with the
Shandong fisherfolk. The camera thus plays up the formalism of court
ritual, with angles and editing to emphasize the effect. When Deng visits
the fishing village, he is more relaxed and is treated as an ally by the
people.[36]

Lin Nong presents both Deng's resolve to continue the battle against
his enemies and the connections between Deng and his men in a word-
less scene unusual in Chinese films, which are noted for their lengthy
dialogue. The sailors hear in the distance one evening the sound of a lute
(*pipa*) being played in an agitated manner. They go to investigate. The
camera cuts to a pair of hands plucking the strings. The audience then
discovers that Deng is playing the instrument, the crashing of the music
reflecting his emotional conflict at being suspended from his duties
through the machinations of his enemies at court. As the sailors respect-
fully approach, unseen by Deng, the music grows at once more regulated

and majestic. Deng is quickening his resolve. A string breaks, Deng stops, and hearing a sound outside his room, flings open the lattice doors. He discovers his men in the courtyard, and the sailors simultaneously find that the lute player is their captain. Together they vow to fight on. The film's use in this scene of a well-known piece of traditional music meshes with the patriotic theme.

The film ends with a cliché, seen also in revolution films. Deng Shichang seizes the helm of his battleship and heads at full speed toward the Japanese flagship. The camera cuts to waves crashing onto rocks, as a heavenly chorus starts up. The noble face of Captain Deng is superimposed on this concluding image. Waves crashing were a favorite device of Chinese directors to represent the tides of patriotism and revolution. It suggests that nature itself is proceeding in the direction in which the film heroes are headed and that their struggle has cosmic dimensions.

Like Deng Shichang in Shandong, Lin Zexu embodies the patriotic ideals of the Guangzhou masses. As one of the films produced to commemorate the tenth anniversary of the founding of the People's Republic of China, *Lin Zexu* (Haiyan studio, 1959) presents a noble portrait of its hero. Here too, the formalism and ritual of court and yamen are contrasted with the grit of mass scenes at the construction of forts and destruction of smuggled opium. Veteran Shanghai director Zheng Junli allows Zhao Dan, in the lead role, to flesh out the script's portrait of Commissioner Lin with small touches, such as his ill-controlled glee at trapping the British ships in the Pearl River estuary.[37] Lin fails to stop the influx of opium, succumbs to bureaucratic intrigue, and is exiled to the far northwest. A final sequence, in which the people's militia of Sanyuanli village traps a party of British redcoats, is interrupted by a shot of Lin on his journey to exile turning to gaze nobly into the far distance, as if he too can see the small triumph of the peasants and fisherfolk he had tried to serve. The Chinese defeat in the first Opium War is not shown. Instead, an off-screen voice reminds the audience that the Sanyuanli skirmish fired the first shots in a century-long battle against imperialism and feudalism. The 1840s militia stand firmly, jaws jutting, as their proud banners wave.

These screen portraits of historical figures often come close to being unconscious and idealized self-portraits of the modern intellectuals who made them. This is particularly apparent in *Li Shizhen* (Shanghai studio, 1956). The movie presents almost sixty years in the life of its hero, from the youth's decision to study medicine to the old pharmacologist's completion of his fifty-two-volume compendium on medicinal herbs. Li eschews scholarly ambition in the official examination system in favor of more practical assistance to the ordinary folk. He generously treats the poor while sternly opposing the corruption and superstition of established and conservative medical practitioners. In the company of his peasant apprentice, Li spends years away from home and creature comforts, collecting specimens for his multivolume compendium. Although he cannot find a publisher, time at least allows him to finish the massive work.

Zhao Dan again plays the historical hero with a nuance that makes his nobility more human than the story might otherwise allow. Coming upon a plant for which he has searched for years, Li gleefully flings himself onto his back in the patch to savor his discovery, crushing the plants in the process. Zhao conveys the growing mental and physical infirmities of old age and Li's frustration at not finding a publisher who might bring his work to a wider audience and thus save more lives at the hands of druggists, who presently rely on inaccurate prescriptions.

Director Shen Fu plays up the painterly quality of his sixteenth-century subject matter. The film in fact starts and ends with a traditional landscape painting. In filming Li on a boat on a river, or searching the mountains for medicinal plants, Shen Fu clearly draws inspiration from classical Chinese painting. Even the crowded urban scenes, as Li looks in vain for a publisher, call to mind the detail and atmosphere of a painting like the famous twelfth-century *Qingming Festival on the River* (*Qingming shanghe tu*). Li's visit to the palace of a prince is presented with camera compositions that are a reminder of earlier Tang court portraits.

This painterly quality, however, contributes to the rather static exposition. Important scene follows important scene, somewhat in the manner of a stage play. This general characteristic of Chinese films derived from the theatrical backgrounds of many filmmakers from the pre-1949 generation, including Shen Fu and Zhao Dan. The emphasis on the film script and the scenarist, rather than on the shooting script and the director, compounded this tendency to present a subject with less fluidity than the medium might otherwise allow.

One small scene includes an interesting illustration of the clarity filmmakers and cultural leaders felt was needed by some viewers. Seated in a rude hut on a mountainside as a snowstorm howls outside, Li Shizhen tries to thread a needle to repair his clothing. An old donkey driver, who has accompanied Li and his apprentice, remarks that if Li were at home, his wife would perform this domestic task for him. The statement seems designed to signal for audiences that the superimposed image of Mrs. Li, which then appears beside the doctor's head, is not a ghost, but a device to indicate that the old pharmacologist is thinking of home.

Deng Shichang, Lin Zexu, and Li Shizhen all appear as noble figures who articulate the patriotic or democratic aspirations of the lower orders. It would be wrong, however, to ascribe this portrayal simply to the requirements of the Party view of historical development. The portrayal of Li Shizhen in particular derives perhaps as much from Chinese intellectuals' self-image as spokespersons for and leaders of the inarticulate "masses." The ever-grateful countryfolk gather silently in awe after Li Shizhen has conducted and won a debate with a conservative druggist. The "masses" hope that Li will find a publisher for his compendium. Li's laying his hands on a poor patient has an almost religious quality. The actor Zhao Dan himself thought up the gesture, in which Li, about to examine the sick woman, first holds his hands up to the rays of sunlight streaming in the window to warm them.

This self-image of the intellectuals' vanguard role for the common people is an ancient one. May Fourth intellectuals, while rejecting much of Confucian morality, unconsciously took on this image of themselves. The Chinese Communist Party, founded two years after the May Fourth incident of 1919 by university professors, schoolteachers, and others, likewise held this self-image, even if Leninism gave it a seemingly modern and scientific caste. Filmmakers, like other intellectuals, continued to subscribe to this view of the role of the educated in Chinese society. The nobility which can be detected in both revolution and historical genre film heroes thus has roots far deeper than cultural bureaucrats' prescriptions.

The stylistic features that these typical and few untypical films shared were outcomes of a nexus of influences. What to a superficial observer might seem simply an artistic response to the overriding concern that literature and art be subordinate to politics often was not so simple. Film artists were not ciphers, and the films they made could not help but reflect their concerns and attitudes. Not infrequently these attitudes were shared by both Party cultural leaders and filmmakers. As Chinese intellectuals and inheritors of the modern May Fourth orientations toward nationalism and social concern, artists and managers were not as dissimilar as much of the political history of Chinese filmmaking might suggest or as Mao indeed had argued in his Yan'an *Talks* twenty years earlier.

As educated Chinese, filmmakers and Party cultural bureaucrats perhaps had more in common with each other than with the audiences they supposedly served. The stylistic concentration on the glossy, exotic, or noble was not solely a response to the political requirements imposed on film art. The emphasis arose also from a degree of unenforced consensus, shared by artists and bureaucrats, about what Chinese audiences were accustomed to seeing in art and were capable of comprehending. The glamour of the presentation of the young men in *The Young People of Our Village*, of Third Sister Liu, or of the revolutionary students in *Song of Youth* derived from a mix of concerns in which the hands of artists and the contributions of politicians are difficult to distinguish. So too, the nobility of revolutionary heroes or ancient intellectuals such as Lin Zexu and Li Shizhen reflected a broad self-image artists and cadres shared.

The apparent simplicity and absence of ambiguity in these films also arose from a consensus between artists and cadres about audiences, and not merely from the political concerns of the Party cultural leadership. Simplicity, moreover, did not rule out the possibility of different levels of appeal, as two May Fourth adaptations, *The Lin Family Shop* and *Early Spring in February*, show. Nonetheless, audiences that had no difficulty with, and indeed delighted in, the rapid transitions of time, space, the earthly, and the supernatural on the opera stage were generally deemed to find disturbing or incomprehensible similar transitions on film screens.

Many artists and cadres seem to have shared this underestimation of "the masses," a catchall term for "them," as opposed to the educated "us." Given the antiquity of this social and intellectual divide, these modern films, in this respect, strongly reflected a national style, even if it was not recognized as such. The great change which the Cultural Revolution effected in Chinese society made recognition of this divide and its style more likely.

Xie Jin's comedy, *Big Li, Little Li, and Old Li,* 1962.

Articulate peasants in the comedy *Li Shuangshuang,* 1962.

Xie Tieli's controversial May Fourth adaptation, *Early Spring in February*, 1963.

An unusual presentation of minorities in *Serfs*, 1963.

A naturalistic representation of peasants in *Jiangnan in the North*, 1963.

The musical version of a minority folktale, *Ashma*, 1964.

(*above & below*) Xie Jin 's homage to film noir, *Stage Sisters*, 1965.

Revolutionary martyrdom in *Red Crag*, 1965.

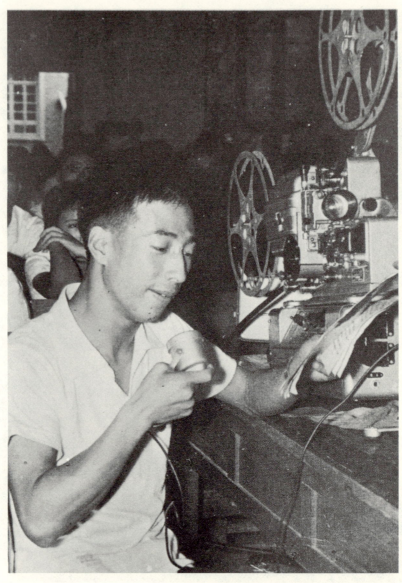

A well-equipped country projectionist in the mid-1960s.

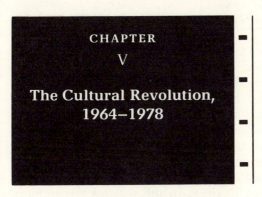

The comfortable presumption that the Cultural Revolution that Mao launched officially in 1966 was simply a distorted and atypical phase of political extremism and forced mobilization, distinct from the years before and after that unfortunate period, is misleading. The Cultural Revolution is significant as much for its continuities with the rest of Chinese history since 1949 as for its disjunctions with what came before and what followed. Until the mid-1960s, three themes had dominated Chinese film history: the tensions between Yan'an and Shanghai, the use of film to help shape a mass national culture, and mutual influences and conflict among Party, artists, and audiences. Out of the destruction and stupidity of the Cultural Revolution these themes were highlighted and eventually modified.

The tensions between a Yan'an-derived view of art and artists and a May Fourth attitude to artistic endeavors, associated with Shanghai, came to a head during these years of political and cultural upheaval. The figures who represented the Yan'an cultural ethos were different from its representatives in the 1950s. Moreover, during the Cultural Revolution these new Yan'an stalwarts were more dominant than any such faction had been in cultural activities in the preceding decade and a half. Ironically, this new group based itself in Shanghai and on the control of the propaganda apparatus in that city. The cultural insurgents repudiated the older, May Fourth cosmopolitan outlook once associated with Shanghai, and tried to eliminate its representatives.

A second theme prominent during the Cultural Revolution derived in part from the first. The efforts at using film to propagate a nationwide mass culture intensified in the late 1960s and early 1970s. Furthermore, the holders of cultural power during these thirteen years sought more self-consciously than their predecessors to establish a sinified film style. This new style eschewed cosmopolitanism and drew its inspiration from the modified Chinese operatic tradition. In this way, the earlier emphasis on combining revolutionary realism and romanticism was taken a step further. While these styles and the cultural powerholders were soundly repudiated after 1976, their forced sinification of film had profound effects on subsequent developments.

During the Cultural Revolution the relationships among Party, artists, and audiences were accentuated and ultimately transformed. Despite appearances, Party cultural officials did not necessarily exercise stronger control than previously. But their actions were definitely more inconsistent and arbitrary than they had been before. Artists were banished or recruited with only limited consistency, and films were criticized or praised in a similar manner. Audiences had little voice in the proceedings. Here again the subsequent changes in the relative strengths of Party, artists, and audiences in the late 1970s and 1980s owed much to the experience of all three groups during the Cultural Revolution. While the Party faction in power changed in October 1976, the prestige of the Party as a whole suffered greatly from the cultural and political posturing of the Gang of Four faction. Film audiences were consequently more critical after 1976 than they had ever been in the seventeen years before 1966.

The political events of 1966–9 gave us the term Cultural Revolution, which is generally applied to the eleven years before 1976. In fact, the Cultural Revolution is best thought of as the years 1964–78. For film, as for all literature and art, the first salvos of what became the Cultural Revolution sounded in mid-1964, when several films were singled out for extended, officially endorsed criticism. Although there were modifications in filmmaking at the beginning of the 1970s, when the so-called radical political leaders moderated their policies somewhat, the regime that had taken the lead in 1966 lasted until late 1976. In October of that year, the Gang of Four, who had attempted to control cultural activities tightly, were arrested by decision of other factions in the Party leadership. The direct effects of that regime lasted in filmmaking for another two years. The years 1964–78 thus form a coherent unit in the history of Chinese film.

Years of shadow war

Change and disruption in the film industry after 1964 reflected, as always, changes in cultural activities in general. The insurgent powerholders during this period called for a "wartime literature." They emphasized the social and political functions of literature and art to an even greater extent than had been usual since Mao Zedong's 1942 Yan'an *Talks*. The ultimate political disgrace of the purveyors of this literature ensured that the official endorsement of their cultural policies did not last.

Filmmaking went through several phases in this long span of fifteen years. In a prologue to the central events of the Cultural Revolution, the lines of conflict were drawn between Yan'anite Party insurgents and

Shanghai May Fourth filmmakers. In 1966, fiction filmmaking stopped completely. When production resumed four years later, the only films made were of the "model performances" endorsed by the new cultural leaders. The scope of the new films widened as the political position of the insurgents weakened in the early 1970s. They lost power in October 1976, and the last Cultural Revolution phase was an epilogue in which filmmakers found it hard to pick up the pieces of their profession after the devastation caused by the previous eleven years.

During the prologue to the Cultural Revolution proper, the insurgent advocates of a militant literature put increased emphasis on the amateur artist and on martial subjects and artists. Jiang Qing and Lin Biao, the chief of the armed forces, headed a Party faction that sought to take control of literature and art. Their immediate power base was in the cultural units of the armed forces. An article in the July 1965 issue of the *Literary Gazette* entitled "Study the PLA's experience in training amateur writers" encapsulated the new emphasis in its very headline.[1] By the end of that year, many of the few new feature films were celluloid versions of stage performances of the new-style operatic morality play, which the rising cultural faction favored. A large proportion of the nondocumentary movies were on military subjects.[2] The emergent leaders gained further influence through a national Forum on Army Literature and Art Work held in Beijing in February 1966.[3]

At this conference Jiang Qing and her supporters made new attacks on the cultural leaders they hoped to supersede. Promulgation in early 1966 of the notion of a seventeen-year "dictatorship of a black line in literature and art" (*wenyi heixian zhuanzheng*) brought together earlier, disparate published criticism of key figures in the older generation of cultural leaders, particularly those with a Shanghai background in the 1930s and 1940s. The earlier criticism in 1964 had included rejection of the films *Early Spring in February*, which was associated with Xia Yan, and *Jiangnan in the North* (*Beiguo Jiangnan*), scripted by Yang Hansheng. By 1966 the list of criticized films had lengthened to include many works that allegedly peddled a "bourgeois" rather than a correct, "proletarian" view of the Chinese past. At the beginning of the Cultural Revolution the critics set these films, which they labeled "poisonous weeds," against the modernized opera, which they offered as models for a new culture.

During 1966, filmmaking ground to a halt. As a former movie actress convinced of her own political importance, Jiang Qing held a high opinion of the significance of film as a medium for purveying what she and her cohorts judged to be negative and positive influences on audiences. The danger of established filmmakers using the medium's power for ends inimical to their own encouraged Jiang Qing and her allies to close down all feature film production for over four years. From 1966 to 1970, no new feature films were released. All but a handful of the movies made in China in the previous seventeen years were banned. During these four years and later, many older artists suffered imprisonment, violence, and physical deprivation. Their less established colleagues underwent political study and self-criticism at interminable meetings while continuing, in the main, to receive their wages. In 1969, however, many artists were expelled from the studios, in the majority of cases going to May Seventh Cadre Schools, which were Maoist labor reform camps for ex-officials.

In 1970 the first new films to appear in a number of years, apart from documentary footage of Mao Zedong surveying assembled Red Guards or floating down the Yangzi River, were celluloid versions of the "revolutionary model performances" (*geming yangbanxi*), the stage epitomes of the new aesthetic. The Beijing studio in October 1970 released *Taking Tiger Mountain by Strategy (Zhiqu Weihushan)*.[4] Over the next three years the model modernized operas *The Red Lantern (Hongdeng ji), Shajiabang, On the Docks (Haigang)*, and others appeared on China's previously empty screens. The model ballets *The White-Haired Girl (Baimao nü)* and *The Red Detachment of Women (Hongse niangzijun)* were also filmed; their stories were based on the 1950 and 1961 films of the same titles.

In January 1974 the studios released new fiction films, as distinct from film versions of stage performances, for the first time in eight years. Later labeled model films (*yangban dianying*), the new releases bore the heavy imprint of the model operas in their stylization of plot, character, and film technique. Their subjects and the reliance on stereotypes were also reminiscent of the first products of the state-owned studios in the early 1950s. Just as at that time self-conscious beginnings were being made in Chinese film, so in the early 1970s the new cultural authorities regarded the new films as exemplars of their militant view of culture. Insistent rhetoricism and heightened but depersonalized emotion were the new norms. Audiences yawned in vast numbers, although they came to the theaters because there was little else to see and staying away might mean accusations of political deviance.[5]

By 1976 it was clear that the political position of Zhang Chunqiao, Yao Wenyuan, Jiang Qing, and their allies was weakening. The massive Qingming festival demonstrations in Beijing's Tiananmen Square and elsewhere in early April were a sign of increasing political tensions and instability. The cultural leaders' response to these changes itself indicated their uncertainty. In filmmaking, over half of the features in production in 1976 were videotaped recordings of traditional operas.[6] This opera was not a throwback, in the face of political challenge, to the earlier reliance on filmed opera as a vehicle for cultural revolution. These fifty old-style operas were made for an audience of one – Mao Zedong.

The last phase of the Cultural Revolution in filmmaking extended beyond the political repudiation of the insurgents. The arrest of the Gang of Four in October 1976 after Mao Zedong's death a month earlier, and the triumph of Party leaders with outlooks not dissimilar from those influential in the early 1960s, promised to allow filmmakers more scope than the strictures under which they had worked during the previous ten years. However, the industry floundered for two more years. New films required time to produce, old scripts needed adjustment, and new ones were urgently sought. Almost a generation of film artists and technical personnel who might have been trained during the eleven years of upheaval was not available, so that reestablishment of a productive film corps took time. Only by 1979, close to fifteen years after the first salvoes of the Cultural Revolution (and thirty years after the establishment of the People's Republic), was Chinese filmmaking in a position to explore new directions in subjects, themes, and styles.

The Yan'an and Shanghai legacies

The Cultural Revolution years marked another downturn, indeed the nadir, in the fortunes of artists and writers who had been active in the film world centered on Shanghai in the 1930s and after the War of Resistance to Japan. The severity of this official rejection, of what had once been praised as the progressive film legacy (*jinbu dianying chuantong*), far exeeded the condemnation associated with the Wu Xun criticism and the Anti-Rightist campaigns. Whereas the earlier critiques of the Shanghai legacy had usually acknowledged some positive features, the post-1964 rejection saw nothing worth saving. Some of the key figures in filmmaking before 1949 lost their jobs, sanity, and sometimes lives in the catastrophe of the late 1960s. In their stead, the official orientation in literature and art represented a resuscitation of the Yan'an legacy. The Gang of Four advocated a wartime literature, with a distinctly rural and martial emphasis in its model performances and later "model" films. Although the insurgents claimed a solid foundation in Marxism–Leninism in its Maoist guise, the model culture owed much to a narrow view of political responsibility derived from the Yan'an experience in the mountain fastness of northern Shaanxi.

The critical attack on Xia Yan in the prologue to the Cultural Revolution clearly reflected this Yan'an versus Shanghai–May Fourth cleavage. Xia, the most prominent of the Shanghai scenarists and dramatists in the 1930s, was closely associated with the 1963 adaptation *Early Spring in February*. Early critics of the film made passing reference to Xia's endorsement of it.[7] A year later, in mid-1965, when published criticism of higher-level literary figures had become more possible, Xia's own 1959 adaptation of Mao Dun's *The Lin Family Shop* came under belated attack. One critic accused Xia of adapting a work with a bourgeois hero under the pretext of bringing great literature to the screen. The film, this critic argued, "turned its back" on the worker/peasant/soldier orientation,

which Mao's Yan'an *Talks* had set as the cultural orthodoxy. Such devia-
tion, the critic warned, could easily become the "antithesis" of the
gongnongbing aesthetic.[8] Xia Yan's *Essays on Film* (*Dianying lunwenji*),
published in 1963 during the relative thaw in cultural and political life,
was criticized in the *Literary Gazette* in the spring of 1966, shortly before
Xia officially fell from grace, and this condemnation was stronger than
the earlier efforts.

The *Literary Gazette* critic argued that Xia divorced himself from the
Party literary and art "battlefront" in three areas: the worker/peasant/
soldier orientation, Party leadership, and the assessment of the 1930s
progressive film tradition. Xia allegedly had shown little sympathy toward workers, peasants, and soldiers, for such persons were absent from
a work such as his 1937 play *Under Shanghai Eaves* (*Shanghai wuyan
xia*). Xia's expressed discontent with the narrowness of subject matter,
formalism, and stereotype linked him, according to this critic, with the
"rightists" of 1957. While the *Literary Gazette* writer stopped short of
arguing that works without worker/peasant/soldier heroes could not
serve post-Yan'an cultural purposes, Xia's sympathies, he suggested, be-
longed elsewhere.

Using the familiar technique of rhetorical illogic, the 1966 critic proceeded from Xia's apparently inadequate response to "rightist" criticism
(by Zhong Dianfei) of his 1956 adaptation of *The New Year's Sacrifice* to
claim that Xia advocated bourgeois individual leadership to replace the
Party's leadership, as "rightists" like Zhong had allegedly sought. Mao's
Yan'an *Talks* provided the ammunition for repudiating Xia's view of the
pre-1949 "progressive film tradition." Whereas a review in *Film Art* in
early 1964 had praised Xia's collection of essays on film as showing his
acceptance, as a leading May Fourth writer, of Party leadership in filmmaking and the Maoist orientation, the *Literary Gazette* writer two years
later strongly disagreed. Mao had called at Yan'an for literature and art to
serve a popular audience of peasants, soldiers, and others. Xia's 1930s
"progressive films" served the urban petit bourgeoisie and intellectuals.
Xia, therefore, like his 1930s colleagues, was no true Maoist.[9]

Similar retrospective arguments about the Maoist credentials of 1930s
filmmakers appeared in critiques of the 1963 *History of the Development
of Chinese Film* (*Zhongguo dianying fazhanshi*). A two-volume work,
edited by Cheng Jihua with the assistance of Li Shaobai and Xing Zuwen,
it covered the years up to 1949, and accordingly emphasized the 1930s
and 1940s Shanghai film enterprise as much as the work of the Yan'an
Film Team, the Northeast Film Studio, and other Party-controlled film
efforts, which had barely begun before 1949. Critics in 1966, however,
found this emphasis unacceptable, for it seemed to suggest that the filmmakers associated with the League of Left-Wing Writers in the 1930s had
already mapped out and started upon the socialist, popularizing direc-

tion outlined by Mao in his 1942 Yan'an *Talks*. Cheng Jihua's rather unconvincing efforts to retrospectively ascribe a proletarian world outlook to late May Fourth Shanghai film artists[10] had been inspired, in the early 1960s atmosphere of cultural relaxation, by Xia Yan's own high estimation of the political significance of the 1930s left-wing film enterprise.[11] After the fall from grace of Xia Yan and other older film artists, the attacks on Cheng Jihua's *History* became more personal, accusing the 1930s film veterans of taking care to "touch up" Cheng's draft manuscript in order to glorify themselves.[12]

The Shanghai–May Fourth associations of most of the films criticized at the beginning of the Cultural Revolution, and the rejection of these films' representations of history, are noteworthy. Yang Hansheng's *Jiangnan in the North*, one of the earliest films criticized, presented an account of land reform and collectivization in a northern Hebei village in the early 1950s with rather more nuance than usual in films on that subject. Yang's script reflects the humanistic concerns of May Fourth artists, rather than the narrowness of Maoist writers. The importance placed on personal motivations, for example, is rare in most post-1949 movies. The hero is a somewhat obstinate Party secretary in the village who has antagonized many of his neighbors by insisting that they dig a series of wells during the winter slack season. Even in the face of near failure, he prefers persuasion, rather than "struggle," to solve the conflicts in the village. His wife, who is slowly going blind in part from the emotional strain, is a strong source of moral authority in the story. Such female characters frequently appear in May Fourth writing. The critics preferred a more simplistic, Yan'an-inspired portrayal of the villagers' struggles, particularly when the subtlety of the script was strengthened by superior direction and acting.[13]

City without Night (*Buye cheng*), a 1957 film scripted by Ke Ling, who had held a high position in the Shanghai cultural apparatus, came under criticism again for its presentation of the career of a Shanghai capitalist from the 1930s to the 1950s. Like *The Lin Family Shop*, *City without Night* was said to encourage sympathy for its bourgeois hero: By 1965, such sympathy was more dangerous.[14] The film, however, perhaps warranted the charges hurled at it. So little time is spent on the hero's repentant acceptance of the new political order at the end of the film that the conversion is unconvincing and does not obliterate the impression of material comfort presented throughout the film, including the scenes from after 1949.

Ke Ling's position high in the Shanghai Party literary organization had protected him from Anti-Rightist criticism of *City without Night* in 1957–8.[15] By 1965, the Maoist literary insurgents were powerful enough to repudiate Ke. They organized Shanghai film circles to discuss the film, an opportunity many filmmakers appear to have seized eagerly in order to disarm their own critics with some appropriate self-criticism. Sun Daolin, who had played the film's hero, spoke of the need for a higher degree of political responsibility in dealing with such topics. Xie Jin, whose own *Stage Sisters* would be attacked less than a year later, went further. "For many years now," Xie argued, "some people in literary circles have used the excuse of writing about things with which they are personally familiar in order to oppose Chairman Mao's directives regarding the need for literary and art workers to go deep among the worker/peasant/soldier masses, to join in the fierce battles, and familiarize themselves with the life of struggle of workers, peasants, and soldiers."[16] What Xie meant in essence was less Shanghai and more Yan'an.

As Shanghai and what it stood for fell from grace, filmmakers and others with stronger Yan'an and "old liberated areas" credentials became more prominent. A writer in the *Literary Gazette* praised at great length the members of two award-winning film projection teams from rural Hebei and Inner Mongolia as "successors in the tradition (*chuantong*) of revolutionary literature and art in the 'old liberated areas'," for which Yan'an had been headquarters.[17] Here was a tradition to set against the 1930s Shanghai legacy. The 1950 film version of the Yan'an folk opera *The White-Haired Girl* reappeared, although not for long, since it was somewhat different in plot and style from the ballet version, which was one of the Cultural Revolution's "model performances."[18]

Existing divisions along Yan'an versus the rest lines within filmmaking ranks once again, as in 1957, allowed for more effective intervention from the Party cultural insurgents. Tian Hua, the star of the film *The White-Haired Girl*, lamented that relations between artists like herself and the masses were not as close as they had been in the base areas during the War of Resistance to Japan.[19] In the same issue of the *Literary Gazette*, Tian's PLA August First studio colleague, the director Yan Jizhou, reminisced on the direct wartime service art workers had given to the fighting troops. Actor and director Cui Wei similarly contrasted his Yan'an-based war experience with what he felt was the dearth of revolutionary heroes in post-1949 films. According to Zhao Ziyue, a veteran of art propaganda work in the Taihang mountains wartime base, modern actors could perform only in big cities, unlike their base-area counterparts, who had been soldiers too.[20]

The punishment meted out by Jiang Qing and her cultural troops against major figures from prewar Shanghai filmmaking found its justification in the rhetoric of total struggle and war. The chief perpetrators of the so-called black line in art and literature since 1949 included Xia Yan, who had lost his deputy ministership of culture in April 1965, Yang Hansheng, writer of *Jiangnan in the North*, and Tian Han, a prominent playwright since the 1930s.[21] The latter died under attack in 1968 at the age of seventy.[22] Jiang Qing appears to have conducted a personal vendetta against several prominent film artists who had known her during her pre-Yan'an days as a Shanghai film actress. The homes of the actor Zhao Dan and of Zheng Junli, codirector of the 1947 epic *The Spring River Flows East*, were ransacked for materials relating to Mao's wife. Zheng's wife and two sons had no news of him from September 1967, when he was placed in custody, until April 1969, when they were allowed to visit Zheng on his deathbed.[23] Cai Chusheng, Zheng's codirector on *Spring River*, also died under the pressure of militant harassment at age sixty-two.[24] One estimate of those from Shanghai film circles who died under attack puts the figure at over thirty.[25] Ironically, not a few of the survivors of this cultural witch-hunt were able to return to work in the early 1970s, when their experience and skills were sorely needed by the perpetrators of these excesses. Nevertheless, the Shanghai studio (a consolidation of the former Haiyan and Tianma studios) was the last to reopen when preparations were made to resume production in 1969–70.[26]

Film and the new mass culture

In rejecting the pre-1949 film legacy and discounting the value of literature and art produced during the seventeen years after that date, the new cultural authorities self-consciously set out to create an alternative mass culture and, as a major part of this, a new film aesthetic. They couched their presentation of this new film style in class conflict and "two-line struggle" terms, but the emphasis was on a national Chinese aesthetic, in contrast to what they perceived as the "bourgeois," cosmopolitan inspiration of the now discredited older filmmakers. Jiang Qing and her allies turned to the modernized "model operas" as the epitome of the new mass culture and the new film style. These operas were models both for the modernization of the operatic arts and for a whole new culture. The characters in the operas were also models of revolutionary behavior. But the results, both in the model performance films and in the feature films made in the early 1970s, indicated that the new film style in many respects was a mere heightening of tendencies typical of Chinese films for at least the previous two decades. Despite their rhetoric, the insurgents cherished an essentially conservative culture, inspired by the quarter-century-old Yan'an experience. Radically new directions could not be expected from them.

Their emphasis on the strong formalism of opera (in its modernized guise) can be seen in the characters, exposition, acting, and film techniques of the operatic and other features made after 1970. In all these respects, the films had antecedents from the seventeen years before the start of the Cultural Revolution. However, all parties had previously rejected this aesthetic rigidity as overreliance on formalism and stereotype. These unwelcome qualities had been the targets of critics in the Hundred Flowers thaw of 1956–7. In the early 1970s, all films shared these now rehabilitated features. Indeed, three movies from the early 1950s, when Chinese film came closest to "socialist realism," were remade in the early 1970s according to the new aesthetic formulas. They were all on military subjects.[27]

The heroes of both the opera films and the later movies appeared without exception in an unrelenting positive light, making them seem lacking in depth – or indeed, in the nonopera films, much interest. The makers of the first model opera film, *Taking Tiger Mountain by Strategy*, integrated medium and close shots in the characters' arias so that, one commentator argued, "the audience is aware of the communion of feeling among the heroic characters themselves, and between them and the other positive characters. In this way the heroes stand out in bold relief."[28] Such care was taken to create this "model" model-opera film that it was filmed three times over a two-year period before the producers were satisfied.[29] The principle animating this film and its successors was the three emphases (*san tuchu*), a concentric emphasis on the positive characters, the band of heroes among them, and the single most inspiring hero. The last-named is unfailingly presented as the initiator of action, fount of knowledge, and unbeatable fighter for Chairman Mao.

The staging and importance of arias in opera lent themselves fairly naturally to the three emphases, although the directors had almost as many options as they had had in tranferring more traditional opera to film. The makers of the model opera films decided to avoid fragmented shots, concentrating instead, in rather static fashion, on the central hero and his or her comrades. Some of the most interminable sequences in Chinese film occur in *On the Docks*, in which the central hero, a female leader of Shanghai dockworkers, guides a younger colleague through an enormous "class education" art gallery. It is a lesson in art appreciation which few viewers can appreciate.

Positive characters, particularly principal heroes, in the nonopera feature films from the early 1970s had much in common with their opera cousins. Zhao Sihai, the leader of a band of steelworkers determined to make a high-quality alloy in *The Fiery Years* (*Huohong de niandai*, 1974), has no doubts as to the correctness of his struggle with engineers, who would rely upon foreign imports. "He recalls how Chairman Mao inspected their steel works four years ago, produces the poster describing Chairman Mao's visit which he kept as a treasure, and ponders the instructions which Chairman Mao gave the steel workers at the time."[30] With the help of his comrade workers Zhao wins over the factory director, exposes the class enemy in the engineering ranks, and produces the new steel. This Maoist zeal extended to small children, including Winter Boy, the hero of *Sparkling Red Star* (*Shanshan de hongxing*, 1974). One of its directors noted:[31]

Practice has proved to us the necessity of learning from the revolutionary operas and ballets and applying them to film: only by depicting the boy at climaxes of the struggles between the two lines and class struggle were we able to portray his heroism in full length, to make his image more inspiring. . . . the evocative power [of a work] is only effective if it enhances the image of the hero: otherwise extraneous incidents are only scattered pearls torn from the string.

The child Winter Boy outwits with ease Japanese commanders and other enemies, while taking the fiery martyrdom of his mother, which he witnesses, as grist for his revolutionary mill.

These feature films, like the model operas (and indeed traditional opera), were peopled with stock characters. The central heroes themselves took on a somewhat homogenized quality, an impression enhanced by the relentless concentration on them by the camera. Their colleagues nearly always included a kind, elderly woman, "Granny," who is perpetually available with a tearful recollection of the bitter past, a young woman eager to join the revolutionary struggle, and an old man who sometimes wavers in loyalty to the cause until the hero puts him right. Class enemies and Japanese, the usual kinds of negative characters in these films, similarly lack depth or nuance, although their evil habits sometimes unwittingly make them seem more interesting than their zealous, but bland, opponents. As an observer noted in 1978: "In these films the goodies are always holding meetings, while the baddies are constantly eating and drinking."[32]

Formalism extended to all elements in these films. The exposition in both the opera films and the ordinary features was typically predictable. The heroes, delineated by the three emphases, not infrequently pass through three crises on the road to inevitable, total triumph. The first crisis might cause some peripheral heroic characters to waver, the second confirms the rightness of the central hero's line, and the third ends in exposure of the enemy and victory for the proletarian forces.[33] Some plot variations were possible. In the 1975 production *Breaking with Old Ideas* (*Juelie*), for example, a teacher whose spectacles and manner suggest he is a backward element undergoes a late but speedy conversion to the cause of educational popularization. Such changes, however, were but sideshows to the main thrust of the plot.

In characterization and plot, therefore, the new films reflected a traditional Chinese lack of concern for artistic originality. Just as a watcher of traditional opera usually knew the story and the characters' fates and attended a show to delight in the familiar and the artifice of the immediate performance, so viewers of these films might bring similar expectations to the cinema. Indeed, a concern for a national style is clearly discernible in the techniques used to transfer the actors' performances to the screen. One director of *Sparkling Red Star*, in discussing technique, made direct reference to the most Chinese of art forms. "Like good poetry or painting, the film must reject all tedious and ineffective frills."[34] This emphasis on plainness is a reminder also of the Yan'an cultural commitment to wartime simplicity (*pusu*), as opposed to the cosmopolitan, more elaborate or refined tastes of Shanghai.

The Cultural Revolution directorial techniques showed a single-minded concentration on the three emphases. *The Red Lantern*, one of the first three model opera films, epitomized this approach. Filming the opera provided more ways than in a stage performance to heighten the prominence of the central hero, an underground Party member and railway signalman named Li Yuhe. "By contrasting front and rear, high and low, at an angle and on the rise, the camera guarantees the predominance of the heroic characters to whom the villains serve only as foils."[35] As this shorthand suggests, villains tend to be shot by the camera from behind, above, and at an angle, thereby cutting them down to size. Heroic Li Yuhe, on the other hand, is most often seen in the foreground, towering over the camera, which frequently zooms in to a closeup. The camera work is so skillful, one commentator noted, that in one scene "Li seems positively to tower over [the Japanese general], although Li is sitting and the Japanese standing."[36] While this commentator cited such directorial sleight of hand as a rejection of "all bourgeois formalism, naturalism and beauty for its own sake," the August First studio makers of *The Red Lantern* under director Cheng Yin consciously created a new formalism "to delineate Li's typical character . . . in a typical milieu." The presentation is a semiotician's delight: "Li's simple coloured clothes seem to denote the intelligence, courage and strength of the working class."[37] This delineation of moral and other qualities by symbolic detail is, of course, typical of traditional opera convention, and indeed of more general Chinese aesthetics.

Such opera-inspired antinaturalism, however, is less expected in fiction films, where the potential authenticity of setting and story make the three emphases somewhat ham-fisted. The typicality of a character in the operatic tradition is not necessarily transferable to heroic figures like the steelmaker Zhao Sihai in *The Fiery Years*. Zhao towers over his enemies, is taller than his comrades, and is always the center of rather static tableaus in group scenes. At climaxes, such as when the steelworkers succeed in producing the new alloy, or when the new dam is dedicated in *The New Doctor* (*Hongyu*, 1975), the hero is surrounded by what has been called a "Chinese chorus."[38] The camera cuts to several similar, straightforward closeup shots of a number of the hero's colleagues expressing group joy, and signaling to the audience how they too should react. Something of operatic acting styles characterizes these films, particularly when actors strike a pose akin to the frozen stance (*liangxiang*) of opera. Without punctuation by opera gong and drum, these gestures seem rather empty, emphasizing the shallowness of the characterization and plot.

Although the cultural authorities and their spokespersons argued that the style of these new features was a repudiation of the "bourgeois," "Hollywood-inspired" styles of the seventeen years before the Cultural Revolution, the stylistic continuities are striking. Since the early 1950s, audiences, film artists, and even Ministry of Culture officials had repeatedly lamented the formalism and stereotype of films. The films of the late Cultural Revolution made a virtue of these faults by claiming their political purposes were correct. In his Yan'an *Talks*, Mao Zedong had himself eschewed naturalism, in a passage inspired by Soviet aesthetic theories: "Literature and art can and ought to be on a higher plane, more intense, more concentrated, more typical, nearer the ideal, and therefore more universal than everyday life."[39] Likewise, the cultural slogan in vogue after 1958 about "combining revolutionary realism and revolutionary romanticism" was antinaturalistic and had allowed for greater acknowledgment of national aesthetic modes, from opera and elsewhere.

The latter slogan continued to provide an underpinning for the Cultural Revolution films, both operatic and fictional. Even their glossiness recalled strongly a typical feature of most pre–Cultural Revolution movies. But this half decade effort at the sinification of film art was a forced one, too closely associated with the political fortunes of a Party faction to endure. Time did not allow the Cultural Revolution film aesthetic to take root, particularly as the makers of even these films had been trained in a more international aesthetic.

Party, artists, and audiences

Unlike the mechanical nature of film plots in these years, unpredictability and unprecedented arbitrariness characterized the continuing tripartite relationship among cultural authorities, filmmakers, and audiences during the Cultural Revolution. Film artists had worked since 1949 by the grace of the Party and had had bitter experiences, particularly during the Anti-Rightist campaign of 1957–8. In the mid-1960s the insurgents took command of the Party cultural apparatus, and work at the studios stopped. The return to Party influence of relative moderates, and a realization, even on the part of the zealots, that eight "model performances" and little else did not amount to much of a public cultural life, helped reopen the studios in the early 1970s. Many of the artists who made the new films had established themselves before 1966, for their expertise was indispensable. Audiences in these years were largely ignored, or lectured at from the screen.

Jiang Qing and her supporters in charge of culture paid as much attention to film as to the model operas. The two were perhaps at opposite poles in terms of native styles, but film offered an opportunity to carry the model performances (which included another distinctly foreign art, ballet) to wider audiences. Film was also an effective tool in the centralization and standardization of culture. The films of the model operas created the definitive versions of these works, and could bring the operas to the whole nation without abuse by local operatic troupes and cultural cadres. There were also negative reasons for the degree of attention Jiang Qing gave to film. As the most foreign artistic medium, staffed by former colleagues from cosmopolitan Shanghai, film was seen as a challenge to the insurgents' cultural policies, unless properly controlled. For these positive and negative reasons, film became even more a tool or medium and less of an art or entertainment than it had ever been during the pre–Cultural Revolution years.

The rise of the insurgents and their history until 1976 provide a warning against viewing the Party as any more monolithic or single-minded than filmmaking circles or audiences. Zhou Yang, China's cultural commissar in the 1950s and early 1960s, critic of many leftist artists in prewar Shanghai and apparent spokesperson for the Maoist, Yan'an-derived view of literature and art with its "revolutionary romanticism" modifications, to the insurgents represented the established, bankrupt cultural leadership. Like the political leadership under Liu Shaoqi, Deng Xiaoping, and others, Zhou Yang's cultural apparatus was toppled by the Jiang Qing–Zhang Chunqiao faction, with support on the ideological front from Yao Wenyuan. The increasing moderation after 1969, once the military had established order among rival local factions, was marked by the rise of a Party group headed by Zhou Enlai. In cultural matters, Jiang Qing and her allies moderated their policies, in part because of changing factional fortunes. The shift to making nonopera feature films, although initiated by the insurgent-controlled Culture Group of the State Council in October 1972, received endorsement from the "moderates." At a 1973 New Year's gathering of Politburo members and film, drama, and music workers, Zhou Enlai complained, with considerable understatement, that for seven years there had been too few movies. "This is a big shortcoming of ours. . . . Fill in this blank with three years of hard work. The masses' needs are urgent."[40]

In his remarks in January 1973 Premier Zhou acknowledged, as Party leaders had done since 1949, the great usefulness of movies. The group, later labeled the Gang of Four, ascribed even greater utility to feature films. The faction headed by Jiang Qing and Zhang Chunqiao sought to use films to gain support for their insurgency. As their grip on cultural and political power encountered challenges, the Gang ordered supporters in the studios in late 1975 to organize the production of films on the theme of those who wanted a restoration of capitalism in China, the "capitalist-roaders in the Party." This charge, resuscitated and leveled at the recently rehabilitated Deputy Premier Deng Xiaoping, was worked into scripts still being written by bringing the settings of film stories closer to the present day, or through other, mechanical adjustments to already somewhat mechanical scripts. Nine of the ten films in production at the Changchun studio in 1976 in this way became "capitalist-roader" films.[41] According to a later claim, in the sixty films planned for 1976, twenty-one basic-level leaders were portrayed as "taking the capitalist road," as were twelve county Party secretaries, nine central department heads and provincial Party secretaries, and a deputy premier. The latter was an obvious reference to Deng Xiaoping.[42]

Money was no object. The twenty-one "capitalist roader" films actually completed in 1976 cost 7.25 million *yuan* (approximately 3.5 million 1976 U.S. dollars) to film, and making copies, which went unreleased, required a further 5.68 million *yuan*.[43] The Film Bureau estimated in 1978 that the fixed capital of the seven major film studios had increased by 184% between 1966 and 1976, in contrast to the great decrease in the number of films produced in those years.[44] The Shanghai studio made three attempts, each costing over one million *yuan*, to film the model opera *On the Docks*. One remake was ordered reportedly because Jiang Qing did not approve of the shade of the central heroine's red scarf.[45] Remakes of six pre–Cultural Revolution films, as "model films" for the 1970s, also consumed an inordinate sum of money by earlier standards. The new versions of *Fighting North and South* (*Nanzheng beizhan*, original 1952), *Scouting across the Yangzi* (*Dujiang zhenchaji*, original 1954), and *Guerrillas on the Plain* (*Pingyuan youjidui*, original 1955) each required three to four times the investment of the originals.[46]

Incorporating the three emphases with the old "socialist realist" stories was clearly an expensive operation, even accounting for some inflation over twenty years and the new versions being in color. Statistics from the China Film Corporation, in charge of national distribution of films, contrast the financial picture of the early 1960s with the mid-1970s. In the five years after 1961, the corporation contributed to state coffers more than 200 million *yuan* over and above expenses. In 1974, the film industry owed the state 4 million *yuan*, and in 1976, 10 million.[47]

It is easier to recount Gang excesses than to analyze the manner in which filmmakers worked under the new cultural leadership. Victors usually provide more information for the justification of their success than on the achievements of the vanquished, so that after 1976, when the Gang fell, the available information was limited and somewhat biased. What is clear is that Jiang Qing and her allies used intimidation and expulsion, and played on filmmakers' ambitions and sense of professionalism to have their say in the studios.

Intimidation of artists and others in the film industry was perhaps the most effective method. Under the slogan of "reorganizing the ranks" (*chongjian duiwu* or *chongxin zuzhi duiwu*), coined by Zhang Chunqiao, representatives of the Gang, such as the worker–soldier propaganda teams (*gongjun xuanchuandui*) at Changchun, set about investigating the political credentials of the creative personnel in the studios. At Changchun the result was that one-third of the 290 middle-level and above Party, managerial, artistic, and technical cadres were judged to have made political mistakes (*luxian cuowu*). Only four of the seventy-four managerial and Party cadres were considered free of blemish.[48] In November 1967 a mass meeting in Shanghai "struggled" against more than two hundred artists and others from the Haiyan and Tianma studios.[49] The Shanghai Film Bureau, in the hands of Jiang Qing's supporters, conducted investigations (*shencha*), itself a sign of its targets' political problems, of 104 out of 108 high-level cadres (of grade 6 rank and above) in 1971 as film production revived. Seven out of eight scenarists were expelled, and thirty-one out of forty-four directors were treated as suitable targets for criticism. Only one of these directors remained at the studio, allegedly as a "negative example" (*fanmian jiaoyuan*) to encourage the others. Likewise only one actor, of twenty-one investigated, continued to be active, as did two of the ten investigated cinematographers.[50]

Mass expulsion was another favored way to "reorganize the ranks." Almost half the artistic personnel at the former Tianma and Haiyan studios in Shanghai were sent from their units after 1970, many undergoing "reform through labor" in factories in the city.[51] The Jilin provincial Party committee, firmly in the hands of the insurgents, in the winter of 1969 sent 521 employees of the Changchun studio to the countryside, about a third of the studio work force. Inducements to leave included the threat of loss of Party membership and withdrawal of grain ration tickets, encouragement to emulate model "volunteers," who knew they would be back in a few months, and (perhaps playing on cadres' habitual expectations of superior treatment) presenting a rosy picture of life at their rural destinations.[52] At about the same time, the Gang ordered that 20 percent of the cadres of the PLA's August First studio be sent away. More expulsions were planned, but the uncertainty after the fall of army chief Lin Biao in mid-1971 put a stop to this "reorganization of the ranks" at the army studio. About a third of the Xi'an studio's cadres were confined or "struggled" (subjected to mass criticism meetings). The Pearl River studio lost 95 percent of its "core cadres."[53]

The picture of Gang control that emerged after 1976 is somewhat blurred regarding the instruments of its power over the studios and the question of supporters among filmmakers themselves. Given the perennial and rigidly vertical nature of industrial and other organization in the People's Republic, officials and other bodies outside the studios had considerable influence on filmmaking. In Beijing the production of *Coun-*

terattack (*Fanji*), an anti–capitalist-roader piece ordered by Zhang Chun-qiao within days of Hua Guofeng becoming acting premier in February 1976, was shared by a number of groups. The Liang Xiao (two schools) writing group, under directions from Chi Qun, who had strong links with Beijing and Qinghua Universities, where the writing group was based, and with the Beijing Film Studio, wrote the script and took care of political questions. Artistic questions were in the hands of the Ministry of Culture, also under Gang leadership and headed by Yu Huiyong and Hao Liang, the original star of *The Red Lantern* model opera. Actual production of the film was the responsibility of the reformed Party committee at the Beijing studio. In the course of the production Chi Qun felt the need constantly to send representatives to the filming group (*shezhi zu*), which seems to have been headed by a Gang supporter.[54]

A similar mixture of remote control and studio allies seems to have characterized Party–artist relations in the other film centers. Xu Jingxian, who held sway in Shanghai over cultural and educational organizations, reportedly sent his own secretary to set up a "reformed" Shanghai Film Bureau. A film group (*dianying xiaozu*) was established at a level above the bureau and the studio. The group issued direct instructions to the studio, circumventing the authority of the bureau and the Shanghai city Party committee.[55]

Reflecting their rising uncertainty about the loyalty of filmmakers and studio managers, the insurgents' intervention from outside the studios continuously increased. In September 1973 the Jilin provincial Party committee dispatched a work group to conduct another reorganization (*zhengdun*) of the Changchun studio, which one group member described as having "the smell of 1957" about it.[56] Feeling their grip slipping in 1976, the provincial Party committee set up a "review team" (*pinglun ban*) at Changchun to examine scripts for fifty days. Scripts written earlier under Gang orders they now judged to be unacceptable. In the confusion, efforts were made to coopt more malleable amateur writers into producing ideas for films.[57]

Just as they had done during the Anti-Rightist campaign, the cultural powerholders made use of tensions among filmmakers and within the studios. A 1978 criticism of the Gang somewhat cryptically accused it of "messing up production relations" in the studios by playing up the divisions between technical personnel, who worked with their hands, and creative people, who worked with their minds.[58] The army's August First studio in Beijing allegedly fell under the personal control of Chen Yading of the Culture Section of the PLA General Political Department, and Zhang Dongliang, who had served as cinematographer in the making of *The Red Lantern* model-opera film at the studio.[59]

Zhang Dongliang was not alone as an experienced film artist making films under Gang auspices, even if his motives may have been untypical.

In a specialized, highly technical medium like film, the insurgent cultural authorities could not "reorganize the ranks" by replacing all experienced film artists with "barefoot filmmakers." This tended to set film apart from most other arts during the Cultural Revolution, when new talent appeared on the national stage to sing, dance, write, or paint. Jiang Qing and her allies depended on the specialist skills of movie directors, cinematographers, and other technical personnel. Actors were a visible reminder of the now condemned pre-1966 films, and like scenarists, were more easily replaced.[60] Xie Tieli, assistant director of the condemned *Lin Family Shop* and adaptor-director of the much-criticized *Early Spring in February*, directed the first of the model-opera films, *Taking Tiger Mountain by Strategy*. Xie Jin, maker of *Stage Sisters* and the original *Red Detachment of Women*, joined him in 1972 to complete *On the Docks*. The watery vistas at the beginning and end of this film, while consistent with the subject matter, were also a reminder of Xie Tieli's favorite directorial device, one used in almost all his films. The cinematographer of *Early Spring in February*, Li Wenhua, served in the same capacity on the ballet film *The Red Detachment of Women*, and went on to direct *Breaking with Old Ideas* in 1975.[61] Apparently, because these filmmakers were relatively young and not tainted with involvement in the jealousies of 1930s Shanghai or wartime Yan'an's Lu Xun Art Academy, they were regarded as more likely to listen to Gang instruction.[62]

But even some veteran filmmakers were also recruited. Sang Hu, a maker of light comedies in Shanghai before 1949, directed the filming of the model ballet *The White-Haired Girl*, and codirected *The Second Spring (Di'erge chuntian)* in 1975.[63] Director Cheng Yin, who had attended the Lu Xun Art Academy in Yan'an and taken up film work in 1948, made the Uighur-language version of *The Red Lantern* in 1975 at the August First studio.[64] In the previous year, Cheng had codirected the model remake of his own *Fighting North and South*, which he had first made in 1952.[65] Although the revival of film classes at the newly established May Seventh Art Academy promised to provide new recruits to film ranks, for the moment the Gang had to depend on those with experience.[66] The compromise, however, was limited. Distrust of film circles lay behind the ten changes in ten years of the leading group (*lingdao banzi*) at the Beijing studio, and the eight changes of leadership at August First.[67]

The motives of the filmmakers with experience in participating in production under Gang auspices are difficult to discern, both from materials of the time and from subsequent repudiation of the Jiang Qing faction. The revival of production offered a chance for artists and technicians to resume practicing their craft, even if they held doubts about the legitimacy of the new cultural authorities. But, like other writers and artists in China, filmmakers wanted to be good socialist artists, rather than uncommitted or apolitical. Good socialism was defined rather differently in the early 1970s, but these professional aspirations of artists allowed little ground for defense against Gang demands.[68] The possibility that some film artists actually found inspiration in the Cultural Revolution should not be discounted, even if after 1976 no one would directly acknowledge this.[69] "Reorganization of the ranks" also provided the means for some filmmakers, especially the underemployed young, to advance their careers at a pace unusual before the removal of more established film figures after 1966. These were the sorts of motivation which had been played upon in the Anti-Rightist campaign of the late 1950s. Above all, the threat of social ostracism, which political fault entailed in China, where employment mobility is also strictly limited, was a heavy burden, particularly with the example of Gang intervention in the studios a fresh and continuing one.

Artists' acquiescence may have been encouraged also by the system of cultural professionalism. To a degree, the Maoist state after 1949 bought off writers, artists, and other intellectuals by providing, at a minimum, material subsistence and generally superior treatment. For writers prepared to serve the regime, there were trips to interesting localities, even abroad (in a society where geographical mobility was severely restricted), sometimes massive royalty revenues on the most popular works,[70] and prestigious appointments to national and local political consultative bodies. The post-1976 rehabilitation of such previously privileged writers, particularly those who had made their reputations in the late May Fourth era, highlighted this central feature of contemporary Chinese cultural life. The position of intellectuals in Chinese society has always been a conspicuous one, whether in disgrace and hounded to death, or in happier times.

Nonetheless, filmmakers resisted some of the cultural insurgents' intervention in their work, especially from 1975 onward, as the power of the Gang in many areas of Chinese life encountered popular resistance. Two films in particular became centers of conflict between Jiang Qing and her supporters on the one hand, and filmmakers on the other. *The Pioneers* (*Chuangye*), a story modeled closely on the opening up of the Daqing oilfield in the Northeast, was completed at the Changchun studio. Jiang Qing, dissatisfied with what seems a typical model film, attempted to have it revised or remade. The filmmakers cleverly appealed to higher authority, with the result that Mao Zedong in the summer of 1975 issued perhaps his first rescript on Chinese film since his 1951 editorial. He ordered that the film be released. The statement was publicized widely after Mao's death. His directive on *The Pioneers*, in contrast to the Wu Xun critique, was a picture of moderation. "Don't nitpick," Mao wrote, "And to list as many as ten accusations against it is going too far. It hampers the adjustment of the Party's current policy on literature and art."[71]

Other evidence of filmmakers' resistance and Gang weakness came in the artists' defense of *Haixia*, about the life of a militia woman in a fishing village on the southeast coast. In 1975 the Gang cultural leaders launched an antiguild (*fan hangbang*) movement in film circles, with *Haixia* as a particular target. The need for an antiguild effort suggests the insurgents realized that filmmakers would not remain docile producers of model films. The movement aimed at eliminating the "cliquish system of the director as the central figure."[72] Granting greater artistic autonomy to production teams, headed by experienced directors, had been a cause advocated during the Hundred Flowers discourse. The Anti-Rightist backlash in 1957–8 had only temporarily put an end to such aspirations. The Gang now attempted to eliminate them. A Shanghai director who had simply argued that "a director should have his own conception (*gousi*) of a work" was charged with advocating "directors as the center."[73] Well-known older directors clearly threatened the influence of the Gang and their protégés.

The makers of *Haixia*, headed by adaptor Xie Tieli and the chief director Qian Jiang, responded, like the producers of *The Pioneers*, by appealing around and above the Gang censors.[74] In a letter to Mao, Xie and Qian complained how representatives of Jiang Qing and Zhang Chunqiao made several visits to the Beijing studio in an attempt to put pressure on the artists. In July 1975 Mao noted on the letter: "Distribute to all comrades in the Politburo."[75] Although *Haixia* was distributed and the Gang put down a peg, the episode serves as a reminder of the dependence of filmmakers on political developments and on the whims of the leadership. During the Cultural Revolution, as in the previous seventeen years, dependence between Party cultural leaders and filmmakers remained mutual. The Party needed the special skills of artists, while the latter could work only at the behest of the leadership. Of the two groups, only the authorities changed during the Cultural Revolution: Filmmaking personnel remained to a large extent constant.

Audiences, the third party in these tripartite relations, had at best an indirect role in the upheavals of the Cultural Revolution. The Party authorities regarded audiences as targets for the filmed model operas and for the later model films. Artists, on the other hand, may have felt they knew audiences better, but were in no position to advocate, on behalf of viewers, changes in film styles and subjects, since the Party leadership, like the emperors of old, was convinced of its direct and unfailing understanding of "the masses." Meanwhile, mass audiences subjected themselves to even larger doses of the formalism and stereotypes, of which they, along with everybody else, had complained during the seventeen years before the Cultural Revolution. Direct comparison by filmgoers with earlier movies was difficult, however, for the 518 films made in the years after 1949 were put into cold storage in 1966. A few, including *The*

Life of Wu Xun, were shown during the following ten years as negative teaching material (*fanmian jiaocai*). In October 1970, for example, five features set in the Korean War were distributed to commemorate the twentieth anniversary of China's participation in the Korean conflict.[76]

Much effort was put into expanding the means of getting the model films (opera and features) to the viewing public. One 1975 report claimed that rural projection units (*danwei*) nationwide had increased four times over the 1965 level. Half of the projection teams were equipped with a newly developed, highly portable 8.75mm projector. In the rural areas of Guangdong Province, countryfolk who had averaged four film viewings a year in 1966 saw ten shows in 1974. The model performances films got most distribution attention. *Taking Tiger Mountain by Strategy* had been watched from its late 1970 release until the end of 1974 by 7.3 billion people, which suggests that every Chinese man, woman, and child saw the film on average over seven times. This figure, of course, bore little relationship to the actual popularity of the film. The lack of much reference to film projection teams in post-1976 criticisms of the Gang tends to confirm this picture of the expansion in distribution.[77]

The apparent silence from audiences, however, was deceptive, for as the film industry in the late 1970s recovered from the earlier disruptions, the importance of audiences increased considerably. This simply reflected wider changes in relations between the Communist Party and Chinese society as an outcome of the catastrophe of the Cultural Revolution.

Aftermath

When in October 1976 the Gang of Four was arrested, these changes in relations between Party and society were perhaps not immediately apparent, and certainly not acknowledged. Party leaders and filmmakers turned their attention to the destructive influence of the Cultural Revolution upheaval, which lingered in both the new films released in 1977 and 1978, and in the industry producing them.

With the fall of the Gang and the cancellation or nonrelease of a number of 1976 productions, new scripts were at a premium. Stories tended to take from two to four years from conception to distribution, so a substantial proportion of the fifty or so new films released in 1977 and 1978 were made from scripts written a few years earlier under Gang auspices. *Battle of Leopard Valley* (*Baoziwan zhandou*), for example, about a self-reliant production movement in the War of Resistance to Japan, was made from a script written in 1973, based on a 1964 play. The script was rewritten ten times in four years, the last extending from March 1977 to January 1978.[78]

Despite such reworking, audiences and filmmakers complained about the quality of the new films. The dull predictability of plot, the false-ness of characterization, the overacting, and the tedious pacing of expo-sition (all objects of complaint in the 1949–66 period, when they were labeled formalism and stereotype) were now put under the new rubric of "gangness" (*bangqi*). The heroine of *Spring Comes Early on the Southern Border* (*Nanjiang chunzao*), one Beijing filmgoer argued, in-dulged in unnecessary heroics. In the best Jiang Qing tradition, she persuades the inflamed masses of the wisdom of her acts with a few well-chosen phrases.[79]

Three types of film helped fill the gap as film production recovered from the years of upheaval. In the two years before January 1979, 300 pre-1966 films were rereleased, while another 100 awaited distribution. Such films served as illustrations, for audiences and filmmakers, of some of the past strengths and weaknesses of Chinese film.[80] Foreign films, from a wider range of countries than before, were distributed, in part to re-inforce among popular audiences impressions of China's comparative material backwardness. In a nation where access to foreign things was limited, audiences flocked to these exotic works.[81] Beginning with the Spring Festival in 1979, some of the classic Chinese films from before 1949 reappeared on screen.[82]

This last move signaled the rehabilitation of the "progressive film legacy," along with its deceased and surviving representatives. In addi-tion to the reemergence of these older figures, the continuity of film per-sonnel in the 1970s should not be overlooked. Even if their work had been severely circumscribed, many of the most active filmmakers before 1966 (including a few who had started in Shanghai films before 1949) had begun to work in the two years before the arrest of the Gang. Studio personnel at criticism meetings condemned those who had been too en-thusiastic in their work under Gang auspices, but in general there seems to have been little disruption of the ranks on this account after October 1976. At the Shanghai studio, for example, those who had actively served as Gang allies in leadership positions had lost their rankings by 1978, and filmmakers who had been used by the Gang had been "helped and criticized." About half the comrades who needed rechecking (*fucha*) had gone through the process by mid-1978.[83] At a national meeting in mid-1978 to draw a formal close to the campaign against Jiang Qing's film world allies, speakers noted that "most workers in the film system are fine or comparatively fine (*hao*)." Only "an extreme minority" could be considered evildoers and supporters of the Gang.[84]

A new film, designed on its release in early 1979 to mark the restora-tion of Chinese cinema, indicated the continuing problems and some of the potential of the film enterprise. *The Great River Rushes On* (*Dahe benliu*) was made as a big-budget blockbuster, written by the creator of the highly popular 1962 *Li Shuangshuang* and starring the creator of that title role. Director Xie Tieli and his colleague Chen Huaikai placed great hopes in the new epic. Audiences soon discovered, however, that parts of the film were not particularly new.

The size of the film was itself reminiscent of the overreach of Cultural Revolution works. *The Great River Rushes On* covers in two parts twenty years in the history of a Henan village. It starts in 1938, when destruction of the Yellow River dikes in the face of Japanese invaders forces the villagers to flee, and ends in 1958, when the village collective takes part in regional efforts to control the river. Part One follows a villager called Li Mai, played by Zhang Ruifang, in her refugee flight to Xi'an, her participation in Communist underground work there, her postwar return with the villagers, and their expulsion of the local landlords. Part Two, a less unified story, marks the first appearance in a Chinese feature film of actors impersonating Mao Zedong and Zhou Enlai, who each visit the region's water conservancy project.[85] The emphasis on the heroine Li Mai, as leader of the villagers and dauntless solver of problems, reminded many viewers of the "three emphases" heroes of earlier movies. In large part the responsibility lay in the script, which in Chinese more than in Western filmmaking provides a rigorous basis for the finished film. Li Zhun had written the first of the two parts in 1975, according to the aesthetic strictures of the day.[86] Small wonder that audiences found too much "gangness" in it.

The Great River Rushes On, however, had strengths that though secondary, were a promise of future developments. The faults of the film indicated the lingering legacy of the Cultural Revolution, but certain directorial embellishments reflected a new awareness of audiences. In one scene on a small boat, Li Mai recounts, with a refreshing earthy humor, her bitter life before 1938 to the New Fourth Army's Commander Qin. In earlier films Commander Qin would have responded by stiffening slightly, clenching one fist, and gazing at an indeterminate point over the camera lens, telling Li Mai that now the Chinese people have Chairman Mao and the Communist Party to lead them to overturn the old order which had caused such misery. Commander Qin does give this standard speech to Li Mai, but not into the camera. As if to spare viewers such a formalist set piece, director Xie takes the camera outside the cabin of the moored boat and onto the bank of the river. Qin delivers the speech as a small figure in the lighted doorway of the cabin, addressing Li Mai within. This indirectness puts less emphasis on the speechgiver and more on the wider context of the statement. Although *The Great River Rushes On* as a whole was a disappointment, parts like this indicated filmmakers' determination to make use of the Party's post-1976 cultural relaxation to strengthen their art and their connections with their long-suffering audiences. The experience of the Cultural Revolution years had wrought profound changes in all three groups.

The Cultural Revolution in filmmaking, as in other areas of Chinese life, far from simply being a highly destructive and aberrant period of disorder, saw the culmination of trends that had been present in the seventeen years before 1966 and that had their origins even before 1949. The use of films to promote a mass national culture had been a prominent feature of Chinese cultural life since 1949. What was new in the Cultural Revolution was the relative narrowness of the officially endorsed mass culture, and the extent to which its strictures were applied to film art. The beginnings of efforts to broaden the range of films and performing arts in late 1975 and 1976 had to take second place to the insistent use of film and other arts in the factional political disputes of these years.

The fortunes of the cosmopolitan Shanghai–May Fourth artistic heritage reached a nadir during these years, but it was a fate that had been presaged during the 1950s, in the Wu Xun and Anti-Rightist campaigns and in the Great Leap Forward. In this respect also the Cultural Revolution repudiation of the Shanghai cultural legacy was much stronger than earlier criticisms. The Yan'an-inspired cultural policies were also less open, during these years, to the vagaries of interpretation and emphasis than the Yan'an cultural line had been at times before 1966.

The Cultural Revolution years confirmed the interdependence of Party cultural leaders and filmmakers, even as many of the latter went to early deaths under unprecedented harassment from the wielders of power. The resumption of film production in the early 1970s saw the return to work of some older and many young film artists and technicians, since they alone could make the films the political leadership invested with such power over viewers. Audiences, whose needs had received haphazard recognition in the decade and a half after 1949, during the Cultural Revolution were treated even more badly as undifferentiated "masses" needing strident guidance from those who knew better. The fruits of this contempt for "the masses" were to ripen in the 1980s.

The Cultural Revolution—style heroine of *Haixia*, 1975.

Zhou Enlai meets the masses in *The Great River Rushes On,* 1978.

One-half of the heroes of the Shanghai comedy *Twins Come in Pairs,* 1979.

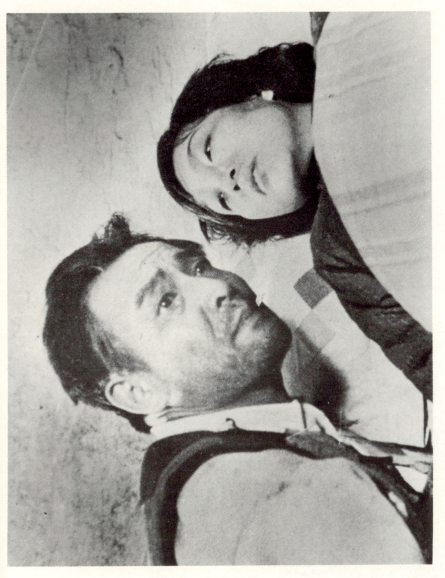

Xie Jin's view of twenty years of political excess, *Legend of Tianyun Mountain*, 1980.

A love story in a war film setting, *The Stars Are Bright Tonight*, 1980.

The effects of the Cultural Revolution on personal lives, *Love and Inheritance*, 1980.

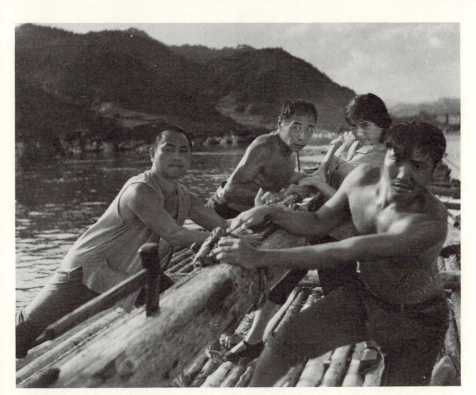

Wu Tianming's symbolic journey in *River without Buoys*, 1983.

Chen Kaige and Zhang Yimou filming *Yellow Earth* (1984), a film heralding China's fifth-generation "New Wave."

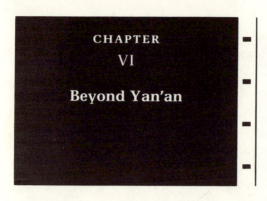

CHAPTER VI

Beyond Yan'an

The "ten-year catastrophe" (as the Cultural Revolution was labeled in the late 1970s) marked as great a transformation in Chinese national life as had the War of Resistance to Japan in the 1940s. Chinese response to this inchoate realization took a variety of forms. The Party leadership, aware of the nation's relative material backwardness, called for resolutely facing the future and the rapid achievement of the Four Modernizations in industry, science, agriculture, and defense. The political public, especially younger citizens who had lost ten years of schooling or career in the Cultural Revolution, was less resolute in embracing the future. Many citizens felt that a proper and sufficient assessment of the past – of the Cultural Revolution and the role of the Party – was a prerequisite for any national advancement. The young Chinese who were active in the Democracy Wall movement of 1978–9 called for a "fifth modernization," a democratization of political life.[1] This new political ferment, although short-lived and circumscribed by elite manipulation, was an attempt at the reassessment of the immediate past which the civil war and Communist victory had provided in the late 1940s, after the national experience of the war with Japan. China in the late 1970s did not erupt in civil war, but the questioning of the period forced considerable readjustment by the nation's leaders.

At the turn of the 1980s Chinese film directly reflected the concerns and problems of the nation as a whole to an extent not seen since the late 1940s. Many of the new films, like contemporary short stories and plays, were set in the Cultural Revolution, or explained their characters' current difficulties by reference to those years. After the sterility of the model operas and the model films, the emphasis on what passed for authentic human feelings and failings, on youthful love and middle-aged frustration, was not unexpected. Chinese filmgoers in the late 1940s saw their own experiences on the screen in *The Spring River Flows East*. In 1980 *Legend of Tianyun Mountain* played a similar role for a large part of what by then was a more heterogeneous film audience.

The Cultural Revolution and its aftermath fostered changes in the

154

tripartite relationship among Party, filmmakers, and audiences which lay behind this film achievement. Most significantly, filmmakers were made more mindful of the tastes and aspirations of audiences. Younger film artists began to play more prominent roles in the film enterprise. Few representatives of the pre-1949 May Fourth generation of artists remained active by the late 1970s, and even those who had become filmmakers after 1949 were reaching the end of middle age. The younger artists, having grown up under the Party government and in many cases been Cultural Revolution activists, had perhaps a better grasp than their older colleagues of audiences' expectations. Filmmakers of all generations had undergone in the "ten-year catastrophe" an experience which they shared with their audiences. The persecution and arbitrary interference by the Party insurgents after 1964 seem to have helped lessen the distance between many film artists, along with other members of the intellectual stratum, and ordinary citizens. No experience comparable to this had occurred since the War of Resistance to Japan and the civil war in the 1940s.

The continuing readjustment of relations between artists and the Party contributed to closer links between the former and their audiences. Clearly, this readjustment was part of broader changes in the position and prestige of the Party in Chinese life. Deng Xiaoping and other leaders realized that the Party could not do everything, and that narrowing the scope of Party intervention in society might also narrow the range of Party responsibility for intractable problems. In cultural matters, the readjustment from the late 1970s was labeled the "second Hundred Flowers." Artists and cultural leaders discussed, more frankly than they had done since 1956–7, the shortcomings of the film system and the need for allowing artists greater creative autonomy.

The official denunciation of a new film, *Unrequited Love (Kulian)*, in 1981 illustrated at once both the limits to this readjustment of Party–artist relations and the inevitability of its continuing. Censors found the film too strong in its condemnation of past political restriction. Although the cultural leadership pulled back from its relative "openness," they generally were still willing to concede that a return to the pre–Cultural Revolution strictures was impossible. Instead, by the mid-1980s the parties involved in the film industry continued their efforts to find a more permanent balance between the Party's requirements, artists' concerns, and audiences' demands.

Policy reassessment

By 1978 the criticism, which the restored Party leadership encouraged in order to repudiate their Gang of Four predecessors and legitimate their own position, had gone beyond this narrow focus to address the whole problem of the relationship between art and politics and filmmaking's problems. Having started with a relatively narrow focus on the Gang, the critics of the late 1970s were in general bolder than their Hundred Flowers predecessors. Soon, however, the distinction between the supposedly aberrant wing represented by the Gang and the rest of the Party became blurred. The boldness encouraged by the initially narrow Gang target provided a momentum to discussion that went beyond the Cultural Revolution years to include an increasingly explicit critique of the Party's cultural leadership in general during the previous three decades. The bold critics in the Democracy Wall movement from the autumn through spring of 1978–9 had counterparts in film circles who shared the aims of democratization and greater autonomy in their own profession.

Younger filmmakers played a conspicuous part in these discussions of the continuing problems of the film enterprise. Generational tensions were as important in film circles as in other areas, where impatient and ambitious younger artists confronted older figures returning to prominent positions. Although there was no major changeover in personnel following October 1976, well-known film artists and leaders of a pre–Cultural Revolution and pre-1949 vintage had much greater influence in the years immediately after 1976. Xia Yan, doyen of the May Fourth generation filmmakers, reemerged in October 1977, at seventy-seven years old barely able to walk, after bad treatment in prison during the "ten year catastrophe." He took up duties as chairman of the Film Association and advisor to the Ministry of Culture. Yang Hansheng, writer of *Jiangnan in the North*, returned to public life in January 1979, serving as vice-chairman of the Federation of Literary and Art Circles. The federation was chaired (after November 1979) by Zhou Yang, who later held a deputy directorship in the Central Committee's Propaganda Department. Zhou returned briefly to something close to the level of influence in cultural policy he had held in the early 1960s. Restoration of the position of older colleagues may have been less obvious at the studio level, for many filmmakers, trained in the 1950s, had already returned to work in the early 1970s.

Although younger filmmakers do not appear to have been demoted, they seem to have had grounds for complaint. In 1977–9, of 140 graduates in acting sent to the film studios, less than half had had a chance to perform on screen. At one studio, most of the over twenty graduates sent there had already abandoned an acting career. Young directors, in 1979 at last given an opportunity to make films, were ill-served by being furnished with less experienced cinematographers, designers, and other specialists than older colleagues.[2] Some younger filmmakers publicly criticized their older colleagues for being too backward-looking after the trauma of the Cultural Revolution. A member of a short-term scriptwriting class at the Beijing Film Academy made this point at a forum of filmgoers. Industry leaders and the Academy, Liu Qing argued, were creating limitations for themselves (*hua di wei lao*, literally, "drawing a circle on the ground and keeping within it") in holding up older films for study and emulation, including Soviet and American films from the 1930s and 1940s, and Chinese works from before 1966. Film leaders put new foreign films last. At the same meeting, a trainee teacher from the Fengtai district endorsed this dissatisfaction with the concentration on the past. "Some leaders keep on stressing that films must achieve the levels reached in the 1950s, and the masses would be satisfied with this. In fact, times have changed and things from the 1950s will not satisfy people's needs. Filmmaking should not create limits for itself, nor stop and fix its gaze backward."[3]

Two young filmmakers in January 1979 made the most comprehensive summing up of the problems in the filmmaking industry. The title of their article, "What's wrong with the movies?" (*Dianying weishenme shangbuqu*), became the heading for a *People's Daily* column that continued for almost six months.[4] Peng Ning and He Kongzhou, artists at the Changchun studio, wanted real change on the part of film management and in the film production system. They feared that some cultural leaders regarded the current policy of liberalization (*fang*, or openness) not as a policy for long-term development, but merely as a temporary post-Gang expedient, to be succeeded by restriction (*shou*, rounding up). Peng and He argued that the lessons of the previous three decades showed the need for openness on the part of the leadership and for boldness from filmmakers. Cultural leaders and studio managers should recognize the artistic peculiarities of filmmakers' work, instead of issuing executive orders on what could or could not be written, and how it should be handled on film.

Peng and He included some concrete suggestions for reform of the film production system, particularly at the studio level. They suggested that the studio head, under Party leadership, and basic level cadres should be selected democratically by the studio employees. To allow artists more say in what was produced, an artistic committee (*yishu weiyuanhui*) should assess the scripts and finished films made by collective creative groups (*chuangzuo jiti*) at the studio. These groups and the studio management, Peng and He argued, should together hold the purse strings and produce the films. Employees' representative assemblies should have the power to assess and approve artistic and management cadres.[5] Peng and He endorsed the concept of "the director as the center of the filmmaking group," which had come under fire both in the 1957 Anti-Rightist backlash and in 1975 from Jiang Qing. They ended their article with a plea for greater efforts in training younger film artists and giving them more opportunities to practice their craft.

Filmmakers, audiences, and the leadership continued to address the problems of the film industry in 1979. In the same January issue of *Film*

Art that Peng and He's article appeared, a 1961 speech by Zhou Enlai to film artists was published for the first time. It offered evidence that, two decades earlier, the spiritual mentors of the current Party leaders had endorsed the need for greater artistic autonomy and less bureaucratic interference.

Many participants in this reformist discourse used the phrase "too many mothers-in-law" (*popo duo*) to characterize the then current film world. Unlike novels and plays, new films still faced a great many obstacles before release. One young filmmaker, who had worked in the industry for only a year, endorsed Peng and He's call for the elimination of bureaucratic management methods. He accused some leaders, often laypersons in matters of art, of wantonly interfering in the writing of scripts and their production. Between script and release, films had to surmount up to ten barriers of studio and higher-level assessment, as had been the case in the past. Unless local and production sections gained more self-determination, audiences would continue to resent the lifeless films the studios produced.[6]

Discussants also reassessed the history of the preceding three decades in an effort to explain the current problems of filmmaking. Li Shaobai, one of the authors of the two-volume 1963 *History of the Development of Chinese Film*, ventured to assess the seventeen years after 1949, which a planned third volume had been designed to cover. Li used a watery metaphor in differentiating two waves and two troughs (*liangqi liangluo*) of film production in the pre–Cultural Revolution years. The surges in production had come when leadership was at its most open, the troughs, when restrictions had been tightest. Filmmakers had been most active in the three years before the *Life of Wu Xun* campaign and in the two or three years at the beginning of the 1960s, after the Anti-Rightist campaign had receded. Although Li refrained from making the connection directly, the two troughs could be ascribed to the actions of Mao Zedong. Li concluded:[7]

The facts tell us that the film industry advances when objective reality, artistic laws and the creative efforts of film workers are respected. On the other hand, our industry falls back when reality is left behind, artistic laws are violated, audiences are treated as idiots [*Adou*], and commands are shot about.

Speakers at the Fourth National Congress of Writers and Artists endorsed the liberalization of the "second Hundred Flowers." In his congratulatory message to the October–November 1979 congress, Vice-Premier Deng Xiaoping noted:[8]

Our writers and artists . . . deserve the trust, love, and respect of the Party and the people. Our contingent of literary and art workers has been rigorously tested by the struggles in this stormy period, and, in general, they have proved themselves worthy of the task. The Party and the people are very pleased to have such writers and artists. . . . Writers and artists must have the freedom to choose their subject matter and method of presentation based upon artistic practice and exploration [*tansuo*]. No interference in this regard can be permitted.

Xia Yan took a less sanguine view. "I nevertheless feel that there are still those who are suspicious and fearful of, or even opposed to, the emancipation of thought [*sixiang jiefang*]." He made a rare reference to factionalism within artistic ranks: "We hope that after the present congress it will be possible to get rid of the personal favoritism of the seventeen-year period and the Cultural Revolution once and for all, to thoroughly wipe out all factors that hinder writing, and to concentrate our main efforts on artistic creativity and theoretical research. . . ."[9]

A forty-nine-year-old army poet and film scenarist made some of the most outspoken remarks at this landmark congress. Bai Hua, who had been labeled a "rightist" in 1958 and had only been fully rehabilitated in early 1979, took exception to the wave of official caution which had occurred in the spring of that year, when many Democracy Wall activists had been arrested. "It cannot yet be said that this is a fairly safe time for writers. Aren't people still writing essays, sending letters, and making speeches asking to lock up so-and-so or to label so-and-so a counterrevolutionary?" Bai noted that "for a long time we have had people pointing at a deer and calling it a horse. Now that the real horse has appeared, people do not recognize it, and they brand the man who calls a horse a horse a heretic." He ended on a strong note:[10]

Let us resolutely resist the sort of "unity" which in the past has been brought into being under the clubs of a certain few. They think that anyone who holds his arms to shield his head is opposed to unity, while those who try to wrest the clubs from their hands are crazed advocates of insubordination and treason. . . . Without courage there can be no breakthrough; without breakthrough there can be no literature.

Bai Hua's remarks took on a somewhat symbolic significance eighteen months later, when clubs began to be raised.

Although by 1980, with the closing down of Democracy Wall, discussions on cultural policy had become less bold, the veteran film actor Zhao Dan wrote a deathbed reminder of the need to address the issues. Under the blunt headline, "Rigid control ruins art and literature," Zhao asked: "Is there anyone who has become a writer because he was asked to by the Party? . . . And who asked Marx to write? . . . Convention is not truth. Still less should corrupt practices be followed as hard-and-fast rules. A good work can never be produced by [passing through] many levels of scrutiny." The publication in *People's Daily* of this statement, from the star of *The Life of Wu Xun*, that "strengthening Party leadership," the usual solution in troubled times, destroyed art, suggests that Zhao's views had some official endorsement. He concluded with the question, "Will this [article of mine] have any effect?"[11]

A partial answer to the concerns expressed by Zhao's question had come already in mid-1980 in a controversy over a film scripted by Bai Hua himself. As a war film, *The Stars Are Bright Tonight* (*Jinye xingguang canlan*, August First studio) had a long cinematic pedigree in socialist China. But in his script Bai Hua did not present much of the major Huaihai campaign of 1948, the setting of the story. Instead, the film centers on the experiences of three youthful soldiers and a young peasant woman who wanders into their midst and falls in love with one of them. This upset some viewers. Chen Yi, a former head of the Culture Section of the People's Liberation Army General Political Department, who had himself been condemned as a "rightist" in 1958,[12] was one of the objectors. In an article, which the *People's Daily* editors published "in the interests of presenting both sides," Chen complained that, by concentrating on the personal story of the youths, the film distorted and diminished the significance of the Huaihai campaign.[13]

The response in defense of Bai Hua and the film was a vigorous affirmation of the new cultural atmosphere of the second Hundred Flowers. At a roundtable discussion on the film organized by the editors of *Popular Film* (at the time China's largest circulation magazine with an estimated readership of 100 million),[14] Chen Yi's objections were condemned. Some discussants saw Chen's remarks as representing a lingering tendency in the new age to fling about old "anti-Party" and "antisocialism" labels. The film was endorsed as one that would not corrupt young persons, a view shared by the Communist Youth League.[15]

Concrete changes in the system of film production were less easy to detect. Just as for the 1950s and 1960s, so in the early 1980s the actual practice of film production in the studios and at higher levels of censorship was difficult to assess. The bulk of the public pronouncements about liberalization by Party leaders, cultural authorities, studio leaders,[16] and artists suggested that adjustments were made in practice as well as in policy.[17] But the sort of artistic autonomy envisaged by Peng Ning and He Kongzhou took time in coming. The lead articles in the December 1980 issues of *Popular Film* and *Film Art* both called for further changes in the production system, involving in particular further devolution of authority to the studio level, to bring the system into line with the spirit of the second Hundred Flowers.[18]

Films of the second Hundred Flowers

The films released in the two to three years after 1979 reflected the changes in the relations among filmmakers, their audiences, and their leadership. The shared experience of the Cultural Revolution brought many artists closer to their audiences than they had been before 1966. The reassessment of Party cultural policy in these years invigorated the growth of stronger artist–audience links. Scriptwriters and directors felt more able to explore social concerns which films from the seventeen years before 1966 had rarely acknowledged. In terms of style also, artists attempted to be more adventurous in the use of film's possibilities. Rejection of the formalism and stereotype of the Cultural Revolution films encouraged artists to create new film characters of more ordinary dimensions who were less prone to rhetorical gesture and speech. This in turn enabled audiences to identify their own concerns and experiences with those of the characters they saw in films. Not since the late 1940s had audiences enjoyed such a wealth of opportunities to recognize themselves on movie screens.

The major concern of audiences and the new films was the Cultural Revolution. The destruction and suffering of the "ten year catastrophe," often in flashback in a story set after those events, were important themes in many of the new films. In response to the discounting of personal feelings by the highly typified "class feeling" of the Cultural Revolution model art, after 1978 most of the new films dwelt notably on love. Films set in the recent Sino–Vietnamese border war, in the latter part of the Gang years, in 1940s Shanghai, or in contemporary times invariably featured a love story. In films set after 1966, the trials of a youthful couple, whose outlooks have in some way been distorted by the Cultural Revolution, were commonly portrayed.

They're in Love (*Tamen zai xiang'ai*, Beijing studio, 1980) is a good example of the new genre. It contrasts the present-day experiences in love of three brothers, children of a high-ranking cadre, a typical family background in many such films. All three sons have suffered because of the Cultural Revolution. The oldest, a doctor, broke up with his doctor fiancée over the political problem of his "class background." The middle son was confined to a wheelchair after being thrown down the stairs of his family's palatial home by Red Guards. With time on his hands, he has taught himself foreign languages and does scientific translations. In the course of the film he inspires his schoolteacher girlfriend to overcome her feelings of inadequacy at work and in love. The youngest brother fell into bad company during the Cultural Revolution, when proper parental guidance was not available, and has continued to be a hooligan (*afei*), using the taxi he drives to impress his ambitious, money-grasping girlfriend. Films like this were a recognition of the destructive effects of the Cultural Revolution on the younger generation, even if the portrait of the two older brothers is somewhat idealized. Near the end of the film, preparations for the joint engagement party of the two senior brothers are interrupted by the arrival of their younger sibling, carrying his newborn child by the money-grubber. His plaintive "I was wrong" (*Wo cuole*) was greeted by at least one young Beijing moviehouse audience with hysterical laughter.

Problems of love and the poisoning of relationships during the Cultural Revolution are the focus of *Love and Inheritance* (*Aiqing yu yichan*, Xi'an studio, 1980). The film contrasts the experiences in love of the son and daughter of the head of an ophthalmology institute. The girl initially imagines that her devotion to her medical career (she too works at the institute) must preclude other, emotional dedications. Moreover, her prospective boyfriend, when a Red Guard, had wrecked her home. She eventually forgives him and they marry, after winning the approval of his parents, who are peasants. Her brother, on the other hand, went astray in the Cultural Revolution years and is being pursued by an ambitious and rapacious young woman, not unlike the youngest brother's girlfriend in *They're in Love*. Before his death the father acknowledges that, in their devotion to the revolution and their work, he and his late wife had tended to neglect the proper education of their children. He leaves them as their inheritance an unpublished research manuscript and a battered case of surgical instruments given him by a martyred comrade at Yan'an. His considerable savings he leaves to the state for research, much to the chagrin of his son's girlfriend, who promptly abandons the youth.

A more direct treatment of the later years of the Cultural Revolution is made in *Reverberations of Life* (*Shenghuo de chanyin*, Xi'an studio, 1979), a cinematic portrayal of the Tiananmen Square demonstrations of April 5, 1976 in memory of Zhou Enlai, which were a direct inspiration for the Democracy Wall movement during the second Hundred Flowers period. For the filming, a replica of the square was built on an airfield near Xi'an. Xiang Kun, who had specialized in playing Guomindang generals and had been labeled a "rightist" in 1957, plays the youthful heroine's father, one of the film's range of rather noble intellectuals, all quietly determined in early 1976 that the popular voice be heard. The love story of his daughter and a composer, intent on writing a musical eulogy to premier Zhou, is the focus of the film. The black and white photography and editing of some tense sequences distinguish this film from its more pedestrian contemporaries, notwithstanding its typical piety toward the memory of the late premier.

Another young director, Wu Yigong, was responsible for a view of the Cultural Revolution in which a love story played a secondary role. *Night Rain on the River* (*Bashan yeyu*, Shanghai studio, 1980) follows a ferry voyage in the early 1970s through the Yangzi River gorges by an assorted group of travelers, including a poet under guard for political offenses. In the course of the film one of the guards, a young woman, begins to realize the injustice of her journey. She, along with the audience, is astonished to learn that her older, security bureau colleague also thinks their detention of the poet is wrong, as does most of the crew. The film ends with the poet somehow set free, tramping the hills above the river with his long-lost little daughter, who happened to be on the boat. Although a brief plot outline seems unconvincing, the film has considerable power. The symbolic qualities of the ship's journey are not wasted, and the somber tone is nicely punctuated by the antics of an elderly passenger, anxious to avoid trouble, who insists on having model opera blaring from the cabin radio and ostentatiously reads political tracts on his bunk. Like *Reverberations of Life*, this film reinforces the view that the vast majority of the people, even persons in positions of considerable authority, did not subscribe to the aims of the Cultural Revolution, but suffered these years in collective silence. The film won several awards in the spring of 1981, including a prize for the scenarist Ye Nan, an army writer.[19]

Two of the most intriguing film treatments of the Cultural Revolution were the work of Yang Yanjin, a Shanghai director in his early thirties who had been in the last class at the Beijing Film Academy before it closed in 1968. *Bitter Laughter* (*Ku'naoren de xiao*, Shanghai studio, 1979) tells of the struggle of a Shanghai journalist in 1975 with his conscience when faced with reporting only good news, instead of exposing the abuses he discovers. His concern for the truth almost causes his marriage to break up, his wife being worried about the future of their small daughter. The exchanges between the couple on their dilemma have an authenticity rarely seen in films made in the thirty years preceding it. Eventually the journalist accepts the dictates of his conscience, but in an almost accidental, rather than heroic, way. One of his reporter colleagues has fewer scruples, and a conversation between the two is overheard by the venal city Party secretary. The good journalist is taken from his family by the police. Until the forced joy of a fireworks and flower-filled denouement, the tone of the film is overwhelmingly somber, and the journalist and other victims are not presented as heroes. One professor has become a pitiful alcoholic under the humiliations he suffers at the hands of Red Guards. This sobriety of tone, in marked contrast to the gloss and heroics of more usual Chinese movies from before the Cultural Revolution, and the somewhat clumsy (though exuberant) use of new technical devices like the split screen, probably account for the film's apparent unpopularity. Many viewers regarded it as a rather foreign work.[20] For these viewers, happy endings should not come as a surprise.

A choice of endings is the most intriguing aspect of Yang Yanjin's second film. *The Alley* (*Xiaojie*, Shanghai studio, 1981) tells the story of a young woman in the Cultural Revolution who, when her intellectual mother is attacked by Red Guards, changes her identity, assuming the guise of a young man. Echoes of the traditional love story of Liang Shanbo and Zhu Yingtai (subject of a popular 1954 Shaoxing opera film, China's first color feature), which involves similar transsexual disguise of one partner, are noteworthy. The scriptwriting narrator of *The Alley* (played by Yang himself) presents viewers with three possible present-day endings: one happy, one tragic, and the third a mixture. Whatever the multiple endings do to the artistic integrity of the work (cinematic reference to Kurosawa's *Rashomon* is not unintended), it amounted to a mutual acknowledgment by the filmmakers and some of their audiences that the simple happy endings characteristic of "socialist realism" were no longer satisfactory.

Other issues in socialist society and human relations in a pre–Cultural Revolution setting were examined in *Longing for Home* (*Xiangqing*, Shanghai studio, 1981), in which a young man, who has grown up with a foster mother in the countryside, goes to the city to be reunited with his real parents, who are important Party officials and veteran revolutionaries. Differences between, and prejudices about, living in urban or rural areas (in the 1950s) are given a prominent place in the film, as are the privileges available to cadres and their offspring. The boy attends a high school for the children of cadres. Lyrical evocation, clearly inspired by traditional landscape painting, of the boy's childhood spent tending water buffalo is contrasted with the bustle, artificiality, and ambition found in cities. The film ends ambiguously, with the boy's decision about whether to remain in the city not clear. Meanwhile his mother has seen the error of her insistence that the boy live with her in town. Interestingly, this is because she recognizes a direct, personal debt to the boy's adoptive mother in the country, whom she now remembers as the young peasant with whom she had left her baby son in the 1930s. As in *The Alley*, the incomplete ending was a new concession to the intelligence of post–Cultural Revolution audiences.

This second Hundred Flowers interest in human feelings and relationships extended also to films with a more distant historical setting. A film centered on the ruling circles of the new Chinese Republic in the 1910s represented a big change in cultural politics. That *Intimate Friends* (*Zhiyin*, Beijing studio, 1981) should dwell on the love between Cai E, the Yunnan warlord, and Fengxian, a courtesan, as well as on their mutual patriotic efforts to save the Republic from president Yuan Shikai's monarchical ambitions, made the work typical of its age. The strengthening affection between warlord and courtesan indeed provides needed momentum for the film, after early expository, political scenes in Yuan's court. In the end, on the death of Cai E in Japan, Xie Tieli and his codirectors show considerable restraint. A single string on the zither Fengxian is playing, on her way to refuge in Hunan, suddenly snaps.[21] Where once, in another context, the film might have cut to shots of crashing waves accompanied by a heavenly chorus (as in the 1962 *Naval Battle of 1894*, for example), *Intimate Friends* ends in a southern Chinese landscape, subtly underlining the patriotic theme and hinting at eventual change arising from the south, where the Communist Party was first successful. The placid, watery context of the last scene also recalls the opening shots of water (around the foundations of Yuan's palace), a favorite directorial device of Xie Tieli, which he had even used in the 1972 model opera film *On the Docks*.

Comedy was not neglected in the films of the second Hundred Flowers, most often in conjunction with a youthful love story. In 1979 the veteran artist Sang Hu, director of the model ballet film *The White-Haired Girl* (1972), and of *The New Year's Sacrifice* (1956), made *Twins Come in Pairs* (*Talia he talia*, Shanghai studio). The film exploits to the full the comic confusion and cinematic trickery of two sets of identical twins, who eventually fall in love. The contrast between the earnest, hard-working couple, giving their all for the Four Modernizations, and their less disciplined siblings, draws a lesson in social morality. A noteworthy feature of this comedy, and many other films made and set in the late 1970s, is the untypical spaciousness and luxury of the characters' accommodations.[22] This luxury, in such 1950s films as *City without Night* and *Loyal Partners*, had been officially criticized in the Anti-Rightist campaign and Cultural Revolution. So-called socialist realism during the 1950s and 1960s seemed to tolerate the idealization only of proletarian reality. A similar idealization of reality seemed to succeed it in films from the 1980s. Seen also in the new television dramas, this new improvement on reality may have been a way to show audiences the putative rewards of achieving the Four Modernizations.

Legend of Tianyun Mountain (*Tianyunshan chuanqi*, Shanghai studio, 1980) combined the themes of love, idealism, and political destruction with an impact not often seen in films made in 1980. For many viewers, this work came closest to reflecting the recent national experience with something like the resonance which had made *The Spring River Flows East* such a significant film for its late-1940s audiences.

In the 1980 film two love stories are intertwined, one happy and the other eventually painful. The happy couple are, ironically, a young engineer condemned as a "rightist" in 1958 for his outspokenness during the first Hundred Flowers discourse and the subsequent Great Leap whose exile in the Tianyun mountains is rendered more bearable by the love of a former colleague, who makes great sacrifices for her husband and her support of his principles. The other couple consists of the engineer's former fiancée and one of the cadres who had criticized the engineer in 1958. In the late 1970s, when the story is narrated, this couple are both high-level officials in the Tianyun district, having themselves been incarcerated during the Cultural Revolution. The cadre refuses, despite his wife's pleas, to reexamine the case of the engineer with a view to reversing the 1958 verdict. The film ends with this marriage in ruins, and the verdict indeed reversed. The engineer's wife does not survive to hear the news. The future lies with the engineer, his former fiancée, the official's wife, and more particularly with two other young people: the inquisitive young woman who served as the initial narrator of the story and the adopted daughter of the engineer.

Youth and love thus are prominent elements in *Legend of Tianyun Mountain*. But Xie Jin, who had directed *The Red Detachment of Women* (1961), *Stage Sisters* (1964), the model opera *On the Docks* (1972), and the especially simplistic *Youth* (*Qingchun*, 1977), combines the themes with a vivid reexamination of Chinese history since the late 1950s. The importance of the individual attitudes, guilt, and courage of the characters is typical of films of the second Hundred Flowers. Motivation for the actions of both the cadre's and engineer's wives, for example, seems to derive from a combination of socialist idealism and personal feelings. All films made under the cultural dictatorship of Jiang Qing, and perhaps most produced in the seventeen years before 1966, strongly discounted the importance of individual characters' emotions. Socialist man (or woman) acted only for objective, socialist reasons. *Legend of Tianyun Mountain* was a reminder of the limitations of this proposition.[23]

These changes in film subjects and themes did not, however, mean that the importance of film as a propagator of a mass national culture had diminished. An emphasis on types and ideals remained strong, as the comparative luxury of accommodations in *Twins Come in Pairs*, and even the outspoken idealism of the inquisitive young woman in *Legend of Tianyun Mountain* suggest. All the films, which still needed central Film Bureau approval before release, were required to serve the purposes of socialist construction, now under the rubric of the Four Modernizations. Television, the medium that might rival film's effectiveness in reaching national audiences, at the beginning of the 1980s was still undeveloped in terms of geographical coverage and audience accessibility.

Cultural authorities and filmmakers continued to express concern for developing a Chinese style in films as part of the medium's national functions. Something of an internationalism of film styles, on the other hand, became apparent in the late 1970s. Here too, cinema reflected broader changes in Chinese society. The so-called opening to the West, which the Dengist leadership initially encouraged, was more vigorous than any such effort in the previous three decades. Its effects were also less controllable than the leadership may have imagined. While it would be easy to exaggerate the importance of international connections in the protest, their significance at the height of the Democracy Wall movement is noteworthy. In some respects, these young activists seemed to have more in common with the Western journalists eager to hear their story than with their poor peasant compatriots who journeyed to Beijing in the winter of 1978–9 and into the new year seeking redress of past wrongs.

Film, after the Cultural Revolution a medium associated increasingly with youth, was also internationalized to a degree. Stylistic borrowings from foreign film, particularly that of Taiwan and Hong Kong, are apparent in many of the movies discussed here. Young lovers wander in flower-filled gardens, as the screen splits into multiple images of spring. Action sequences are more tightly edited than in most pre–Cultural Revolution films, and even martial art (*wushu*) sequences occur in some features.[24] In a sense Chinese films by the early 1980s had to cater to more youthful tastes, which were expanding and changing under exposure to a much greater variety of foreign, Western movies.[25]

Unrequited Love

The official criticism of a film in internationalist style on a patriotic theme, which in many respects resembled other works about the Cultural Revolution, paradoxically defined the limits of criticism. *Unrequited Love (Kulian)* was a script by Bai Hua, who had been so outspoken at the Fourth Congress of Writers and Artists, and the young Peng Ning, who had coauthored a seminal 1979 article on the need for "artistic democracy." Before the film, titled *The Sun and the Man (Taiyang he ren)* and directed by Peng Ning, could be released, it came under fire. A "special commentator" in *Liberation Army Daily (Jiefangjun bao)* in April 1981 criticized the film and Bai Hua for exceeding the limits of recent cultural liberalization. To this critic, the patriotism of the film did not seem to include an equal loyalty to the Communist Party. Curiously, very little happened immediately in public, which seemed to indicate a new climate for literary debate. In the past the *Liberation Army Daily* article might have been the first salvo in a "campaign" against the film and what it was taken to represent. In the autumn of 1981, however, two well-known, strategically placed critics revived the public controversy over *Unrequited Love*. It became the focus for further and more cautious redefinition of the limits of change in films and cultural policy in general.

Unrequited Love draws strongly on a romantic and humanist strain in Chinese literature. The script, for example, makes several direct references to Qu Yuan, the third-century-B.C. poet and patriot who committed suicide rather than serve an unjust ruler.[26] Ling Chenguang, the artist hero of the film, paints a portrait of Qu Yuan for display at the April 5, 1976 Tiananmen Square demonstrations in memory of Zhou Enlai and against what became the Gang of Four. At the end of the film Ling dies in an attitude similar to Qu Yuan's portrait. Flights of geese, in the arrowhead formation of the Chinese pictograph for man (*ren*), punctuate the film at ten points. The theme song reads:[27]

Oh,
Smiling gaily amid the deepest hardships
Marching forward boldly
We will write the word "man" across the sky.
Oh! The glory of it! It is the strongest symbol in the universe.

The film traces, through flashback from late 1976, the career of Ling Chenguang, a painter, and emphasizes his patriotism. As a small boy in the 1920s, he befriends a schoolgirl, Chen Juanjuan. At the Chen home, Juanjuan's mother plays a Chopin nocturne while Ling Chenguang thrusts a muddy hand out to greet Mr. Chen, a scientist who has spent most of his life abroad. When Ling eventually goes abroad, it is unwillingly, having been "shanghaied" to crew a cargo steamer. In the United States in the 1940s Ling prospers as an artist. His arrival at an exhibition of his paintings is like that of a movie star at a premiere. Flashbulbs pop, young women seek his autograph, and chauffeurs snap to attention. When the ragged country woman whom he had loved many years ago inexplicably turns up at the American gallery, Ling takes her home to his mansion, complete with black maid. Once home, having not seen each other in many years, they each dramatically pull out from their breasts a newspaper with the news of the founding of the People's Republic of China.

Ling Chenguang and Lüniang decide to return to their homeland and abandon the material comforts of life in the West. Back in China, Ling's struggles are initially artistic, to capture on canvas the optimistic spirit of the times. The off-screen narrator notes: "This is a torment mixed with joy and sweetness. We would willingly endure it for two lifetimes." The scene immediately jumps twenty years to Ling's 1976 torment as an outcast in the marshes.[28] Meanwhile, during the Cultural Revolution, Ling's friends begin to suffer political persecution. Xie Qiushan, a poet who returned to China on the same boat as Ling, departs for a May Seventh cadre school, reciting in a poem: "Since you want to put me in fetters and handcuffs, why do you have to smile?" Xie returns some time later to find a letter of notification that his wife has died. In voiceover, she is heard stating, on the ship which brought them back from America twenty-five years earlier, "It will be all right as soon as we get back to China. Everything will be fine."

Soon afterward Ling Chenguang's daughter suddenly tells her father that she is going to marry an overseas Chinese and emigrate. This provides the opportunity for direct comment. Xingxing angrily asks her father: "Dad, you love your country. Through bitter frustrations, you go on loving her. . . . But, father, does this country love you?" Ling reels from his painting and makes no reply. Ling's childhood sweetheart, Juanjuan, returns on a visit from abroad, dressed entirely in white, perhaps to indicate recent widowhood. This further contrived encounter allows Ling Chenguang to affirm that he has no regrets about returning to China twenty-five years earlier. Later, when an old general urges his friend Ling to flee Beijing, Ling responds: "Living in post-Liberation China, can we still become fugitives? Living under socialism in our native land, do we still have to run away?"

The film ends with a mixture of hope and not a little ambiguity. It is after October 1976, for the search party looking for the fugitive Ling Chenguang in the marshes includes the historian Feng, who had earlier spent time there with Ling in order to save a precious manuscript from destruction. Clutching the page proofs of the book, Feng calls out: "We are now in a time when a correct view of history is possible!" The poet Xie cries out eloquently: "Brother! These are not the fires of hell! This is the radiance of humanity drawing closer to you! Brother! We are not demons. We are men." The old general, also in the search party, affirms that the nation needs and loves Ling. The film cuts to a high aerial shot of a huge question mark stamped out in the snow. The dot at its base is the frozen corpse of the artist, his hands raised imploring to the heavens, like his earlier portrait of Qu Yuan. His eyes are fixed open. Aerial views of Chinese landscapes, which may have been intended to recall similar shots in the widely distributed post-Gang documentary in memory of Zhou Enlai, follow as Ling Chenguang's voice repeats a passage heard at the very beginning of the film:

If [these images] were no more than the products of a painter's imagination, we could rip them apart, deface them, throw them away! But they are none of these. This is our motherland! . . . We have walked untold millions of miles, suffered immeasurable hardships, but we have won the sacred right to say, "I love this land, my motherland."

Yet another flight of geese in the form of the "man" character climbs across the sky. The film's final image is of a solitary reed standing tall against the wind.

The critics in 1981 were probably correct in their assertion that *Unrequited Love* went beyond most contemporary films in its portrayal of the past. The critics, who had been silent when the script was published in 1979, now objected to what they perceived as the failure of Bai Hua and Peng Ning to make a proper distinction between the regimes of the Guomindang and Gang of Four on the one hand, and the Communist Party regime on the other. The film focuses attention on the similarities between two eras, which the Communists saw as antithetical. At one point the narrator states: "Everybody has fond memories of China in the 1950s. Everything was new, everything was firm, especially the people's will to do everything possible to make the country strong and prosperous. How strong was our determination! What a perfect beginning for the new China!" Party leaders and others nervous about the public standing of the regime might naturally feel that the narrator was contrasting the 1950s as much with 1981 as with 1976 of the story's setting. Filmic devices added to the blurring of distinctions. Shots of Ling Chenguang being fired at by Guomindang thugs on a Shanghai street are rapidly intercut with Ling being shot at in the marsh thirty years later. The poet

Xie refers to fetters and handcuffs in his 1975 farewell poem. Ling had worn these bonds when press-ganged by Guomindang troops.

Also of concern to critics of the film were implications in *Unrequited Love* about Mao Zedong before the Central Committee decision of June 1981, which attempted to put Mao in his proper, historical place. At a Chan (Zen) temple, an old monk explains to the young Ling Chenguang that the once gilded Buddha statue has been blackened by the incense of worshipers. "You will find, my child," the priest observes, "that in this world the actual result is often the exact opposite of the good intention."

The critics of *Unrequited Love* were relatively restrained, compared with their predecessors in the Anti-Rightist campaign or the Cultural Revolution. The April *Liberation Army Daily* commentator condemned the script not as anti- (*fan*) socialist, but as "expressing hostility toward" (*chouhen*) communism and socialism, apparently a less severe charge. The April criticism was not followed up directly by other major newspapers, as had been typical in the past. The April writer even hoped that Bai Hua might "understand his mistakes in method, clear up his thinking, and hereafter write works of use (*youyong*) to the socialist nation and people."[29] In early May, in response to readers' concern, its editors noted, the *Beijing Evening News* (*Beijing wanbao*) published a report on Bai Hua's situation in Wuhan from his local Party committee. He was said to be writing as usual.[30] Later the same month Bai Hua was among thirty-five recipients of awards announced by *Poetry Magazine* (*Shikan*) for poetry written in 1979–80.[31]

Despite its apparent moderation, the April army criticism of *Unrequited Love* provoked a lot of unpublished concern among filmmaking and other literary circles. The response of the Party leadership indicated a degree of uncertainty about how to assert control over artists who produced works like this film.

The reported remarks which Hu Yaobang, the general secretary of the Central Committe, made at a forum on filmmaking in early May 1981, implied that the concern expressed over the criticism of Bai Hua had come as something of a surprise to the Party leadership. Hu spoke of the need to allow such countercriticism, and of the neccessity to avoid putting an issue like *Unrequited Love*, however well-founded the case against it, in every newspaper and magazine at once. Care should be taken also to distinguish between a writer and his or her work. It would seem that attacks like those on filmmakers in 1957 and 1966 would not be repeated. Perhaps not sufficiently aware of post–Cultural Revolution changes in the relative boldness and prestige of Party and artists, Hu Yaobang concluded by arguing that the *Unrequited Love* issue could be brought to a swift and tidy end by a few well-chosen words on it by local Party leaders in cultural and other enterprises.[32]

The Bai Hua episode by this time had become part of the Party concern over bourgeois liberalist tendencies (*zichanjieji ziyou qingxiang*) among intellectuals. At a conference on problems on the ideological front, called in August 1981 by the Propaganda Department, Hu Qiaomu argued that the presentation in *Unrequited Love* of a one-sided view of the Cultural Revolution showed that a lot of people held similar attitudes. The portrayal of the Cultural Revolution in films was of particular concern because films had great influence, especially on the young. In Hu Qiaomu's view, films lacked the means to explain subtleties which other literary forms allegedly possessed. Hu emphasized that the Bai Hua problem should be solved within literary and art circles themselves.[33]

The *Unrequited Love* criticism, however, provided an occasion for several cultural leaders to force a reassessment of the cultural liberalization of recent years. Two such leaders revived the criticism in the public media with a widely republished article in the October 1981 issue of the *Literary Gazette*. They were Huang Gang, an orthodox literary journal editor and film critic since the 1950s, and the writer Liu Baiyu, a deputy chairman of the Writers Association and head of the Culture Section of the PLA General Political Department. Both the April and October articles on *Unrequited Love* were thus closely associated with the army and its discontent with the liberalizing trends, in this and other areas of Chinese life, over the previous three years. The October article was a more forceful reiteration of the first critique six months earlier. Peng Ning was here first publicly named as cowriter of the film's script.[34]

But by the end of 1981 it was clear that most of the Party leadership wanted to put the *Unrequited Love* business behind them. In the National Day (October 1) issue of *Red Flag*, the Party's theoretical journal, an article entitled "Films should contribute toward developing socialist spiritual civilization" put *Unrequited Love* in the broader context of film's social purpose, as perceived by the Party. The writer's main concern was the vulgar commercialism which he detected in recent love films. *Unrequited Love* was thus not unique in having a bad influence on young viewers; more films were needed on orthodox, revolutionary martyrs, the writer argued.[35]

Bai Hua made further "self-criticism" in late November 1981 in the form of a letter to the editors of the *Liberation Army Daily* and the *Literary Gazette*, the two journals which had published the major critiques of *Unrequited Love*. The letter received widespread publicity in December.[36] In his letter Bai Hua wrote that he had been wrong to confuse the fate of writers and artists in feudal society, since the time of Qu Yuan, with artists' problems under "leftist" mistakes in the new China. In so doing, he had ignored the strength of the Party and the people during the "ten year catastrophe" and had exaggerated the power of the Gang of Four. The parallels drawn between worship of Mao and feudal idols were also wrong, Bai confessed. These mistakes, likely "to cause those people who had doubts about the Party and the socialist enterprise to feel more hopeless," Bai Hua ascribed to his "contradictions in world outlook." Addressing a closing session of a ten-day conference on feature film production, Party General Secretary Hu Yaobang on December 27, 1981, declared that the *Unrequited Love* episode had been satisfactorily settled.[37]

The upshot of the episode appeared to confirm the eclipse of the Yan'an cultural view, a decline which the excesses carried out in its name during the Cultural Revolution had hastened. The critics of the film, such as Huang Gang and Liu Baiyu, cherished a view of the form and style of literature derived from Mao's Yan'an *Talks*, in the version in which they had been made the basis of cultural orthodoxy in the 1950s. In the 1980s Huang and Liu's persistence in questioning the standards used by literary circles to judge a work like *Unrequited Love* arose from an awareness that the Yan'an view was under threat. Their hopes to use the film, much as *The Life of Wu Xun* had served in 1951, as a touchstone to strengthen Yan'an orthodoxy in film and intellectual circles in 1981 were unfulfilled.

The internationalist setting and style of *Unrequited Love*, despite its insistently patriotic theme, could be said to derive more from the cosmopolitan, Shanghai cultural heritage. This modified May Fourth inspiration of romantic nationalism helps account for the film's unsurprising, but to some cultural leaders alarming, distinction between patriotism and the Communist Party. The film was representative of broader changes in Chinese cultural development, in which the simplification of policies, themes, and styles sanctioned by the Yan'anite vision were replaced by a more ready recognition of complexity and change. But by the 1980s May Fourth, already sixty years old, also required modification to remain relevant.

Striking a balance

As the fortieth anniversary of Mao Zedong's Yan'an *Talks* passed, the Party cultural leadership sought to strike a balance between moderation and control. Hu Yaobang, Zhou Yang, and others hoped to establish a medium position between what they saw as the excesses of *Unrequited Love* and the desire on the part of some leaders, notably associated with the military, to impose the sort of restriction that Mao's *Talks* had helped rationalize in the 1950s. Cultural leaders of all persuasions and filmmakers seemed more aware than these conservatives of the changes in the relations among Party, artists, and audiences which the Cultural Revolution had wrought. The preeminence of the Party, which had characterized cultural life in the 1950s and 1960s, had to be modified to recognize the importance of artists and the demands of readers and viewers.

Divisions within the cultural leadership itself threatened the achievement of a compromise between Party and artistic requirements. On the one hand were leaders such as Liu Baiyu, who had coauthored the article which revived the *Unrequited Love* criticism in late 1981. At a national forum on writing on military subjects, Liu spoke of the "unhealthy [influence of] the viewpoint of 'abstract, eternal human nature' " which had arisen in recent years. This label was reminiscent of the Party insurgents' arguments in 1964, which they backed with reference to Mao's writings, that there was no human nature beyond class nature.[38] Leaders of this persuasion apparently sought to return to simpler times, when what Mao said was treated as gospel.

The group that emphasized the need for continued moderation in cultural policy appeared stronger. Speakers at a forum on Mao Zedong's thinking on literature and art, convened in 1982 on the eve of the fortieth anniversary of the Yan'an *Talks*, referred to the erroneous tendency on the part of some in the Party "to take a metaphysical and dogmatic approach, to blindly insist that 'every sentence [which Mao wrote] is truth'."[39] Huang Gang, who had coauthored a major *Unrequited Love* critique with Liu Baiyu, in late 1982 was reportedly dismissed from his editorship of *The Age* (*Shidai de baogao*), along with a number of military writers he had recruited to that periodical.[40]

The dominant group showed its flexibility in the new assessment of Mao's *Talks* after forty years. Ironically, Zhou Yang, exponent of Mao's literary policy in the 1950s, made the acknowledgment that times had changed. "Some comrades rigidly adhere to old slogans and in this way fall out of step with the progress of the times." In a confession that some of his listeners might have felt self-righteous, Zhou went on, "Though I have always been loyal to Mao Zedong Thought (*Mao Zedong sixiang*), loyalty does not necessarily mean correctness." Zhou and other discussants now emphasized the May Fourth context of Mao's Yan'an remarks and sought to downplay the differences between May Fourth writers and Mao, thereby ignoring, of course, much of the cultural history of the three decades of the People's Republic.[41]

In the 1980s the charge of distance from the masses, which Mao had made in Yan'an against May Fourth intellectuals, had less validity. Zhou Yang himself made hyperbolic claims in this regard: "The intellectuals have become part of the laboring people, a part of the working class. It is wrong, therefore, to treat them in the old manner."[42] Other participants at the reassessment of the Yan'an *Talks* shared this view. "The initial prosperity that has been brought about in writing and artistic creation since the downfall of the Gang of Four is precisely the result of literary and art workers closely integrating themselves with the masses."[43] This statement could be interpreted in two ways. To old-fashioned cultural leaders, it was a reiteration of the old leveling view that artists should submit to the masses', meaning in reality to the Party's, literary fiat. To more liberal cadres, Zhou's words could be read as official recognition of the importance of the Cultural Revolution as marking a turning point in Chinese life, when intellectuals did indeed come closer to common people.

Xia Yan, the doyen of Chinese filmmakers and one of the few surviving May Fourth generation writers, urged artists to sustain the progress made since the late 1970s:[44]

We are meeting at a time of fine weather. There is neither cloud nor frost. But one can say that there is still a problem of ecological balance. . . . For a long time things were carried too far in felling and destroying flowers and trees in the cultural garden. . . . Today, we have fortunately entered a period of stability and unity, and cannot return to a time in which trees and people are raised in surroundings of wild wind and rain . . . the most important thing is to energetically plant trees and create forests, and open up and increase the sources of energy.

Xia Yan ended these remarks, to the postponed second plenary session of the fourth committee of the Federation of Literary and Arts Circles, with brave words: "Let us be united, arouse our enthusiasm, talk less nonsense, do more concrete things, and realistically apply ourselves for ten years. . . ."[45]

The same mid-1982 meeting adopted a ten-point Literary and Art Workers Pact which was both a post–*Unrequited Love* reassertion of Party control and a reflection of the hope that divisions within artistic ranks would not again allow wanton interference. Point seven read in part: "Oppose ultraindividualism, liberalism, factionalism and sectarian bias. Old, middle-aged, and young writers should respect, love, learn from, and help each other." The ecological balance Xia Yan urged was in part the responsibility of artists themselves. In 1951, 1957, and 1964, factionalism had made political intervention in cultural circles more possible and more destructive. As the May Fourth generation of filmmakers, and even those trained in the 1950s, gave way to younger colleagues, the older grounds for factional alignment became less important. Nonetheless, within artistic ranks divided still by competition for blessing from a still divided Party leadership, factions could not be easily avoided.

Shanghai and Yan'an

By the mid-1980s the parties in the troika which made up the Chinese film enterprise had reached a degree of adjustment that reflected a drawing back from the relative openness of the late 1970s and first years of the new decade. The structure of control under the Party had reasserted itself; film artists resigned themselves to the new conditions; and audiences, perhaps tired of the films exposing the evils of the Cultural Revolution, found escapism, China-made or imported, more attractive. Meanwhile, a new generation of filmmakers, trained in an international style, began to emerge to buck this trend with films of unprecedented quality and power. Finding audiences and pleasing censors, however, proved difficult.

However, there could be no return to the destructiveness of the Anti-Rightist years, let alone the sterility of the early 1970s. Mass audiences knew this, filmmakers hoped for it, and most of the Party apparatus acknowledged, at least indirectly, the limitations of their fiat.

Not all the organizations of control, however, appeared to share this resignation to changing circumstances, as China opened its political and cultural borders to an extent not seen for the previous three decades, and indeed since the May Fourth era, or even the Mongol Yuan dynasty (1206–1368) of Marco Polo's time. The campaign against "spiritual pollution" from abroad, launched in late 1983 by the head of the Party's Propaganda Department, was an indication of the lack of consensus at the top over the directions the nation was taking in foreign relations and in domestic policy. The fate of the campaign, however, gave comfort to citizens and artists who saw the limitations of statist interference at the old level which had been characteristic since 1949.

In the autumn of 1983 Deng Liqun, director of the Propaganda Department, was reported to have earlier complained about the pernicious influence of Western popular music, fashions, and literature on China's young people. The complaints were widely publicized by the media during the following months, as young people and intellectuals, those most influenced by foreign tastes, wondered if a liking for makeup, new hairdos, and free verse might blight their political records. Despite apparent support from the highest levels of political and military leadership during the winter, the "spiritual pollution" campaign petered out by the spring of 1984. Public indifference and resentment of such nativism caused considerable embarrassment to the top leadership, who decided that they were flogging a dead horse.

That the horse had been dusted off and trundled out was an indication, nevertheless, of the persistence of Yan'an-inspired attitudes to the outside world and conceptions of the relationships between Party leadership and society. Leaders like Deng Liqun seemed to ignore the great transformation in the prestige and influence of the Communist Party which the disastrous years of the Cultural Revolution had wrought. One of the most common responses to the campaign against "spiritual pollution" was astonishment that men like Deng could conceive of their word having a cleansing effect on popular tastes and attitudes throughout Chinese society. Leaders in Yan'an, in the mountain fastness of northern Shaanxi far from the cosmopolitan indiscipline of Shanghai, had self-consciously created the matrix for a new society. They had cherished a view of the Party's all-encompassing power for reform. In 1984, such a view seemed a naive throwback to simpler times.

Conversely, the fading of the criticisms directed against foreign pollution indicated that the internationalization of Chinese culture, which had been characteristic of the most liberalized years after the the the end of the Cultural Revolution, would continue. In contrast to the Yan'an nostalgia of leaders like Deng Liqun, the continuing openness to foreign interchange represented the persistence toward the end of the century of Shanghai openness. Bell-bottomed trousers and a fascination with Western dance styles were superficial evidence of the longevity of an eagerness to participate in the world community.

Two films, made at this time, can be said to have represented these two streams, Yan'an and Shanghai, in the 1980s. One was, ironically, in the style of the great May Fourth film adaptations of the pre-1966 period. The other, more Shanghai-representative, was in many respects a cinematic revival of the "mandarin duck and butterfly" genre of popular urban fiction of the pre-1949 era.

Bao Father and Son (*Baoshi fu zi*, 1983), a screen version of a 1934 short story by Zhang Tianyi, has the look and feel of two earlier May Fourth adaptations, *Early Spring in February* (1963) and *The Lin Family Shop* (1959). The painstaking attention to period re-creation, the slow pacing, and the respectful treatment of a modern classic are all characteristics the 1983 film shares with its predecessors. Xie Tieli, the director of *Bao Father and Son*, had directed *Early Spring* and served his apprenticeship as assistant director on *The Lin Family Shop*.

The film presents the relationship between old Bao, a servant in a big household, and his young son, in whom the father has placed all his hopes. The young Bao attends a modern-style, Western school. Father and son are convinced this will guarantee their future social advancement. The older Bao foresees a traditional future for his son. He will become an official, and in the old filial manner, ensure the rise of all those associated with him, especially his family. The younger Bao's mind is filled with more modern dreams of a Westernized life-style, after the fashion of his prosperous schoolmates, toward whom young Bao feels an overwhelming inferiority.

Departing somewhat from the short story's spirit, the film's contrast between parent and child parallels the contrast between Chinese and Western values which critics of "spiritual pollution" stressed. In writing the original story fifty years earlier, Zhang Tianyi humorously satirized both major protagonists, the father for his old-fashioned and venal views of the benefits of a political career, and the son for his ludicrous dreams of rising above his station to become a Brylcremed "young master" like his classmates. Xie Tieli in his film adaptation, as with his protagonists in *Early Spring*, fails to eschew a sympathetic presentation of the older Bao. The old man is an honest servant and proud father. He draws the sympathy of viewers in his efforts to find the funds for his son's school expenses and his pathetic refusal to see the worthlessness of much of what the boy does. The younger Bao is satirized in a manner similar to the short story, when he constantly fusses over his appearance and dreams of dancing with the rich girl he thinks he loves. When presented alongside the pitiable figure of his doting, old-fashioned father, the son's worship of foreign fashions and flashy displays of wealth is seen as not just laughable, but also ultimately destructive. The viewers' sympathy remains with the father. It is a contrast with appeal to the opponents of "spiritual pollution" from the West.[46]

Nevertheless, after watching the failure of father Bao's dreams, when his son is expelled from the high school which had guaranteed him a career in the modernized bureaucracy, viewers might conclude that solutions to the problems of China's relations with Western culture are not easy to find. As a representative of more traditional, Chinese values, Bao senior may engage sympathy, but his selfish and corrupt ideals do not have much appeal. The conflict between Chinese and Western bourgeois values *Bao Father and Son* addresses is not amenable to the rejectionist solutions the proponents of the campaign against "spiritual pollution" seemed to embrace. Nativism, which was a strong component of the Yan'an legacy since the 1940s, in the 1980s had little attraction in a social and political climate that placed growing emphasis on pragmatism and openness to new, even foreign, solutions. Yan'an had become increasingly irrelevant.

The nature and critical success of another film produced in the mid-1980s suggested that the Shanghai legacy in contemporary Chinese culture was alive and well. *Under the Bridge (Daqiao xiamian*, Shanghai studio, 1983) received a Ministry of Culture prize as one of the best films of the year. It also appears to have been popular with audiences. Although a rather ordinary artistic effort, in contrast at least to *Bao Father and Son, Under the Bridge* has an appeal which Xie Tieli's film strains for and never achieves.

Like many 1930s and 1940s films, *Under the Bridge* combines elements of the incongruent twin strains of the Shanghai cultural heritage: May Fourth literature and urban fiction of the "mandarin duck and butterfly" variety, popular before the War of Resistance to Japan. The film tells a contemporary story, set in Shanghai, of the romance between two educated young people who eke out a living as sidewalk vendors. Qin Nan returned to the city in 1979, after more than a decade in the countryside on a state farm. Like many of her contemporaries when they came back from Cultural Revolution rural exile, she cannot find a job. She makes do by operating a sewing machine, which she has bought on credit, on the street. The young man who eventually falls in love with her is also a private "entrepreneur." Gao Zhihua has set up a bicycle-repair stand outside his home. He is now thirty-one and still single, which his mother finds disappointing. Mrs. Gao's visions of a role as grandmother and mother-in-law are clouded by the appearance of Dongdong, whom Qin Nan acknowledges as her own child. After initial hesitation, and in the face of the censure of old-fashioned neighbors, Gao Zhihua and Qin Nan resolve to make a future together.

In contrast to the simplistic moralism of *Bao Father and Son*, *Under the Bridge* presents its moral message in a more popular form. As the outline of the story suggests, the emotionalism and melodrama typical of popular fiction in most countries and eras, and certainly characteristic of Chinese fiction in the first four decades of this century, is given considerable play in the film. The heroine is a woman with a past, in this case a lengthy romance which culminated in a brief affair, a pregnancy, and rejection by Dongdong's father after he emigrates to join relatives in Canada. She is a filial daughter, taking care of her father, who was widowed when Qin Nan's mother committed suicide to escape Cultural Revolution political persecution. In a film in which characters cry rather frequently, there are other somewhat stereotypical characters. Gao Zhihua's best friend, another unemployed youth, takes one risk too many in trying to make a living, and ends up on a prison farm. Gao promises to take care of his friend's sister during his absence, but it is Qin Nan who looks after the girl, a talented painter and stone seal carver, who is confined to her small room because she has been crippled since childhood. A modern element in the story is the care the young woman also receives from the neighborhood Party secretary. The crippled girl's parents are unable to help: Her mother died under political pressure, and her father went mad during the Cultural Revolution.

May Fourth elements are less obvious than these melodramatic features in *Under the Bridge*, although they underpin the theme of the film. The portrayal of idealistic young people, eager to serve the nation but thwarted by the social conservatism of their neighbors, puts the protagonists in a May Fourth mold. Gao Zhihua and Qin Nan at the end of the film finally declare their love for each other:

"Do you believe in fate?"

"Fate? If our country does well, then we shall do well. That's our fate."

The camera tracks up over the table at which the couple sit, pans up over the rooftops of the neighborhood, and finally into the sky over Shanghai.

If much of the story and narrative of *Under the Bridge* reflects a Shanghai sensibility, the city provides an authentic setting for the film. In the past most films on contemporary subjects were set in ersatz cities, unidentifiable as any particular place. *Under the Bridge* starts and ends with shots of Shanghai, and has scenes in its streets and on its waterfront, with sights and sounds that convey the flavor of the place. Some of the characters speak Mandarin with a southern accent, and very minor characters are even heard speaking Shanghai dialect.

The conglomeration of May Fourth, popular, and Shanghai elements in *Under the Bridge* gives the film something of the feel of a Chinese movie from the 1930s. It is a film about ordinary people whose only real heroics, once the story's melodrama is cut away, is surviving with a sense of personal integrity in a sometimes hostile world. Such classics of the Shanghai cinema as *Street Angel* (*Malu tianshi*, 1937) and *Crossroads* (*Shizi jietou*, 1937) come to mind when watching *Under the Bridge*.[47]

These 1930s predecessors emerged from a social context in which people had barely heard of Yan'an and could not foresee the indigenous, would-be-national and revolutionary legacy the town would represent. The artistic success of the 1980s film, its winning plaudits in Beijing, and the popular appeal of *Under the Bridge* suggest that for artists, cadres, and audiences, China's modern, would-be-internationalist, Shanghai heritage in the 1980s was more attractive. In 1985 *The Life of Wu Xun*, the film that had served as a target in 1951 for official condemnation of this heritage, was restored to respectability.[48]

A new film that in many ways managed to combine the Yan'an and international legacies announced the emergence of a new generation of filmmakers in the second half of the 1980s. *Yellow Earth* (*Huang tudi*, Guangxi studio, 1984) was made by Chen Kaige and Zhang Yimou, 1982 graduates in their thirties from the Beijing Film Academy's first post–Cultural Revolution degree class.[49] It was the best film China had produced since 1949.

Little happens in the film: In 1939 a soldier comes to a village to collect folk songs, which, in the dour poverty of northern Shaanxi Province, seems singularly inappropriate. He tells the daughter of the family where he is billeted about the new treatment of women in the Communist capital at Yan'an, about a hundred miles away. The soldier leaves. The girl, married at thirteen to an older man to whom she had been betrothed since infancy, goes looking for Yan'an. She apparently drowns. In a huge raindance at the end, the peasants continue to seek solutions from the gods, rather than from themselves or from Mao Zedong and his army in Yan'an.

The freshness of *Yellow Earth* is apparent in the first few minutes of the film. With unexpected framing, limited dialogue, closely edited images, and local music, a poor village wedding is presented. Grays, blacks, blues, and occasional ironical reds dominate in the carefully modulated color scheme. Here is a film which knows it is a film. Its youthful makers were perhaps the first generation of Chinese film artists who saw cinema as a sufficient art in itself. Their predecessors had consistently, if unconsciously, regarded film as second to literature, often as a substitute for literary art or as a means to popularize great writing.

The fifth generation, represented to such dazzling effect in *Yellow Earth*, was trained by exposure to a wider range of world cinema than its predecessors. The new artists were products of the Cultural Revolution years, when their lives and education had been disrupted and they had gained a knowledge of society rare among intellectuals since the May Fourth era.

Chen and Zhang chose a visual style that looks international but has deep Chinese roots. Perhaps only from being familiar and comfortable with film art from abroad did the makers of *Yellow Earth* feel free to explore the possibilities in their own tradition. The framing of the landscape shots, for example, is strongly reminiscent of traditional Chinese landscape painting. Earth, mountain, or rock fills four-fifths of the frame; the sky is allowed just the strip at the top of the screen. Human figures are overwhelmed by nature. As largely static shot follows shot, viewers are reminded of turning the pages of a Chinese picture book or comic story.

Another distinctly Chinese aspect of the film is its pace and simplicity. The minimal story unfolds at a slow pace, as image piles upon image. Many filmmakers in China in the 1980s were anxious to deflect criticism that Chinese films were too slow and lacked excitement, particularly when compared with films from abroad. The makers of *Yellow Earth*, in contrast, decided to ignore this general tendency toward faster pacing. The results initially may not have worked well at the box office, but as art they are brilliant.

But art is not enough. *Yellow Earth* is a strongly political film. Its achievement lies in the use of film art to suggest its political points. The screen allusions to traditional landscape painting, the slow pace, the static nature of much of the imagery, and the lack of much action all combine for thematic, as well as artistic, effect. Unlike films on the Chinese revolution that attempt through a good deal of heroics and a contrived realism to assure audiences of the importance of the events, *Yellow Earth* takes an indirect path. The value of the subsequent revolution in land ownership, the position of women, and general social attitudes is here implied by the force of the film's presentation of people stuck on an earth that will not give them a livelihood. Although the story takes place in 1939, there is a carefully crafted timelessness about the film. On the banks of the Yellow River, in the very heartland of Chinese civilization, peasants have been enduring lives of despair and resignation for centuries.

Some critics in China, continuing to cherish an exaggerated assessment of the power of films to change people's attitudes, took exception to *Yellow Earth*. The depiction of bare subsistence caused some alarm, even though the story is clearly identified at the beginning as happening in 1939. This feeling that the film was too harsh, and not *mei* (beautiful) was shared by many ordinary viewers as well as cultural bureaucrats. The latter further objected that the Communist solution to these peasants' problems is only implied. The Red Army headquarters at Yan'an is simply seen in a strange sequence of massed drum dancers. This is how the girl Cuiqiao imagines Yan'an. Indeed Yan'an, and all that it implies in terms of heroism and austerity, may have become similarly remote and the stuff of dreams for the generations, including the makers of *Yellow Earth*, born after the Communist victory in 1949. Likewise, the final extra-ordinary sequence of the raindance attracted the attention of critics who naively imagined that to present something on screen, without clear sig-nals of disapproval (villains with green faces, and the like) is to endorse it. These pettifoggers should have seen the sequence for what it is: a final, most effective expression of the need for change through revolution.

This film, like the other features from the hands of this fifth generation of filmmakers, could not expect to have mass appeal. However, particu-larly after it had won several awards and high praise at a number of international film festivals, Chinese audiences began to pay more atten-tion to *Yellow Earth*, which was given limited rerelease. Young viewers were especially interested in the fifth generation's new films and aware of their critical success abroad. A measure of *Yellow Earth*'s unexpected appeal was its fifth place in the best film category of *Popular Film*'s 1986 Hundred Flowers readership poll.[50]

Yellow Earth represented the newest generation in the film enterprise in China. The first two generations learned their craft from watching Hollywood films in Shanghai, and in the 1930s and 1940s went on to experiment, with some remarkable results. The third generation, under a political leadership and artistic policies shaped in the wartime headquar-ters at Yan'an, turned their backs on Shanghai and sought models in Moscow. The Cultural Revolution disrupted the artistic maturation of the fourth generation, who had just begun their careers when it began. The generation of Chen Kaige and Zhang Yimou, the fifth, had an opportunity at film school to learn from international cinema to an extent not possi-ble, even in Shanghai, before the 1980s. Indeed their film can be read broadly as a presentation of the impact of outside ideas on a hitherto largely closed community, a metaphor for China in the 1980s and this generation's place in it. *Yellow Earth* is as international as the older Shanghai film and artistic tradition, and yet its message and setting derive from Yan'an. Art thrives on paradox; politics, Mao might have added, flourishes on contradiction.

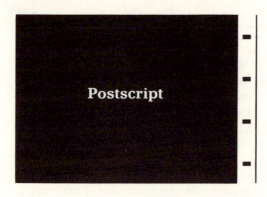

Postscript

Having taken power at the center, the leaders of the Communist Party, like their predecessors as rulers of China, presumed that they had also taken leadership of the culture which formed the basis of the political entity. They could then effect a cultural transformation. As in the past, however, the leaders' presumption of control of culture led to conflict between the censors and cultural workers. The Anti-Rightist campaign and the Cultural Revolution, when political and cultural authorities asserted their leadership with devastating results, were the most obvious instances of such conflict. Culture could not be revolutionized as easily as had been the case, apparently, with political life.

A study of filmmaking in contemporary China suggests that a fuller understanding of Chinese cultural history since 1949 can be gained by acknowledging the importance of the interaction of Party, artists, and audiences. This is not to deny the importance of conflict between the first two groups. But a wider focus pays proper attention to the points of resemblance between the Party cultural leadership and artists, as well as to the context in which these groups operated. An emphasis on a great divide between Party and artists can too easily encourage a presumption that each group was more monolithic and united than was the actual case. In reality, cultural practitioners, filmmakers included, were as riven by factional and personal jealousies as the leaders of the Party. In a cultural enterprise in which the blessing of the authorities could be so important, competition for that blessing encouraged rivalry. It is accordingly difficult to present a picture of brave artists nobly resisting the Party cultural diktat.

On the other hand, as in any nation, perhaps a greater divide separated the intellectuals of both the Party and artistic ranks from the bulk of their political and cultural audiences. This distinction, between the educated "us" and the mass "them," was as ancient as the linkage of cultural with political leadership. Film, as the most popular medium in terms of audiences and yet the most highly specialized in terms of production, uniquely illuminates this cultural divide. Much of the nobility invested in educated film characters reflects one side of this gap.

The weakness of artists in relation to cultural authorities was in part because of the weakness of their connections with their audiences. Party leaders, in contrast, presumed to speak for the mass "them," much as emperors in earlier times had claimed a mystical and direct connection with the people. Mao Zedong in Yan'an in 1942 had called writers "heroes without a battlefield, remote and uncomprehending." As the medium that could most effectively connect the political and cultural leadership with the greatest number and range of people, film was a battleground for educated, elite heroes seeking access to the rest of society.

The importance of the Cultural Revolution years lies in their effect on this cultural divide. To an extent not seen since the War of Resistance to Japan, the Cultural Revolution was an upheaval of national dimensions. Large numbers of people, particularly the educated young, had an opportunity to travel, rare under a regime usually offering its citizens about as much geographical mobility as a medieval or peasant society. This experience on such a scale meant that the Cultural Revolution had a profound impact on the perceptions of both the educated, political public and the wider population. The questioning of the regime, which the Democracy Wall movement in the late 1970s represented, was addressed as much perhaps to the problems of bridging the gap between the educated elite and the masses as to the narrower problems of the position of the Party. Many young people in particular had seen the alienation of the elite from the rest of society during the Cultural Revolution years and their exposure to rural society during forced rustification or to urban workplaces. A few tried to cross the divide, to articulate truly popular grievances and seek redress of elitist abuse of power. Most educated political activists, however, do not seem to have perceived the cultural divide.

The films of the post–Cultural Revolution era in turn illuminated some of these changes. The Cultural Revolution differentiation of Party and masses was paralleled by a growing distinction drawn by intellectuals, including filmmakers, between political powerholders and themselves. The tendency to harangue audiences, seen in films of the 1950s, 1960s, and early 1970s, gave way to readier acknowledgment of more ordinary, personal concerns. Two films directed by the forty-five-year-old Wu Tianming were representative of this change of direction. *River without Buoys* (*Meiyou hangbiao de heliu*, Xi'an studio, 1983) concentrated to an unprecedented extent on the psychological responses to political events of three men on a raft during the Cultural Revolution. Wu's *Life* (*Rensheng*, Xi'an studio, 1984) explored a young man's conflict between a city future and a rural love in a northern Shaanxi setting, not far from Yan'an. The integrated artistic achievement of these two films, whose director had also become head of the Xi'an Film Studio, was cause for optimism about the future of Chinese films.[1]

Pessimists, on the other hand, noted the huge drop in film attendance after 1980, and began to wonder about the future of filmmaking in terms not of Party control, but of audience interest. Urban audiences dropped by 2 billion between 1980 and 1983, and urban film revenues by 25 million *yuan* (about 8 million U.S. dollars) per year in the same period.[2] Reasons for this challenge to film's preeminence included vastly increased levels of television ownership and the availability of other entertainment, particularly imported from abroad. Filmmakers identified improvement of quality and increased relevance to their viewers as guarantees of film's future. The Party leaders seemed to agree, and reformed the distribution system to discourage unpopular films and reward more successful movies with wider circulation and thus greater return for the studios (and perhaps even the filmmakers) that made them. The shifting of the Ministry of Culture's Film Bureau to a new Ministry of Radio, Film, and Television in early 1986 reflected the rapid rise of television to challenge the importance of film as the most popular medium, and the politicians' continuing concern to ensure control of both.[3] Student demonstrations in favor of political rights later that year and the sputtering of the ensuing Yan'an-inspired campaign against "bourgeois liberalization" through 1987 showed how difficult shaping cultural change had become.

The empty rhetoric, which had done so much to discredit the prestige of the political and artistic leadership, in the 1980s had to give way to a more meaningful cultural discourse. The makers of *Yellow Earth*, the film that signaled the emergence of a fifth generation of filmmakers and a Chinese New Wave, carefully constructed an ambivalent ending in which the promise of the Party may not be easily fulfilled. Most of the heroes of the past by then had left the cultural battlefield. Some Chinese began to realize that the real battlefield was perhaps even larger and less easy to conquer than earlier heroes had imagined.

Appendix: Feature film production, 1949–1986

	Changchun	Beijing	Shanghai	Other studios[a]	Musical subtotal	Annual total
1949	6	0	0	4	(0)	10
1950	13	5	2	6	(1)	26
1951	1	3	6	7	(0)	17
1952	2	2	1	3	(0)	8
1953	4	2	1	3	(1)	10
1954	8	2	13	1	(6)	24
1955	10	1	11	1	(6)	23
1956	15	4	19	2	(11)	40
1957	14	4	18	5	(10)	41
1958	30	8	49	14	(8)	101
1959	26	9	26	18	(18)	79
1960	16	10	12	21	(16)	59
1961	5	4	7	10	(7)	26
1962	5	7	7	14	(11)	33
1963	9	5	15	10	(10)	39
1964	8	6	7	7	(5)	28
1965	11	9	10	13	(20)	43
1966	1	3	1	7	(4)	12
1967	0	0	0	0	(0)	0
1968	0	0	0	0	(0)	0
1969	0	0	0	0	(0)	0
1970	0	1	0	1	(2)	2
1971	1	1	0	0	(2)	2
1972	1	1.5	1.5	1	(5)	5
1973	3	0.5	0.5	0	(4)	4
1974	5	4	4	4	(6)	17
1975	5	6	6	8	(7)	25
1976	7	7	13	10	(14)	37
1977	6	2	4	7	(2)	19

	Changchun	Beijing	Shanghai	Other studios[a]	Musical subtotal	Annual total
1978	9	9	9	18	(5)	45
1979	14	11	11	26	(10)	62
1980	16	11	19	37	(9)	83
1981	16	10	19	60	(11)	105
1982	19	10	21	64	(8)	114
1983	18	12	20	77	(16)	127
1984	21	17	20	85	(11)	143
1985[b]						127
1986[b]						125

[a]Until 1953 includes private studios in Shanghai.
[b]Studio figures are not available.

Sources: Calculations based on *Zhongguo yishu yingpian bianmu* (for 1949–79), *Zhongguo dianying nianjian 1981–5* (for 1980–4), and DZDY and DYYS (for later years).

Notes

The following source abbreviations are used in the ensuing notes; complete details for these and for all works cited by author and date are given in the bibliography.

Cheng Jihua   *Zhongguo dianying fazhanshi*
DYYS   *Dianying yishu*
DZDY   *Dazhong dianying*
Hua'nan . . . Wu Xun   Hua'nan renmin chubanshe, ed., *Wu Xun yu 'Wu Xun zhuan' pipan*
Nianjian   *Zhongguo dianying nianjian*
RMDY   *Renmin dianying*
RMRB   *Renmin ribao*
Sanshiwunian   *Zhonghua renmin gongheguo dianying shiye sanshiwunian, 1949–1984*
Siren bang . . . hui   *"Siren bang" shi dianying shiye de sidi. Wenhua bu dianying xitong jiepi "siren bang" zuixing dahui fayan huibian*
WYB   *Wenyi bao*
Zhonghua   *Zhonghua quanguo wenxue yishu gongzuozhe daibiao dahui jinian wenji*

I. Film and Chinese society before 1949

1. For an introduction to the variety of modern Chinese theatrical forms, see Colin Mackerras (1975), *The Chinese Theatre in Modern Times*. On opera and more, see the encyclopedic work of Tao-Ching Hsü (1985), *The Chinese Conception of the Theatre*.

2. Jay Leyda's *Dianying: Electric Shadows* (1972/1978[?]) offers an invaluable, though often impressionistic, account of the rise of film in China. Its pioneering contribution to Chinese film study cannot be overestimated.

3. The importance of French films in the Chinese market declined during the war, but American films gained a preeminence they never lost until the 1950s.

4. These figures are from E. T. Way (1930), "Motion Pictures in China," pp. 2–3.

5. These statistics are drawn from Way (1930, p. 1); Wilbur Burton (1934),

"Chinese reactions to the cinema," p. 594; Rudolf Löwenthal (1938), "Public communications in China before July 1937," p. 47.

6. The 1929 figures are from Way (1930), pp. 8–9; and the 1932 picture based on "Motion pictures in the Far East," (1932, p. 532).

7. See C. J. North (1927), "The Chinese motion picture market," pp. 13, 17, 20, 23; "Motion pictures in the Far East," (1932, pp. 532, 535). In Japan, *katsuben* (also known as *benshi*) served a similar announcer-narrator function for foreign and Japanese films even into the sound era, but turned the service into a performing art.

8. The Chinese titles and the names of the makers of all films mentioned in this study are listed chronologically in the filmography.

9. See E. Perry Link, Jr. (1981), *Mandarin Ducks and Butterflies*.

10. This plot summary is drawn from the standard history of Chinese filmmaking before 1949: Cheng Jihua, Li Shaobai, and Xing Zuwen, eds. (1963), *Zhongguo dianying fazhanshi* [History of the development of Chinese film; hereafter abbreviated Cheng Jihua] I: 237–9.

11. Tang Na in *Shidai dianying* (June 1934), quoted in Cheng Jihua I: 239. Tang Na was Jiang Qing's third husband. Mao Zedong was her last.

12. C. J. North (1927, pp. 7–8). This use of films was not just a 1920s phenomenon: In late 1984 *Gazing into My Eyes* (*Kanzhe wode yanjing*, Shanghai studio) used a love story about a fashion designer to present the proper use of modern, Western styles; DZDY 11:pictorial section (November 1984).

13. On the Commercial Press film venture see Cheng Jihua I: 29–40. The Press sold its film enterprise to another company, which collapsed within a year.

14. See Sun Yu, "Huiyi 'Wusi' yundong yingxiang xia de sanshi niandai dianying," *Dianying yishu* [*Film Art*] 3:7–9, 36 (March 1979). This article has been translated in Tony Rayns and Scott Meek, eds. (1980), *Electric Shadows: 45 Years of Chinese Cinema*, pp. T2–7.

15. The only history of Chinese film published in the People's Republic and the most substantial history of film before 1949 published anywhere, Cheng Jihua's *Zhongguo dianying fazhanshi* encourages exaggeration of the importance of leftist artists by emphasizing their role in the 1930s. Cheng also tends to identify these artists with the Communist Party to an extent not uniformly apparent in the period before 1949.

16. For an outline of the studios discussed below, see Scott Meek, "An outline history of the film industry in China," in Rayns and Meek, pp. A2–5, and Cheng Jihua I: 203–45 (Mingxing), 245–71, 457–83 (Lianhua).

17. The filmmakers invited peasant experts to the studio to advise the actors and directors; Cheng Jihua I: 210.

18. Cheng Jihua I: 210.

19. For an outline of the film, see Cheng Jihua I: 344–5.

20. The film is discussed in Cheng Jihua I: 341–4.

21. Both government and party each controlled a studio in Chongqing; Cheng Jihua II: 41, 59. A similar division between state and Party cultural apparatuses was preserved after 1949 in the form of the State Council's Ministry of Culture and the Communist Party's Propaganda Department.

22. Cheng Jihua II: 59. The Northwest (Xibei) film studio, established in 1935 by warlord Yan Xishan at Taiyuan in Shanxi Province, attracted some ex-Shanghai leftists. The studio, after revival in 1937, ceased production in 1939; Cheng Jihua II: 66–71.

23. Cheng Jihua II: 122, 74.

24. One such artist was the playwright Shi Dongshan; Cheng Jihua II: 128–9.

25. On the Hong Kong activities of ex-Shanghai filmmakers, see Cheng Jihua II: 75–86.

26. Cheng Jihua II: 94–119. See also Sato Tadao, "Il cinema di Shanghai sotto l'occupazione giapponese (1939–1945)," in *Ombre elettriche: Saggi e richerche sul cinema cinese*, pp. 72–80.

27. *The Lute*, however, ends with the couple reunited. For a translation of this work, see *The Lute. Kao Ming's P'i-p'a chi*, Jean Mulligan, trans. (New York, 1980). I am indebted to Patrick Hanan for pointing out the parallels between the film and this particular traditional story.

28. Leo Ou-fan Lee suggests this in Chris Berry, ed. (1985), *Perspectives on Chinese Cinema*, p. 1.

29. Cheng Jihua II: 199–203.

30. Cheng Jihua II: 159.

31. Cheng Jihua II: 235.

32. Cheng Jihua II: 208.

33. Cheng Jihua II: 251–2; interview with Sun Daolin, Shanghai Film Studio, December 1980.

34. Cheng Jihua II: 319. Fei Mu also moved to Hong Kong, where he died in 1951. He was partially rehabilitated by the Chinese cultural authorities in the 1980s.

II. Yan'an and Shanghai

1. Most of what follows on the Yan'an film effort is based on the chronicle in Cheng Jihua II: 337–63. See also Yuan Muzhi (1962), *Jiefangqu de dianying*.

2. A camera was donated by Joris Ivens, the Dutch documentary film pioneer, during a visit to China in 1938; see Ivens (1970), *The Camera and I*.

3. See Introduction in Bonnie McDougall (1980), *Mao Zedong's "Talks at the Yan'an Conference on Literature and Art:" A Translation of the 1943 Text with Commentary*, pp. 3–54.

4. The following three quotations from Mao's Yan'an *Talks* come from McDougall, pp. 59–60, 84, 60, respectively.

5. McDougall, p. 78.

6. The above account is drawn from Cheng Jihua II: 381–6; Yuan Muzhi (1950), "Guanyu jiefangqu dianying gongzuo," in *Zhonghua quanguo wenxue yishu gongzuozhe daibiao dahui jinian wenji* [hereafter cited as Zhonghua], pp. 200–4; DZDY 18:16–17 (September 1954). This latter source claims that the Manchukuo studio was not equipped with modern machinery.

7. Cheng Jihua II: 392–3; interview with Chen Qiang, who played the father, Beijing, November 1980.

8. Cheng Jihua II: 393–4.

9. In an interview in Beijing in May 1986, Cheng Jihua disagreed forcefully with this view, pointing out that the film leadership came from artists who had gone to

Yan'an during the War of Resistance to Japan. The Yan'an–Shanghai differentiation is more, however, a question of mentality than one of personalities. In this book the two place names are used as shorthand for a range of somewhat different perceptions of the function of art and artists in society.

10. Cheng Jihua II: 403; *Renmin ribao* [RMRB], 23 April 1949, p. 2. The leftist filmmakers at work in Beijing included Jin Shan, writer-director of *On the Sungari River*. Beiping city became Beijing later in 1949.

11. Cheng Jihua II: 402.

12. The takeover in Shanghai is chronicled in Cheng Jihua II: 404–5. See also RMRB, 5 June 1949, p. 1. On Xu Tao see DZDY 5:10–11 (March 1954).

13. For these speeches, see Zhonghua, pp. 35–67, 69–97.

14. Zhonghua, pp. 203–4.

15. Zhonghua, pp. 248–72.

16. For the list of officers, see Zhonghua, pp. 584–5.

17. RMRB, 17 January 1950, p. 3.

18. The regulations are reprinted in RMRB, 12 July 1950, p. 3. On the Film Bureau, see also *Wenyi bao* [WYB] 10:28 (February 1950).

19. RMRB, 12 July 1950, p. 3.

20. RMRB, 17 January 1950, p. 3; 18 September 1950, p. 3; 5 February 1951, p. 3.

21. WYB 3:37 (February 1952).

22. WYB 3:37 (February 1952).

23. WYB 8:34 (April 1952); RMRB, 2 April 1952, p. 3; 9 April 1952, p. 3.

24. RMRB, 10 July 1950, p. 4; 3 January 1951, p. 3; see also RMRB, 5 May 1950, p. 3.

25. RMRB, 4 December 1955, p. 1. The average county population, excluding the urban centers, where there was usually a cinema or hall for picture shows, numbered one, two, or several hundred thousand.

26. See WYB 19–20:59 (October 1959), and DZDY 18:8 (September 1954). The Ministry of Culture 1953 annual report gives a slightly lower figure for that year: RMRB, 12 January 1954, p. 3. For the 1954 figures, see DZDY 10:28–9 (May 1955).

27. DZDY 5:2–3 (July 1952); DZDY 10:28–9 (May 1955).

28. DZDY 4:2–3 (July 1952).

29. DZDY 1–2:66,67 (May 1952). Some rural middle-school students reportedly had to be pushed to watch movies; DZDY 3:26–7 (February 1953).

30. RMRB, 8 May 1950, p. 4; DZDY 7:33 (April 1953).

31. In the first half of 1950 the state lent 48 billion *yuan* (roughly a quarter of a million 1952 U.S. dollars) to private film companies to help particularly money-making exports and distribution of films during the peak box-office period of the Spring Festival. The regulations on licensing and censorship, promulgated in mid-1950, were intended, according to a Ministry of Culture spokesperson, particularly to encourage the private filmmakers. See RMRB, 12 July 1950, p. 3, and 27 July 1950, p. 3.

32. RMRB, 20 May 1951, p. 5. The fate of the film will discussed at length later in this chapter. On the absorption of the studios, see also RMRB, 27 July 1950, p. 3, and RMRB, 12 July 1950, p. 3.

33. RMRB, 25 January 1952, p. 3. This new company does not appear to have produced any films.

34. DZDY 3:3 (February 1953).
35. See Richard Taylor (1979), *The Politics of the Soviet Cinema*, and Jay Leyda (1960), *Kino: A History of the Russian and Soviet Film*, chap. twelve.
36. A survey in July of that year estimated that 67 of every 100 movies (foreign and Chinese) was obscene (*yinhui*), although the criteria used to make this alarming judgment were not spelled out; RMRB, 21 September 1949, p. 2. In April 1949, 64% (124 films) of the 194 films shown in Shanghai cinemas were American. Sixty-two films were Chinese made, and 8 films were from the Soviet Union: Zhongguo dianyingjia xiehui dianyingshi yanjiubu (1985), *Zhonghua renmin gongheguo dianying shiye sanshiwunian, 1949–1985* [hereafter cited as Sanshi-wunian], p. 335.
37. RMRB, 19 March 1951, p. 3.
38. RMRB, 19 March 1951, p. 3.
39. One source for Shanghai puts the attendance of American films at 52% of audiences in March 1950, at 14% in September, and at 10% in November; RMRB, 3 January 1951, p. 3. Another source claimed that in the autumn of 1950 American movies still attracted 52% of filmgoers, presumably in Shanghai; WYB 3:27 (November 1950).
40. RMRB, 3 January 1951, p. 3.
41. DZDY 1–2:6 (May 1952).
42. RMRB, 3 January 1951, p. 3. See also RMRB, 19 March 1951, p. 3. In Shanghai, attendances in May 1950 at state-studio films averaged 25,600 for each film's run; at private studios' films, 12,300; and 5,900 for American and other foreign films.
43. The Northeast studio released the first three Soviet features in 1949; RMRB, 1 March 1950, p. 3. Forty-three Soviet films were dubbed in 1950; RMRB, 18 February 1951, p. 3. See also DZDY 3:24 (February 1954).
44. WYB 2:34 (October 1949). On new audiences, see also RMRB, 20 July 1952, p. 2; 14 February 1952, p. 4; and 14 September 1952, p. 2.
45. WYB 3:27 (November 1950).
46. RMRB, 14 February 1952, p. 4.
47. RMRB, 11 November 1951, p. 2.
48. RMRB, 3 July 1952, p. 3; DZDY 1:31 (January 1953). On local problems, see RMRB, 5 August 1952, p. 2; DZDY 1:32–3 (January 1953).
49. RMRB, 12 January 1954, p. 3.
50. WYB 1:18–19 (October 1950); WYB 7:7 (April 1952); DZDY 7:25 (April 1955); DZDY 5:26–9 (July 1952); DZDY 14:29 (July 1953).
51. RMRB, 18 February 1951, p. 3. One such expert was Sergei Gerasimov, who had briefly come under a cloud in Moscow on account of his 1948 film *Young Guard*; see Mira Liehm and Antonin J. Liehm (1977), *The Most Important Art: Soviet and Eastern European Film after 1945*, pp. 55–6.
52. DZDY 11:17–21 (June 1955).
53. See Liehm and Liehm, pp. 47–75. Zhdanov had disappeared from public life in 1949. Requirements for a set percentage of color films may also help account for the slump in Soviet production.
54. RMRB, 1 June 1949, p. 4.
55. Zhonghua, p. 205; RMRB, 25 September 1949, p. 5. The editors of the *Literary Gazette*, the major journal of cultural policy, expressed similar sentiments in

March 1951, at the beginning of a special "China Film Month," featuring films from the three state-owned studios; WYB 10:3–4 (March 1951).

56. RMRB, 31 July 1949, p. 4.

57. RMRB, 8 January 1950, p. 5; 9 July 1950, p. 5. Zhong Dianfei was prominent in the Hundred Flowers criticism of 1956–7 and a victim of the subsequent backlash; see Chapter III.

58. RMRB, 24 June 1949, p. 4.

59. RMRB, 28 April 1950, p. 3. See also RMRB, 30 April 1950, p. 5. The appeal of minorities films is discussed in Chapter IV. Soon after release *Spring Rays* was renamed *Victory of the Inner Mongolian People* (*Neimeng renmin de shengli*), apparently to deemphasize the love element in the film.

60. WYB 5:14 (June 1951). On Sha Meng's background, see DZDY 17:26 (September 1954). The script was by Feng Xuefeng, who in 1954 became the target of a major campaign of criticism. For a report on the problems of creating new-style films in 1950, see WYB 6:8–14 (July 1951).

61. Work came to a virtual stop in 1953 and 1954 because of lack of scripts; DZDY 24:30–2 (December 1954).

62. WYB 4:3–4 (February 1953); DZDY 5:2–3 (July 1952).

63. WYB 12:4–5 (June 1953).

64. RMRB, 12 January 1954, p. 3.

65. On the Northeast, see DZDY 18:16–17 (September 1954); on Shanghai, see DZDY 18:19–21 (September 1954).

66. These resolutions were reproduced in full, to reassure a film-hungry public that the highest authorities were concerned about the problem, in RMRB, 12 January 1954, p. 1. Encouraging younger writers to write scripts was a good move, for it was perhaps easier for youthful talent to make a name in film writing than in other, more established, literary genres.

67. See, for example, WYB 9:3–7 (May 1953), and WYB 13:21–5 (July 1954). On script problems, see WYB 12:3–4 (June 1953).

68. WYB 6:32 (March 1955). See also DZDY 6:28 (March 1955).

69. See, for example, the review by Zhong Dianfei in DZDY 4:16–18 (February 1953). *Gate No. 6* (*Liuhao men*), directed by Lü Ban, told a similar before and after story, in this case about Tianjin transport workers.

70. See Li Shizhao, ed., *Wu Xun xiansheng de zhuanji* (Shanghai, 1948); Duan Chengze, ed., *Wu Xun xiansheng huazhuan* (Chongqing, 1938 and 1944); Zhang Mosheng, *Wu Xun zhuan* (Shanghai, 1946 and 1949).

71. Hua'nan renmin chubanshe bianjibu, ed., *Wu Xun yu 'Wu Xun zhuan' pipan* [hereafter Hua'nan . . . Wu Xun], p. 11.

72. The fullest account of the Wu Xun episode by Sun Yu is his "Dui biandao dianying 'Wu Xun zhuan' de jiantao," in Pei Wenzhong and others (1952), *Wode sixiang shi zenmeyang zhuanbian guolai de*, pp. 177–95. The quote is from p. 186. See also Sun Yu, "Biandao 'Wu Xun zhuan' ji," *Guangming ribao* [*Guangming Daily*], 26 February 1951, p. 4.

73. Kunlun had already invested 700 million *yuan* (over 30 thousand 1952 U.S. dollars) in the project; WYB 3:16–17 (February 1952).

74. *Guangming ribao*, 5 December 1949, p. 3. The articles included a poem by Tao Xingzhi and an essay by a writer of the pictorial biography.

75. Pei Wenzhong, pp. 186–7.

76. *Guangming ribao*, 26 February 1951, p. 4. See also Xia Yan, "Cong 'Wu Xun zhuan' de piping jiantao wo zai Shanghai wenhua yishujie de gongzuo," RMRB, 26 August 1951, p. 3.

77. RMRB, 26 May 1951, p. 3.

78. The *People's Daily* editorial (by Mao), which officially launched the campaign against the film, included a list of forty articles in praise of the movie which had been published after the film's release; RMRB, 20 May 1951, p. 1.

79. WYB 1:7–11 (April 1951).

80. See, for example, WYB 2:26–7 (May 1951); WYB 4:4–16 (June 1951); RMRB, 16 May 1951, p. 3.

81. The editorial is translated in *Selected Works of Mao Zedong* V: 57–8. Official acknowledgment of Mao's authorship came in 1966.

82. Hua'nan . . . Wu Xun, pp. 9–29.

83. McDougall, p. 78.

84. Hua'nan . . . Wu Xun, p. 26.

85. RMRB, 26 August 1951, p. 3.

86. Zhang Yu, "Dui Xia Yan tongzhi guanyu 'Wu Xun zhuan' wenti de jiantao yihan," WYB 4:29–32 (December 1951).

87. RMRB, 26 May 1951, p. 3; DZDY 1–2:7 (May 1952).

88. See, for example, RMRB, 17 June 1951, p. 5; DZDY 1–2:7 (May 1952).

89. See WYB 8:11–16, 17–20 (August 1951). Zheng had starred in the 1934 film *The Highway* (see Chapter I).

90. RMRB, 14 July 1951, p. 3.

91. RMRB, 23 July 1951, p. 3. See also articles in each issue of RMRB, 24–8 July 1951, p. 3. The investigation team included a youthful Zhong Dianfei, whose fate in 1957 will be discussed in Chapter III.

92. RMRB, 8 August 1951, p. 2 and p. 3.

93. Xia Yan, "Jiuzheng cuowu, gaijin lingdao, jianjue guanche Mao Zedong de wenyi fangzhen," WYB 11–12:8–10 (June 1952).

94. Chen Bo'er, "Gushipian cong wu dao you de biandao gongzuo," WYB 1:3–5 (March 1950).

95. Hua'nan . . . Wu Xun, p. 26.

96. RMRB, 26 August 1951, p. 3.

97. Jia Ji, "Tan dianying gongzuozhe de sixiang gaizao," WYB 14:9–12 (July 1952). Jia Ji's examples of the work of wrong-thinking filmmakers were all films from the private Shanghai studios.

98. Hua'nan . . . Wu Xun, p. 18.

99. WYB 14:10 (July 1952). See also DZDY 3:28 (June 1952).

100. The Shanghai figures include workers at the Scientific and Educational Film Studio, established in 1953; DZDY 13:26 (July 1953). The Northeast studio figures are from DZDY 18:16 (September 1954).

101. The director Cheng Yin, for example, who in 1952 became the secretary-general of the central Film Bureau, had been a member of Marshal He Long's drama troupe in the Communist-held base areas in the War of Resistance to Japan; DZDY 1:34–6 (January 1954). So too had been the director Lin Nong.

102. See the listing of officers in Zhonghua, pp. 584–5. On the 1953 meeting, see WYB 19 (October 1953) issue.

103. See the table on the ages of delegates in Zhonghua, p. 558. The large delegation from the People's Liberation Army cultural ranks contributed to this youthful median age.

104. DZDY 16:4–5 (August 1955). Wang Rong was described in criticism sessions as a "disuniting element" in film ranks.

105. DZDY 19:3 (October 1953).

106. DZDY 6:16 (August 1952).

III. Beyond Shanghai

1. For an interesting discussion of the evolution of mass culture in China, see Leo Ou-fan Lee and Andrew J. Nathan, "The Beginnings of Mass Culture: Journalism and Fiction in the Late Ch'ing and Beyond," in David Johnson, Andrew J. Nathan, and Evelyn S. Rawski, eds., *Popular Culture in Late Imperial China* (Berkeley, 1985), pp. 360–95.

2. On radio, see Alan P. L. Liu (1971), *Communications and National Integration in Communist China*, pp. 118–29.

3. The Hong Kong film industry, with a chiefly local and Southeast Asian audience, has not always produced films exclusively in Cantonese. From the mid-1950s through the late 1970s Mandarin films were the predominant mode, with subtitles in Chinese characters. This was largely because the Hong Kong industry was dominated in those years by Mandarin speakers from Shanghai and elsewhere. British feature films, for example, gained a great deal of variety in the 1950s when characters with regional accents became more important.

4. The staff of the studio numbered about 300 in 1959, over 500 in 1965, between 700 and 800 in 1972, and in 1980 had reached 1,100; interview with management cadres, Pearl River Film Studio, December 1980. See also *Zhongguo dianying nianjian, 1981* (Beijing, 1982) [hereafter Nianjian 1981], pp. 472–3, and Sanshiwunian, pp. 141–2.

5. Interview at Pearl River Film Studio, December 1980. Between its founding and 1980 the studio had dubbed only 7 or 8 films into Cantonese. Most "dubbing" was simply providing a sound tape for playing during a screening. By 1980 some films were made in minorities' languages. Uighur actors in 1980 performed *Effendi* for cameras at the Beijing studio in their own language. The usual absence of synchronous sound recording in all Chinese studios meant no one could hear the actors' original lines. Sound is added later, for most audiences in Mandarin, and in Uighur and other languages for Xinjiang minority viewers. (Visit to Beijing Film Studio, October 1980.)

6. Sanshiwunian, pp. 162–7; Nianjian 1981, pp. 474–5; interview at studio, April 1986.

7. As an economy measure, Emei closed down for three years after 1962: Sanshiwunian, pp. 176–8; Nianjian 1981, pp. 475–6.

8. The two feature studios were revived in 1971 and 1975, respectively: Sanshiwunian, pp. 215 (Xiaoxiang), 208–9 (Guangxi); Nianjian 1981, pp. 477, 478.

9. Sanshiwunian, pp. 191–3 (Tianshan), 204–6 (Inner Mongolia); Nianjian 1981, pp. 479, 480. The Inner Mongolia studio, for example, dubbed 21 features and animated films between 1972 and 1976, and reopened as a full studio in 1979: Sanshiwunian, p. 206.

10. Interview at Shanghai Film Studio, December 1980; see also Sanshiwunian, pp. 103–4.
11. Interview at Shanghai Film Studio, December 1980, and Sanshiwunian, p. 104.
12. DZDY 18:16–17 (September 1956); RMRB, 30 October 1959, p. 7.
13. WYB 15–16:61 (August 1960).
14. RMRB, 30 October 1959, p. 7.
15. WYB 15–16:61 (August 1960).
16. RMRB, 14 December 1962, p. 2.
17. The figures here are drawn from RMRB, 3 June 1958, p. 7; 4 December 1955, p. 1; 28 April 1960, p. 7.
18. This count, in fact, may have been generous: RMRB, 15 May 1958, p. 7.
19. RMRB, 23 December 1959, p. 4; 3 June 1958, p. 7; 14 December 1962, p. 2.
20. RMRB, 23 December 1959, p. 4.
21. DZDY 4:5 (April 1962).
22. RMRB, 7 November 1963, p. 6.
23. RMRB, 22 February 1957, p. 7.
24. Nianjian 1981, p. 486; interview at Beijing Film Academy, Zhuxinzhuang, November 1980. In addition, film studios in Changchun and Shanghai conducted training programs from 1958 to 1960, in part to provide specialist staff for the expansion of the studios in the late 1950s: DZDY 10:30 (May 1960); DZDY 11:25, 30 (June 1960).
25. Chinese adoption of this and other Soviet literary theories is discussed in D. W. Fokkema (1965), *Literary Doctrines in China and Soviet Influence, 1956–1960*, although Fokkema treats Chinese use of socialist realism with rather more respect.
26. Zhou Yang, "Xin min'ge kaituo le shige de xin daolu," *Hongqi* [*Red Flag*] 1:33–8 (June 1958); Zhou Yang, "Jianli Zhongguo ziji de Makesizhuyi de wenyi lilun he piping," WYB 17:7–12 (September 1958). Jia Ji, the 1951 critic of *The Life of Wu Xun*, wrote also of the new revolutionary realism, in WYB 1:26 (January 1959).
27. RMRB, 3 June 1958, p. 7.
28. RMRB, 2 February 1960, p. 7.
29. RMRB, 2 February 1960, p. 7.
30. RMRB, 28 August 1961, p. 7.
31. On the origins of the "middle character" concept, see a critical collection of materials in WYB 8–9:15–20 (September 1964). The outstanding example of a middle character on film is Li Shuangshuang, who is discussed, along with comic and historical films, in Chapter IV.
32. WYB 8:4 (April 1959).
33. Leyda, *Dianying* (1972/1978 [?], p. 231), emphasizes the tears shed in the film (and novel), an aspect perhaps more obvious to a viewer who cannot understand the dialogue. May Fourth adaptation, including *The New Year's Sacrifice*, is further discussed in Chapter IV, and its fate in Chapter V.
34. Opera films enjoyed a brief revival during the War of Resistance to Japan as vehicles for the disguised expression of patriotic sentiments.
35. On post-1949 opera reform, see Zhao Cong (1969), *Zhongguo dalu de xiqu*

gaige, and Daniel S. Yang (1968), "The traditional theatre of China and its contemporary setting: An examination of the pattern of change within the Peking theatre since 1949."

36. RMRB, 7 October 1956, p. 8.

37. RMRB, 21 March 1958, p. 8.

38. DZDY 8:23–4 (August 1962). Real and false settings could both be used in an opera film, if carefully done. See also Zhang Junxiang, Sang Hu, and others (1959), *Lun xiqu dianying.*

39. RMRB, 2 August 1961, p. 7; RMRB, 5 June 1959, p. 8.

40. Some of the revolutionary model operas later promulgated during the Cultural Revolution were also done in Cantonese versions.

41. RMRB, 26 April 1957, p. 7.

42. Zhong Dianfei was accused in 1957 of saying this; WYB 19:8 (August 1957).

43. [Zhong Dianfei], "Dianying de luogu," WYB 23:3 (December 1956).

44. The vigor of cultural commissar Zhou Yang's denial in 1957 that the studio was split up in response to criticisms of overcentralization tends ironically to confirm the interpretation presented here; WYB 19:8 (August 1957). The soup remark can be found in WYB 36:11 (December 1957).

45. DZDY 2:30–1 (January 1957).

46. WYB 19:8 (August 1957). These tensions between expert artists and lay producers are not unknown in film industries throughout the world.

47. Quoted in WYB 36:11 (December 1957), and in DZDY 17:7 (September 1957).

48. DZDY 3:15 (February 1958).

49. See, for example, RMRB, 22 May 1957, p. 7. *Crows and Sparrows* is discussed briefly in Chapter I.

50. WYB 11:1–2 (June 1957).

51. RMRB, 22 May 1957, p. 4. The Association replaced the filmmakers association established at the First Congress of Writers and Artists in 1949.

52. Luo Dou, "Changying de diyige shengyin," WYB 11:1–2 (June 1957). Luo was 27 years old; WYB 23:11 (September 1957). On Beijing film actors' similar frustrations, see DZDY 12:23–4 (June 1957).

53. WYB 36:11 (December 1957). The accused actor was Shi Hui.

54. DZDY 3:15 (February 1958). Zhang was a Communist Party member.

55. RMRB, 12 December 1958, p. 7. The quote reads literally "you can eat for life."

56. DZDY 1:32–3 (January 1958).

57. RMRB, 2 April 1957, p. 7.

58. WYB 23:3–4 (December 1956).

59. RMRB, 26 April 1957, p. 7.

60. After the discrediting of the makers of this film in 1957, film comedy on contemporary subjects was not attempted until the 1960s.

61. DZDY 6:26–7 (March 1957).

62. An early review of the film can be found in WYB 19:14 (October 1957). For a criticism of the bourgeois elements in the film, see RMRB, 3 December 1957, p. 8.

63. WYB 36:11 (December 1957); DZDY 23:26 (December 1957). For a brief account of the fate of Shi Hui, see *Zhongguo dianyingjia liezhuan* II, 77 (1982).

64. See, for example, DZDY 19:3–7 (October 1957).

65. DZDY 17:7 (September 1956).

66. DZDY 18:5–7 (September 1957); DZDY 17:7–8 (September 1957). Lü Ban was even alleged, by "an old Party member," to have joined the Party in pursuit of a female member. He died in November 1976, at age sixty-three.

67. WYB 20:11–12 (August 1957). The beginning of the shift in literary policy to revolutionary realism and romanticism allowed this otherwise startling refinement of the status of the *gongnongbing* policy.

68. WYB 29:14 (October 1957). This statement recalls Deng Xiaoping's celebrated remark, used against him during the Cultural Revolution, that the color of a cat was immaterial so long as it caught mice.

69. Guo had criticized bureaucratic leadership in the studios: WYB 36:11 (December 1957).

70. DZDY 14:25–6 (July 1957).

71. DZDY 12:21 (June 1958). The film was criticized by Huang Gang in RMRB, 21 May 1958, p. 7.

72. DZDY 1:13 (January 1958).

73. WYB 13:36–39 (July 1958).

74. RMRB, 2 December 1958, p. 7; interview with Chen Huangmei, Turin, March 1982. As newly appointed head of the Film Bureau, Chen was perhaps making ritual obeisance to the Yan'anites in the Party leadership with this unusually bitter article.

75. RMRB, 4 March 1959, p. 7. The secretary, Yuan Wenshu, dated his letter in Shanghai, perhaps signaling that his response could be seen as on behalf of Shanghai film circles. Chen's letter carried no place of composition. Four months later, an article in *People's Daily* titled "We need this type of film review" lavished praise on a recent and rather ordinary review in *Popular Film* by Chen Huangmei, as if to restore his reputation; RMRB, 22 July 1959, p. 8.

76. DZDY 7:15 (April 1958).

77. DZDY 6:21–2 (March 1958).

78. RMRB, 3 June 1958, p. 7; DZDY 11:22 (June 1958).

79. DZDY 23:28 (December 1958).

80. RMRB, 7 October 1958, p. 6.

81. DZDY 3:14 (February 1958). Among the first to "go down" was Tao Jin, star of the 1947 classic *The Spring River Flows East* and director of the 1957 "rightist" comedy *Nurse's Diary* (*Hushi riji*) at the Shanghai Jiangnan studio.

82. RMRB, 3 June 1958, p. 7.

83. RMRB, 3 June 1958, p. 7.

84. DZDY 5:28 (March 1958).

85. DZDY 6:21 (March 1958).

86. DZDY 1:7 (January 1960); Chen Huangmei, in RMRB, 30 October 1959, p. 7, noted that 171 feature films had been made between 1949 and 1957.

87. The original plan is mentioned in DZDY 1:16 (January 1958). The final number for 1958 is calculated from *Zhongguo yishu yingpian bianmu* I, 353–408. From the same source it appears that Changchun produced 30 features in 1958 (pp. 309–42), and the Beijing studio a mere 8 (pp. 343–52).

88. RMRB, 2 February 1960, p. 7. Television, with its potential for news coverage, only began in Beijing in late 1958, and in other centers later.

89. Reports on assistance can be found, for example, in RMRB, 6 July 1958, p. 2; 8

July 1958, p. 7; 4 September 1959, p. 7; DZDY 14:16 (July 1958). The Nantong "studio" is described in the 15-part outline history of Chinese film since 1949 by Xue Yan and Li Tao in the Hongkong monthly *Nanbeiji [The Perspective]* 5:82 (May 1977).

90. RMRB, 2 February 1960, p. 7. These films cost an average of 57 thousand *yuan*.

91. RMRB, 5 October 1958, p. 2; 3 November 1959, p. 4. At the same time a more careful effort was put into 18 feature films made to commemorate the tenth anniversary of the founding of the People's Republic; RMRB, 2 February 1960, p. 7.

92. DZDY 6:6, 12–13 (March 1960). See RMRB, 7 April 1960, p. 8, for a review by Jia Ji. This film was made during a revival of the Leap in early 1960, in part in response to criticism of the Leap expressed in mid-1959 by Marshal Peng Dehuai and to Sino-Soviet inter-Party tensions: see Roderick MacFarquhar, *The Origins of the Cultural Revolution. 2:The Great Leap Forward 1958–1960*, pp. 293–325.

93. See, for example, RMRB, 5 October 1958, p. 2; DZDY 7:27 (April 1960). The catalogue of 1949–79 films, *Zhongguo yishu yingpian bianmu*, published in 1982, reverses the relative importance of documentary and art by labeling these films "artistic documentaries" (*yishuxing jilupian*).

94. RMRB, 5 October 1958, p. 2. Chen Huangmei listed the film in the *Literary Gazette* as one of the ten best of the whole period 1949–58; WYB 19–20:56 (October 1959). Jia Ji reviewed it in *People's Daily*; RMRB, 24 October 1958, p. 8.

95. DZDY 22:7 (November 1958).

96. Cai Chusheng applied these four faults (falseness, obviousness, wordiness, and roughness) to all films made since 1949, but especially those since the Great Leap; DZDY 8:5–6 (August 1961).

97. WYB 7:17–19 (April 1960). "Modern revisionism" was a codeword for the Soviet Communist Party.

98. DZDY 6:26–7 (March 1960); DZDY 24:20–1 (December 1960).

99. The speech was published widely in early 1979 in a number of periodicals; see, for example, WYB 2:2–18 (February 1979). An English translation of excerpts can be found in *Chinese Literature* 6:83–95 (June 1979).

100. WYB 13–14 issue (July 1960). The first Congress had been held in July 1949, and the second in September 1953. The third had been postponed, with the start of the Anti-Rightist campaign in 1957, until 1960.

101. WYB 2:2 (February 1979).

102. DZDY 8:7–8, 26 (April 1960).

103. WYB 5–6:33–47 (May 1962).

104. DZDY 1:5 (January 1962).

105. RMRB, 3 May 1962, p. 2.

106. See, for example, WYB 4:2–9, 11 (February 1960).

107. DZDY 7:20 (July 1961); WYB 3:29–31 (March 1961).

108. DZDY 10:9 (October 1962).

109. The review originally appeared in *Beijing Daily* (*Beijing ribao*); RMRB, 4 August 1963, p. 6.

110. Qu Baiyin, "Guanyu dianying chuangxin de dubai," DYYS 3:52, 53, 54, 56 (June 1962).

111. RMRB, 14 March 1961, p. 4. A similar reluctance to leap to condemnatory conclusions is apparent in reported debates on *Daji and Her Father* (*Daji he tade fuqin*, 1961). The *Literary Gazette* published 14 short articles on the film in one issue: WYB 12:17–31 (December 1961). See also WYB 7:15–21 (July 1961). Zhou Enlai, in his July 1961 speech, made reference to the criticism of the film; WYB 2:4–5 (February 1961).

112. Quoted in a later, 1966 criticism of Qu Baiyin; DZDY 6:31 (June 1966).

113. DZDY 6:31 (June 1966).

114. DZDY 4:17 (April 1961). The groups had been established during the Hundred Flowers and appear to have lasted until the mid-1960s; see for example, DZDY 21:21 (November 1958) and RMRB, 31 August 1960, p. 7.

115. DZDY 12:6–8 (December 1962). The veteran actress Wu Yin also returned to work at this time.

116. WYB 7:6–9 (July 1961). Satirical comedy reappeared on screens in 1959, although *Master Qiao Mounts the Sedan* (*Qiao laoye shang jiao*) was based on a folktale and had an ancient setting, unlike the criticized, contemporary 1956 comedies; DZDY 11:16 (November 1960).

117. The viewers' selections included the musical *Third Sister Liu* (*Liu Sanjie*), the comedy *Li Shuangshuang*, which are discussed in Chapter IV, and another modern musical, *Red Guards of Lake Hong* (*Honghu chiweidui*); DZDY 4:5–6 (April 1962); DZDY 5–6:19 (June 1963).

118. DZDY 10:25 (October 1962).

119. DZDY 10:2–3 (October 1963).

IV. Film genres, 1956–1964

1. See Fokkema, pp. 46–7, 77–81, 262–7.

2. This Chinese aesthetic tendency to prettify can be seen also in films made in Taiwan and Hong Kong under more commercial than political imperatives.

3. The assessment of the signifiance involves necessarily arbitrary decisions. A statistical gloss for this ordering might be found through a content analysis of *Popular Film* for these years. From the point of view of most filmmakers in this period, the May Fourth adaptation and history genres would be closer to the top of the list, and minorities films somewhat lower.

4. Interview with Huang Zongjiang, Beijing, November 1980.

5. A Tibetan actress even played one of the Han nurses; Huang Zongjiang interview. The main players had attended drama school in Shanghai, and so had some training.

6. There was apparently some debate among the filmmakers and in the Film Bureau about including these last words. Proponents argued that it was fitting because, to many Tibetans, Mao Zedong had become something of a living Buddha.

7. *Nongnu: cong juben dao yingpian* (1965) includes articles by the filmmakers, and many stills.

8. The scenes of singing and dancing youths caused *Ashma* to be strongly criticized as a "hippy" film during the Cultural Revolution. Elsewhere the film comes close to parody when, for example, Ashma is surrounded by the flames most often associated with revolutionary martyrdom. Most of the actors in the film appear to be Han Chinese.

9. Like many other minorities films, the filmmakers of *Visitor on Ice Mountain* included an advisor on customs. One of the most effective sequences in the film, using montage and unusual camera angles, is a brief flashback to the hero's childhood before 1949. The logic would seem to be that film techniques should be sober and straightforward, like life itself, when dealing with postrevolutionary events.

10. The film was selected by *Popular Film* readers as a favorite of 1961, in the first Hundred Flowers film poll conducted in the spring of 1962.

11. Xie Jin (1962), "Daoyan chanshu," in *Hongse niangzijun: cong juben dao yingpian*, pp. 256–7, 258, 260.

12. Xie Jin, " 'Hongse niangzijun' daoyan chuangzuo zhaji," *Hongse niangzijun: cong juben dao yingpian*, pp. 273–4.

13. Interview with Chen Qiang, Beijing, November 1980.

14. *Stage Sisters* was criticized at the beginning of the Cultural Revolution, in part because it appeared at a time when reformed modern opera, rather than the Shaoxing musical drama presented in the film, was being advanced as the only acceptable opera form.

15. Interview with Yang Mo, Cambridge, Massachusetts, May 1981.

16. In contrast, Western viewers tend to grow restless at the rather static prison scene.

17. The 1951 film is discussed in Chapter II.

18. For a discussion of audience response to "typical" characters in novels of this period, see Joe C. Huang (1973), *Heroes and Villians in Communist China: The Contemporary Chinese Novel as a Reflection of Life*, pp. 320–8.

19. The story is much simplified in the ballet. Simplification of plot is also true of another Cultural Revolution ballet, *The White-Haired Girl*, drawn from the Yan'an-period opera and its 1950 film version.

20. Another sports story, *Girl Diver* (*Nü tiaoshui duiyuan*, Changchun studio, 1964), from a far less assured director, illustrates the deterioration in filmmaking that set in during the year of its production. The film is crammed with dialogue and badly acted. Reifenstahl-like diving sequences are its only interest.

21. Interview with Li Zhun, Cambridge, Massachusetts, October 1982.

22. The film took the best feature, script, and actress awards in the second Hundred Flowers readership poll conducted by *Popular Film* in 1963. Director Lu Ren, in an article on the film, wrote of the deliberate emphasis on the beauty (*mei*) of "hard work, [correct] ideology, the times and the social system"; see Lu Ren, " 'Li Shuangshuang' de daoyan fenxi he gousi," in *Li Shuangshuang: cong xiaoshuo dao yingpian* (Beijing, 1963), p. 227.

23. The film received the awards for cinematography, music, and art direction in the second Hundred Flowers poll.

24. For a discussion of the background to the Third Sister Liu legend and its adaptation, see Wai-fong Loh, "From romantic love to class struggle: some reflections on the film *Liu Sanjie*," in Bonnie S. McDougall, ed. (1984), *Popular Chinese Literature and Performing Arts in the People's Republic of China, 1949–1979*, pp. 165–76.

25. See DZDY 1:11–12 (January 1962); DZDY 2:19–21 (February 1962); DZDY 8:20–3 (August 1962).

26. Another musical film, the dance drama (*wuju*) *Small-Sword Society* (*Xiaodao hui*, Tianma studio, 1961), in its hybrid mix of Western music and dance to relate the story of a Shanghai uprising during the nineteenth-century Taiping rebellion, anticipated much of the Cultural Revolution model ballet.

27. This is not to underestimate Xia Yan's restraint in the adaptation. A guiding principle, he later wrote, was to preserve the cool surface and strong emotional heart of Lu Xun's work; see Xia Yan (1959), "Zatan gaibian," in *Zhufu: cong xiaoshuo dao dianying*, p. 119.

28. From the shooting script in *Zhufu: cong xiaoshuo dao dianying*, pp. 55, 114. Xiang Lin's wife in the film does indeed ask the question about death which starts the short story, but at the end of the film and to herself. Xia Yan argued that the off-screen narrator made the film easier to comprehend for viewers unfamiliar with the short story; see *Zhufu: cong xiaoshuo dao dianying*, p. 123.

29. At least one reviewer objected to this addition, in an otherwise favorable review; RMRB, 22 October 1956, p. 7. Xia Yan defended the doorstep scene in *Zhufu: cong xiaoshuo dao dianying*, pp. 121–2.

30. Critics complained later that Lin is not shown directly exploiting the "masses," only smaller shopkeepers. His relations with his assistant also drew fire by allegedly emphasizing Lin's paternal concern for the young man, instead of the class exploitation in the relationship. Criticism of the film is discussed in Chapter V.

31. This watery beginning, along with the final scene in which Lin's boat sails away, may have been the work of deputy-director Xie Tieli. Almost all Xie's own later films start and end with a shot of water, a directorial signature rare in modern Chinese films.

32. See Chapter V. Patrick Cavendish makes an excellent analysis of the changes made between novella and film script in Jack Gray and Patrick Cavendish (1968), *Chinese Communism in Crisis: Maoism and the Cultural Revolution*, pp. 90–2.

33. This appears to be the volume called *February, early spring* mentioned in Peter R. Moody (1977), *Opposition and Dissent in Contemporary China*, p. 116.

34. The 1956 film adaptation of *Family* (*Jia*), referred to in Chapter III, also illustrates this difficulty in keeping an unsympathetic distance from May Fourth works.

35. The contemporaneous and much more free film treatment of a Mao Dun short story in the 1933 *Spring Silkworms*, discussed in Chapter I, is noteworthy here.

36. The somewhat theatrical grouping of the massed fisherfolk, and in other scenes with large numbers of people, is noteworthy and a further indication of the stage-inspired nature of much of Chinese film directing in the 1950s and 1960s.

37. The film was codirected by Cen Fan, who went on to make *The Dream of the Red Chamber*.

V. The Cultural Revolution, 1964–1978

1. WYB 7:2 (July 1965).

2. See, for example, the pictorial center pages of DZDY June, September–December 1965, and January, February 1966.

3. Although this forum did not receive much publicity at the time, it acquired great retroactive significance once the faction which promoted it had secured power in culture and the media. Given his military background, it is difficult to imagine army commander Lin Biao's interest in cultural matters being more than political.

4. RMRB, 30 September 1970, p. 2.

5. This assessment of audience reactions is based in part on the present writer's observations as a student in Beijing in 1974–6.

6. Based on the listing of films in *Zhongguo yishu yingpian bianmu* II: 1039–120.

7. WYB 8–9:30 (September 1964).

8. WYB 6:2–5, 14 (June 1965).

9. WYB 3:3–17 (March 1966). See also the long critique of Xia by the May Fourth poet He Qifang, in RMRB, 1 April 1966, pp. 5–6.

10. See particularly Cheng Jihua I, 291–2, 402–3.

11. RMRB, 19 April 1966, p. 6.

12. See, for example, RMRB, 19 April 1966, p. 6; *Jiefangjun wenyi* [*Liberation Army Literature and Art*] 10:17–23 (May 1968); *Chinese Literature* 6:95–100 (June 1968).

13. For a convenient summary of the film script, see Gray and Cavendish, pp. 96–8. Criticisms of the film can be found in RMRB, 30 July 1964, p. 6; 6 September 1964, p. 7; 8 September 1964, p. 6; WYB 8–9:31–5 (September 1964); DZDY 8–9:18–22, 28 (September 1964). At this early stage in what became the Cultural Revolution, a dissenting view could be published; see RMRB, 24 August 1964, p. 6. For Yang Hansheng's later recollection of the criticism, see the author's postscript in *Yang Hansheng dianying juben xuanji* (Beijing, 1981), pp. 325–6. In a conscious parallel with the Wu Xun affair, an investigation team went to the district in which the film is set. The *People's Daily* editors prefaced the publication of the team report by acknowledging the problems of investigating the settings of fiction; RMRB, 15 November 1964, p. 7.

14. WYB 7:19–34 (July 1965). Ke Ling had been chief editor of *Popular Film* and head of the Shanghai Film Art Research Institute in the 1950s.

15. The 1965 charges had been presented before; see WYB 17:35–7 (September 1958). The seemingly nostalgic presentation of wealthy life styles was reminiscent of the 1957 *Loyal Partners*, discussed in Chapter III.

16. DZDY 6:29 (June 1965). Another film subjected to large-scale criticism was one aptly titled *City Besieged* (*Bing lin chengxia*, 1964), based on a 1959 play, which presented its characters with a subtlety not unlike *Jiangnan in the North*. Relations between officers and other ranks, in both the Guomindang and Communist armies, were treated with exceptional naturalism. For criticisms of the film, see WYB 5:57–8 (May 1966); *Chinese Literature* 11–12:142–53 (December 1969).

17. WYB 11–12:44–7 (December 1964).

18. DZDY 10–11:52–3 (November 1964).

19. WYB 9:15–16 (September 1965).

20. WYB 9:14–15, 13–14, 16, respectively (September 1965).

21. Zhou Yang was an exception among the "black liners," having been a critic of many in 1930s Shanghai leftist literary circles and an eager proponent of Mao's Yan'an *Talks* in the 1950s. To the insurgents, however, he represented the cultural establishment.

22. See his biography in Nianjian 1981, p. 233, and in *Zhongguo dianyingjia liezhuan* II: 55–6.

23. Huang Chen, Zheng's wife, recalled these events in *'Siren bang' shi dianying shiye de sidi. Wenhuabu dianying xitong jiepi 'siren bang' zuixing dahui fayan huibian* [hereafter Siren bang . . . hui] (Beijing, 1978), pp. 200–2, and in televised testimony at the trial of the Gang of Four in Beijing, December 1980.

24. See Cai's biography in Nianjian 1981, pp. 231–2; and in *Zhongguo dianying-jia liezhuan* I: 338–49.

25. Siren bang . . . hui, pp. 204–6.

26. Siren bang . . . hui, pp. 72–3.

27. Siren bang . . . hui, pp. 171, 183. Three other remakes were based on films made on the eve of the Cultural Revolution.

28. *Chinese Literature* 2:87 (February 1971).

29. Nianjian 1981, p. 713.

30. *Chinese Literature* 5:123 (May 1974).

31. *Chinese Literature* 2:94 (February 1975).

32. Siren bang . . . hui, p. 82.

33. For an interesting analysis of the narrative structure of several films from the early 1970s, see Chris Berry (1982), "Stereotypes and ambiguities: An examination of the feature films of the Chinese Cultural Revolution," pp. 37–72.

34. *Chinese Literature* 2:95 (February 1975). See also RMRB, 14 August 1974, p. 3.

35. *Chinese Literature* 5:102 (May 1971).

36. *Chinese Literature* 5:102 (May 1971).

37. *Chinese Literature* 5:105, 106 (May 1971). Hao Liang, the opera actor who created the stage portrayal of Li Yuhe, rose high in the Culture Group of the State Council, which replaced the Ministry of Culture during the Cultural Revolution.

38. Berry, "Stereotypes and ambiguities," pp. 46–7.

39. Mao Zedong, *Selected Works* III: 82; compare with the slightly less emphatic original text in McDougall (1980), p. 70.

40. Nianjian 1981, p. 713.

41. Siren bang . . . hui, p. 95. Much of what follows is based on this source, published in 1978 for internal distribution (*neibu*). It provides the most comprehensive account available of the Gang years, with detailed articles by representatives of each of the major film studios and of other organs in the film industry.

42. Siren bang . . . hui, p. 22.

43. Siren bang . . . hui, p. 184.

44. Siren bang . . . hui, p. 179.

45. Siren bang . . . hui, p. 183.

46. Siren bang . . . hui, p. 183.

47. Siren bang . . . hui, p. 174.

48. Siren bang . . . hui, pp. 88–9.

49. Siren bang . . . hui, p. 204.

50. Siren bang . . . hui, p. 40.

51. Siren bang . . . hui, pp. 72, 205.

52. Siren bang . . . hui, pp. 89, 90. Another source says over 55 percent of Changchun cadres were incarcerated or expelled from the studio; Sanshiwunian, p. 45.

53. Siren bang . . . hui, p. 107 (August First); Sanshiwunian, p. 167 (Xi'an); Sanshiwunian, p. 143 (Pearl River).

54. See Siren bang . . . hui, pp. 56–69, especially pp. 56–7.

55. Siren bang . . . hui, pp. 72–3.

56. Siren bang . . . hui, pp. 91–3. The Gang supporters were strongest in the educational film, feature film, and script editing sections of the studio.

57. Siren bang . . . hui, p. 95.

58. Siren bang . . . hui, pp. 181–2.

59. Siren bang . . . hui, pp. 109, 111–12.

60. Some actors did reappear on screen. Guo Zhenqing, for example, who had played the hero in the original 1955 version of *Guerrillas on the Plain*, played the central role in Changchun's 1974 feature *Iron Giant (Gangtie juren)*. Zhu Xijuan, who had played the lead in the 1961 *Red Detachment of Women*, appeared in a 1974 production. Such a popular actress as Zhang Ruifang, the original Li Shuangshuang, was appearing on screen by 1976, as were Xie Fang, who had played Miss Tao in *Early Spring in February*, and the actors Wang Xin'gang, Yu Yang, and even Xiang Kun, whose fortunes had taken a temporary plunge in the Anti-Rightist campaign.

61. Li was the scenarist and director of *The Scout (Zhencha bing)*, which, in an interview in Beijing in November 1980, Cheng Jihua named as the first new nonopera feature film to be made after the studios resumed production. See also *Guangming ribao*, 16 September 1973, p. 4.

62. Interview, Beijing Film Studio, October 1980. The same was true of Li Jun, director of *Serfs*, who codirected *Sparkling Red Star*, and whose remarks on that film are quoted above. Li had directed his first film in 1957.

63. See Sang Hu's article on the making of the ballet film; *Chinese Literature* 7:96–8 (July 1972).

64. This apparent, but circumscribed, regionalist concession even in the "model performances" is noteworthy. *Shajiabang* and other model operas were also produced in Cantonese versions.

65. Cui Wei, who had directed *Song of Youth* in 1959, directed *The New Doctor* in 1975. Lin Nong, director of *Naval Battle of 1894* (1962) and the criticized *City Besieged* (1964), made film versions of two Hao Ran novels during the Cultural Revolution, *Bright Sunny Skies (Yanyangtian)* in 1973 and *The Golden Road (Jinguang dadao)*, Part I, in 1975.

66. Interviews at the Film Research Institute, Ministry of Culture Literature and Art Research Academy, Beijing, and at the Beijing Film Academy, Zhuxinzhuang, November 1980. The initial film specialties at Jiang Qing's Academy were sound recording and lighting.

67. Siren bang . . . hui, p. 179.

68. This point is made in Gray and Cavendish, p. 148.

69. "Some were willing to sell their artistic consciences, but they were extremely few."; Siren bang . . . hui, p. 73.

70. The size of royalties is indicated in Appendix 2 of Lars Ragvald (1978), *Yao Wenyuan as Literary Critic and Theorist*.

71. Nianjian 1981, p. 713. The English translation is from *Chinese Literature* 1:1 (January 1977). The directive is dated July 25, 1975. Jiang Qing found fault with the film reportedly because the central hero was based on a real-life figure of whom she did not approve.

72. *Renmin dianying* [*People's Film*; RMDY] 5:16 (May 1978).

73. Siren bang . . . hui, p. 73.

74. Qian Jiang had been the cinematographer for the original 1950 film version of *The White-Haired Girl*, for *The Lin Family Shop*, and for *On the Docks*. The other *Haixia* directors were Chen Huaikai and Wang Haowei. Chen prefers his personal names rendered Huaikai, rather than (the strictly correct) Huaiai: interview, Beijing, May 1986.

75. Nianjian 1981, pp. 713–14; RMDY 1:12–15(January 1978); RMDY 2–3:30–7(March 1978); RMDY 5:16–17(May 1978). The actor Chen Qiang played an old man in the film. His question to young people in the film, "What do you know about guns?" was later cited as an example of disguised criticism of the Gang; interview, Beijing Film Studio, October 1980. The Gang allowed limited release of the film, reportedly in order to recoup some of its costs; Siren bang . . . hui, p. 169.

76. Nianjian 1981, p. 713. These films included a 1964 adaptation of the May Fourth writer Ba Jin's Korean War novel *Heroic Sons and Daughters* (*Yingxiong ernü*). It starred Tian Fang, who later died under Gang pressure in 1974, at age sixty-three.

77. Figures are drawn from *Hongqi* 6:50–3 (June 1975). See Siren bang . . . hui, pp. 164, 174, 175. See also, for example, RMRB, 30 June 1974, p. 4; *Guangming ribao*, 23 July 1971, p. 2; *Guangming ribao*, 13 May 1976, p. 2.

78. RMDY 4:13–14 (April 1978). In early 1979 there were only about 40 trained scriptwriters in the then seven feature film studios; RMRB, 12 March 1979, p. 3.

79. RMDY 8:13 (August 1978). See also, for example, RMDY 9:2–3 (September 1978); RMDY 1:14 (January 1978).

80. RMRB, 27 January 1979, p. 3.

81. RMRB, 23 January 1979, p. 3; DZDY 1:10–12 (January 1979); RMDY 12:7–9 (December 1978). About thirty foreign films, from the film centers of North Korea, Vietnam, and Albania, had been shown during the eleven years of the Cultural Revolution; Siren bang . . . hui, p. 170. In 1979 the foreign films included Peckinpah's *Convoy* and recent Japanese features. For further details, see Paul Clark, "The Film Industry in the 1970s," in Bonnie S. McDougall, ed. (1984), *Popular Chinese Literature and Performing Arts in the People's Republic of China, 1949–1979*, pp. 189–90.

82. DZDY 2:12–13 (February 1979); RMRB, 23 January 1979, p. 3; DZDY 4:7–8 (April 1979). These films had also enjoyed revivals during the first Hundred Flowers and in the early 1960s, two periods of relative cultural liberalization.

83. Siren bang . . . hui, p. 83.

84. Siren bang . . . hui, p. 15; see also p. 73.

85. The idea to include Mao and Zhou was apparently Xie Tieli's own. It may have been in response to Jiang Qing's earlier objection that the hero of *The Pioneers* had been based on a real-life figure (interview with scenarist Li Zhun, Cambridge, Massachusetts, October 1982).

86. Scripts of the two parts can be found in RMDY 5–6:65–96 (June 1977), and RMDY 7:36–64 (July 1977). The film was expensive by Chinese standards, reportedly costing well over one million *yuan* (about 500,000 1978 U.S. dollars) to make.

VI. Beyond Yan'an

1. For discussion of these changes, see Roger Garside (1981), *Coming Alive. China After Mao*; Victor Sidane and Wojtek Zafanolli, eds. (1981), *Procès politiques à Pékin: Wei Jingsheng, Fu Yuehua*; Andrew J. Nathan (1985), *Chinese Democracy*.

2. DZDY 4:3 (April 1979).

3. DZDY 3:8 (March 1979). The Beijing Film Academy reopened four-year degree classes in 1978.

4. RMRB, 21 January 1979, p. 3; reprinted in DYYS 1:28–33 (January 1979).

5. One implication was that these committees might censure cadres for their actions under the Gang regime.

6. RMRB, 14 May 1979, p. 3. See also RMRB, 13 February 1979, p. 3; 22 January 1979, p. 4.

7. RMRB, 14 May 1979, p. 3. Direct public criticism of Mao had not yet begun when this article appeared in May 1979.

8. Translation from Howard Goldblatt, ed. (1982), *Chinese Literature for the 1980s: The Fourth Congress of Writers and Artists*, pp. 8, 13–14. *Tansuo* (*Exploration*) was the name of a well-known unofficial magazine from the Democracy Wall movement, which by then had been closed down under Deng's orders.

9. Translation from Goldblatt, pp. 161, 165. One major area of research and discussion was "modernism," seen as a change from "socialist realism." For an excellent analysis of debates on literary theory in this period, see D. E. Pollard, "The controversy over modernism, 1979–84."

10. Goldblatt, pp. 63, 59, 66–7. This talk of clubs and hands shielding heads was reminiscent of Qu Baiyin's relatively bold remarks of 1962; see Chapter III.

11. RMRB, 8 October 1980, p. 5. Translated in *Chinese Literature* 1:107–11 (January 1981). No mention of this article was made at a memorial meeting for Zhao, chaired by Zhou Yang and addressed by Xia Yan and others, which the present writer attended in Beijing, October 1980.

12. See WYB 5:21–4 (March 1958).

13. RMRB, 30 July 1980, p. 5. For Bai Hua's response, see RMRB, 3 September 1980, p. 5.

14. Interview with editors of *Popular Film* and *Film Art*, Beijing, November 1980. Readership numbers declined drastically in the mid-1980s, as film attendance slumped and other magazines attracted readers.

15. DZDY 10:1–5 (October 1980).

16. Studio leaders held the first of what became annual national meetings in February 1979; DZDY 3:24 (March 1979).

17. This was confirmed in interviews at the Beijing, Shanghai, and Pearl River studios in October–December 1980.

18. DZDY 12:1 (December 1980); DYYS 12:1–3 (December 1980). See also DZDY 11:1 (November 1980).

19. Wu Yigong was supervised in directing the film by the veteran artist Wu

Yonggang, director of the 1934 film *The Goddess*, discussed in Chapter I. Wu Yigong in 1984 became head of the newly formed Shanghai Film Corporation, management body for the Shanghai Film Studio, Shanghai Animation Film Studio, and other film enterprises in the city.

20. These impressions were gathered in interviews with filmmakers and viewers in Beijing and Shanghai in late 1980, and in interviews with Yang Yanjin, Shanghai, December 1980.

21. The film's title comes from an ancient poetic comparison of close friendship with a pair of stringed instruments in harmony.

22. Interview with Sang Hu, Turin, Italy, March 1982.

23. This emphasis on personal motives was a major concern of published criticism of the film in the spring of 1982, almost eighteen months after its release. The *Literary Gazette*, in the spirit of the "double hundred" policy, the editors noted, published in April an article that expressed disquiet at the alleged magnification of the Anti-Rightist campaign's errors in the film, particularly in the portrayal of the private motives of the Party cadre who had condemned the engineer. In June a vigorous defense of the film appeared. See WYB 4:76–80 (April 1982); WYB 6:55–60 (June 1982). See also the review of the film by the newly rehabilitated "rightist" Zhong Dianfei in *Guangming ribao*, 24 April 1982, p. 5.

24. See the hilarious mock "formula" for making one of the new films, by a disgruntled reader of DYYS 2:39 (February 1983). Martial arts films enjoyed a brief period of prosperity (1982–4), before coming under an official cloud for being "vulgar" and encouraging youthful excesses.

25. Xie Jin's 1982 feature, *The Herdsman* (*Muma ren*), had a somewhat contrived international story with a strong patriotic theme. The herdsman of the title had been labeled a "rightist" in 1958 and exiled to the Northwest. In the late 1970s he meets his father, president of a large American chemical company, after thirty years. He declines the chance to join his father in favor of remaining in the land of his birth. The screenplay was by Li Zhun, writer of *Li Shuangshuang* and *The Great River Rushes On*.

26. For a study of the Qu Yuan legend, see Laurence A. Schneider (1980), *A Madman of Ch'u: The Chinese Myth of Loyalty and Dissent*.

27. The script of *Unrequited Love*, first published in China in *Shiyue* (*October*) 3:140–71, 248 (September 1979), was reprinted in the Hong Kong magazine *Zhengming* (*Debate*) 6:82–98 (June 1981).

28. Qu Yuan committed suicide by leaping into the Miluo River in the marshlands of northern Hunan Province.

29. The April criticism was reprinted in *Beijing ribao* (*Beijing Daily*), 20 April 1981, p. 2. The April 1981 *Liberation Army Daily* commentator cited *Night Rain on the River* as a film which showed how the "broad masses" were "basically unsympathetic" toward Lin Biao and the Gang of Four.

30. *Beijing wanbao*, 8 May 1981, p. 3. The criticism of *Unrequited Love* had provoked protests by students at Beijing and Fudan universities. What the reports of Bai Hua's condition did not describe was his writing project of the summer of 1981. Set in the Spring and Autumn period (722–418 B.C.) and drawn from the *Annals of Wu and Yue* (*Wuyue chunqiu*), the new play contrasted the careers of two loyal ministers to the king of Yue. After helping expel the forces of the Wu state, one minister, Fan Li, withdraws from public life, acknowledging loyalty to his principles over that to his king. Wen Zhong, on the other hand, sees loyalty to the state as outweighing the insults he must bear to remain in the court of the king of Yue. The play was staged in Beijing in the summer of 1983.

31. *Shikan* 7:7 (July 1981). His poem was one of eight prizewinners classified as political lyrics (*zhengzhi shuqingshi*). Titled "The spring tide is in sight" (*Chunchao zaiwang*), it had been published in RMRB, 17 March 1979, p. 6.

32. Excerpts from Hu Yaobang's speech were reprinted in *Zhengming* 8:16 (August 1981).

33. Hu Qiaomu's August speech was published in the Party organ *Red Flag* (*Hongqi*) 23:2–22 (December 1981). Hu named Peng Ning as co-author of the film script. The April *Liberation Army Daily* commentator had not mentioned Peng.

34. The article was reprinted in RMRB, 7 October 1981, p. 5. A reported change in *People's Daily* editors was linked with the earlier nonpublication by that newspaper of the April *Liberation Army Daily* article. Hong Kong sources claimed that Liu Baiyu had also written this first article.

35. *Hongqi* 19:29–33 (October 1981).

36. RMRB, 24 December 1981, p. 4. The letter, dated November 25, was published the previous day in *Liberation Army Daily* and in the January 1982 issue of the *Literary Gazette*. Bai Hua returned to publication in May 1982 with an article in *Yangcheng ribao* (*Yangcheng [Guangzhou] Daily*), 21 May 1982, p. 2, on a trip to Cangshan and Erhai in Yunnan, his old stamping ground in the early 1950s. See also a report on Bai Hua's recent activities in WYB 10:51 (May 1982).

37. *Guangming ribao*, 30 December 1981, p. 1. Zhou Yang made similar statements at this time. Attention in the media turned to concern at the strong emphasis on love in films and literature in recent years; see *Qishi niandai* (*The Seventies*) 1:78–80 (January 1982).

38. RMRB, 21 April 1982, p. 5.

39. *Guangming ribao*, 20 May 1982, p. 1.

40. *Mingbao* (Hong Kong), 22 October 1982, p. 5.

41. RMRB, 23 June 1982, p. 5.

42. RMRB, 23 June 1982, p. 5.

43. *Guangming ribao*, 20 May 1982, p. 1.

44. RMRB, 25 June 1982, p. 4.

45. RMRB, 26 June 1982, p. 1. The plenary session had been postponed in 1981 because of the Bai Hua business. The "pact" was designed to reinforce general cultural policy, made up of the "double hundred" slogan and the Four Basic Principles: upholding Marxism–Leninism–Mao Zedong Thought, proletarian dictatorship, Party leadership, and socialism.

46. The unexpected contemporary relevance of the film perhaps explains the curious prologue which precedes the title and credits. Xie Tieli is briefly seen talking to the seventy-eight-year-old Zhang Tianyi. The director, we are told, was anxious to ensure the film's authenticity. The prologue suggests that Zhang's original story condemned only the abject fascination with Western tastes of the younger Bao. Critics of "spiritual pollution" in the 1980s, it is implied, had their predecessors in the 1930s.

47. For a masterful discussion of literature and art in 1949–79, and of artists and change since May Fourth times, see Bonnie S. McDougall, "Writers and performers, their works, and their audiences in the first three decades," in McDougall (1984, pp. 269–304).

48. At a meeting of the Tao Xingzhi Research Society in September, Hu Qiaomu, the Party's chief ideologue, declared the 1951 criticism of the film initiated by Mao Zedong "extremely superficial, extremely excessive and also extremely crude." Wu Xun himself deserved further assessment by historians, rather than politicians. Tao Xingzhi had been a pre-1949 admirer of Wu Xun's example of reformism. The same meeting marked the establishment of the Tao Xingzhi Foundation, a private educational effort in the Wu Xun tradition: RMRB, 6 September 1985, p. 1.

49. Chen is the son of Chen Huaikai, assistant director of *The New Year's Sacrifice* (1956), and codirector of *Song of Youth* (1959), *Red Flower of Tianshan* (1964), *Haixia* (1975), *The Great River Rushes On* (1978), *Intimate Friends* (1981), and numerous prize-winning opera films.

50. *Yellow Earth's* vote total was a fifth that of the most popular film, and less than a half the total for the fourth placed: DZDY 7:2 (July 1986).

Postscript

1. Xi'an, under Wu Tianming, was selected as the one film studio in which to apply the experimental managerial responsibility system for factories and other units, giving considerable and unprecedented executive power to the manager rather than Party committees. For a fascinating picture of Wu Tianming and his impact on the Xi'an studio, see the two-part reportage by the eminent writer Liu Binyan, "Meishang yinmu de gushi: ji Xi'an dianying zhipianchang changzhang, daoyan Wu Tianming," RMRB, 7 and 8 August 1986, p. 8. In a Party response to the December 1986 student demonstrations, Liu was expelled from the Communist Party in early 1987. *People's Daily*, for which he wrote, subsequently received thousands of letters in Liu's support.

2. Shao Mujun, "Chinese film amidst the tide of reform," *East–West Film Journal* I, 1:59–68 (December 1986). See also reports on much larger declines in DZDY 9:2–3 (September 1985) and Sanshiwunian, p. 344. For an interesting analysis of audience interest in Zhangjiakou City in Hebei Province, see the article by Dai Baiye in DYYS 11:10–17 (November 1984).

3. By the mid-1980s the entire film system under the Film Bureau, including the distribution apparatus, employed about half a million people. (Interview at Film Bureau, Beijing, May 1986.)

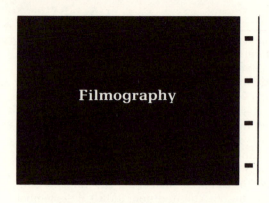

Filmography

This chronological listing includes all Chinese films mentioned in this study. Chinese characters for the titles are included. Complete information can be found in Cheng Jihua (for films made before 1949), *Zhongguo yishu yingpian bianmu* (for films from 1949 to 1979), and Nianjian (for 1979–84 films). Abbreviations: d, director; s, scenarist.

1926

Three Shanghai Girls *(Shanghai hua)*
上海花
d, s: Wang Fuqing
Guoguang studio

1931

Singsong Girl Red Peony *(Genü hong mudan)*
歌女红牡丹
d: Zhang Shichuan
s: Hong Shen
Mingxing

1933

Sister Flowers *(Zimei hua)*
姊妹花
d, s: Zheng Zhengqiu
Mingxing
Spring Silkworms *(Chuncan)*
春蚕
d: Cheng Bugao
s: Xia Yan
Mingxing

1934

The Goddess (Shennü)
神女
d, s: Wu Yonggang
Lianhua

The Highway (Dalu)
大路
d, s: Sun Yu
Lianhua

1937

March of Youth (Qingnian jinxingqu)
青年进行曲
d: Shi Dongshan
s: Tian Han, Xia Yan
Xinhua

Street Angel (Malu tianshi)
马路天使
d, s: Yuan Muzhi
Mingxing

Crossroads (Shizi jietou)
十字街头
d, s: Shen Xiling
Mingxing

1947 and 1948

The Spring River Flows East (Yijiang chunshui xiang dong liu), 2 parts
一江春水向东流
d, s: Cai Chusheng, Zheng Junli
Lianhua/Kunlun

1947

Along the Sungari River (Songhuajiang shang)
松花江上
d, s: Jin Shan
Changchun

Eight Thousand Li of Clouds and Moon (Baqianli lu yun he yue)
八千里路云和月
d, s: Shi Dongshan
Kunlun

1948

Spring in a Small Town (*Xiaocheng zhi chun*)
小城之春
d: Fei Mu
s: Li Tianqing
Wenhua

Leave Him to Fight Old Jiang (*Liuxia ta da lao Jiang*)
留下他打老蒋
d, s: Lin Qi
Northeast

1949

A Life of Hope (*Xiwang zai renjian*)
希望在人间
d, s: Shen Fu
Kunlun

Tears of the Pearl River (*Zhujiang lei*)
珠江泪
d: Wang Weiyi
s: Chen Canyun
Nanguo

Crows and Sparrows (*Wuya yu maque*)
乌鸦与麻雀
d: Zheng Junli
s: Chen Bochen and others
Kunlun

Bridge (*Qiao*)
桥
d: Wang Bin
s: Yu Min
Northeast

Returning to Our Own Ranks (*Huidao ziji duiwu lai*)
回到自己队伍来
d, s: Cheng Yin
Northeast

Boundless Light (*Guangmang wanzhang*)
光芒万丈
d: Xu Ke
s: Chen Bo'er
Northeast

Daughters of China (*Zhonghua nüer*)
中华女儿
d: Ling Zifeng, Zhai Qing
s: Yan Yiyan
Northeast

White-Coated Fighter (*Baiyi zhanshi*)
白衣战士
d: Feng Bolu
s: Wang Chenzhi
Northeast

1950

Zhao Yiman (*Zhao Yiman*)
赵一曼
d: Sha Meng
s: Yu Min
Northeast

The Life of Wu Xun (*Wu Xun zhuan*)
武训传
d, s: Sun Yu
Kunlun

Spring Rays in Inner Mongolia (*Neimeng chunguang*)
内蒙春光
d: Gan Xuewei
s: Wang Chenzhi
Later called *The Mongolian People's Victory* (*Neimeng renmin de shengli*)
Northeast

The White-Haired Girl (*Baimao nü*)
白毛女
d: Wang Bin, Shui Hua
s: Shui Hua, Wang Bin, Yang Runshen
Northeast

1951

Shangrao Concentration Camp (*Shangrao jizhongying*)
上饶集中营
d: Sha Meng, Zhang Ke
s: Feng Xuefeng
Shanghai

A Married Couple (*Women fufu zhi jian*)
我们夫妇之间
d, s: Zheng Junli
Kunlun

Platoon Commander Guan (*Guan lianzhang*)
关连长
d: Shi Hui
s: Yang Liuqing
Wenhua

1952

Dragon's Beard Ditch (*Longxu gou*)
龙须沟
d, s: Xian Qun
Beijing

Gate No. 6 (*Liuhao men*)
六号门
d: Lü Ban
s: Chen Ming
Northeast

Fighting North and South (*Nanzheng beizhan*)
南征北战
d: Cheng Yin, Tang Xiaodan
s: Shen Ximeng, Shen Mojun, Gu Baozhang
Shanghai

1953

Scouting across the Yangzi (*Dujiang zhenchaji*)
渡江侦察记
d: Tang Xiaodan
s: Shen Mojun
Shanghai

1954

Liang Shanbo and Zhu Yingtai (*Liang Shanbo yu Zhu Yingtai*)
梁山伯与祝英台
d: Sang Hu, Huang Sha
s: Xu Jin, Sang Hu
Shanghai

1955

Song Jingshi (*Song Jingshi*)
宋景诗
d: Zheng Junli, Sun Yu
s: Chen Bochen, Jia Ji
Shanghai

Dong Cunrui (*Dong Cunrui*)
董存瑞
d: Guo Wei
s: Ding Hong, Zhao Huan, Dong Xiaohua
Changchun

Guerrillas on the Plain (*Pingyuan youjidui*)
平原游击队
d: Su Li, Wu Zhaodi
s: Xing Ye, Yu Shan
Changchun

1956

The New Year's Sacrifice (*Zhufu*)
祝福
d: Sang Hu
s: Xia Yan
Beijing

Family (*Jia*)
家
d: Chen Xihe, Ye Ming
s: Chen Xihe
Shanghai

Hua Mulan (*Hua Mulan*)
花木兰
d: Liu Guoquan, Zhang Xinshi
s: Henan *Yu* Opera Academy writing group
Changchun

Before the New Director Arrives (*Xin juzhang daolai zhi qian*)
新局长到来之前
d: Lü Ban
s: Yu Yanfu
Changchun

The Man Unconcerned with Details (*Buju xiaojie de ren*)
不拘小节的人
d: Lü Ban
s: He Chi
Changchun

Li Shizhen (*Li Shizhen*)
李时珍
d: Shen Fu
s: Zhang Huijian
Shanghai

1957

Girl Basketball Player No. 5 (*Nülan wuhao*)
女篮 5 号
d, s: Xie Jin
Tianma

Loyal Partners (*Qing chang yi shen*)
情长谊深
d, s: Xu Changlin
Tianma

Unfinished Comedy (*Wei wancheng de xiju*)
未完成的喜剧
d: Lü Ban
s: Luo Tai, Lü Ban
Changchun

Braving Wind and Waves (*Chengfeng polang*)
乘风破浪
d: Sun Yu, Jiang Junchao
s: Sun Yu
Jiangnan

Nurse's Diary (*Hushi riji*)
护士日记
d: Tao Jin
s: Ai Mingzhi
Jiangnan

City without Night (*Buye cheng*)
不夜城
d: Tang Xiaodan
s: Ke Ling
Jiangnan

1958

Steel Man and Iron Horse (*Gangren tiema*)
钢人铁马
d: Lu Ren
s: Fei Liwen
Haiyan

Loving the Factory as One's Home (*Ai chang ru jia*)
爱厂如家
d, s: Zhao Ming
Jiangnan

The Big Wave (*Julang*)
巨浪
d: Liu Qiong, Qiang Ming
s: Ai Mingzhi
Haiyan

A Revolution in Twenty Days (*Ershitian ge ge ming*)
20天革个命
d: Ge Xin
s: Li Hongxin
Tianma

Huang Baomei (*Huang Baomei*)
黄宝妹
d: Xie Jin
s: Chen Fu, Ye Ming
Tianma

1959

Lin Zexu (*Lin Zexu*)
林则徐
d: Zheng Junli, Cen Fan
s: Ye Yuan
Haiyan

Song of Youth (*Qingchun zhi ge*)
青春之歌
d: Cui Wei, Chen Huaikai
s: Yang Mo
Beijing

Master Qiao Mounts the Sedan (*Qiao laoye shang jiao*)
乔老爷上轿
d: Liu Qiong
s: Tian Nianxuan, Liu Qiong
Haiyan

Five Golden Flowers (*Wuduo jinhua*)
五朵金花
d: Wang Jiayi
s: Zhao Jikang, Wang Gongpu
Changchun

The Young People of Our Village (*Women cunli de nianqing ren*), Part I
我们村里的年轻人（上集）
d: Su Li
s: Ma Feng
Changchun

The Lin Family Shop (*Linjia puzi*)
林家铺子
d: Shui Hua
s: Xia Yan
Beijing

1960

Third Sister Liu (*Liu Sanjie*)
刘三姐
d: Su Li
s: Qiao Yu
Changchun

For Sixty-one Class Brothers (*Weile liushiyige jieji xiongdi*)
为了六十一个阶级兄弟
d: Xie Tian, Chen Fangqian
s: Xie Tian, Chen Fangqian, and others
Beijing

A Revolutionary Family (*Geming jiating*)
革命家庭
d: Shui Hua
s: Xia Yan, Shui Hua
Beijing

Menglongsha Village (*Menglongsha*)
勐垅沙
d: Wang Ping, Yuan Xian
s: Luo Shui
August First

1961

The Red Detachment of Women (*Hongse niangzijun*)
红色娘子军
d: Xie Jin
s: Liang Xin
Tianma

Daji and Her Father (*Daji he tade fuqin*)
达吉和她的父亲
d: Wang Jiayi
s: Gao Ying
Emei and Changchun

Red Guards of Lake Hong (*Honghu chiweidui*)
洪湖赤卫队
d: Xie Tian, Chen Fangqian, Xu Feng
s: Mei Shaoshan, Zhang Jing'an and others
Beijing and Wuhan

Small-Sword Society (*Xiaodao hui*)
小刀会
d: Ye Ming
s: Zhang Tuo, Bai Shui, Zhang Lin, Shu Qiao, Li Qun
Tianma

1962

Naval Battle of 1894 (*Jiawu fengyun*)
甲午风云
d: Lin Nong
s: Xi Nong, Ye Nan, Chen Ying, Li Xiongfei, Du Li
Changchun

Big Li, Little Li, and Old Li (*Da Li, xiao Li he lao Li*)
大李、小李和老李
d: Xie Jin
s: Yu Ling, Ye Ming, Xie Jin, Liang Yanjing, Wu Li, Jiang Rongquan
Tianma

Fire on the Plain (*Liao yuan*)
燎原
d: Zhang Junxiang, Gu Erji
s: Peng Yonghui, Li Hongxin
Tianma

Li Shuangshuang (*Li Shuangshuang*)
李双双
d: Lu Ren
s: Li Zhun
Haiyan

The Dream of the Red Chamber (*Honglou meng*)
红楼梦
d: Cen Fan
s: Xu Jin
Haiyan and Jinsheng (Hong Kong)

1963

What's Eating You? (*Manyi bu manyi*)
满意不满意
d: Yan Gong
s: Fei Ke, Zhang Huan'er, Yan Gong
Changchun

Early Spring in February (*Zaochun eryue*)
早春二月
d, s: Xie Tieli
Beijing

Serfs (*Nongnu*)
农奴
d: Li Jun
s: Huang Zongjiang
August First

Visitor on Ice Mountain (*Bingshan shang de laike*)
冰山上的来客
d: Zhao Xinshui
s: Bai Xin
Changchun

Jiangnan in the North (*Beiguo Jiangnan*)
北国江南
d: Shen Fu
s: Yang Hansheng
Haiyan

1964

Ashma (*Ashima*)
阿诗玛
d: Liu Qiong
s: Ge Yan, Liu Qiong
Haiyan

Red Flower of Tianshan (*Tianshan de honghua*)
天山的红花
d: Cui Wei, Chen Huaikai, Liu Baode
s: Ou Lin
Xi'an and Beijing

Girl Diver (*Nü tiaoshui duiyuan*)
女跳水队员
d: Liu Guoquan
s: Geng Geng
Changchun

City Besieged (*Bing lin chengxia*)
兵临城下
d: Lin Nong
s: Bai Ren, Lin Nong
Changchun

Heroic Sons and Daughters (*Yingxiong ernü*)
英雄儿女
d: Wu Zhaodi
s: Mao Feng, Wu Zhaodi
Changchun

1965

Stage Sisters (*Wutai jiemei*)
舞台姐妹
d: Xie Jin
s: Lin Gu, Xu Jin, Xie Jin
Tianma

Red Crag (*Liehuo zhong yongsheng*)
烈火中永生
d: Shui Hua
s: Zhou Hao
Beijing

1970

Taking Tiger Mountain by Strategy (*Zhiqu Weihushan*)
智取威虎山
d: Xie Tieli
s: Beijing Beijing Opera Troupe
Beijing

The Red Lantern *(Hongdeng ji)*
红灯记
d: Cheng Yin
s: China Beijing Opera Troupe
August First

1971

The Red Detachment of Women *(Hongse niangzijun)*
红色娘子军
d: Pan Wenzhan, Fu Jie
s: China Dance Drama Troupe
Beijing

Shajiabang *(Shajiabang)*
沙家浜
d: Wu Zhaodi
s: Beijing Beijing Opera Troupe
Changchun

1972

The White-Haired Girl *(Baimao nü)*
白毛女
d: Sang Hu
s: Shanghai Municipal Dance School
Shanghai

1972 and 1973

On the Docks *(Haigang)*, two versions
海港
d: Xie Tieli, Xie Jin
s: Shanghai Beijing Opera Troupe
Beijing and Shanghai

1973

Bright Sunny Skies *(Yangyantian)*, Part I
艳阳天（上集）
d: Lin Nong
s: Collectively adapted from the Hao Ran novel
Changchun

1974

Shajiabang *(Sagabong),* Cantonese version
沙家浜
d: Yu Deshui
s: Beijing Beijing Opera Troupe Shajiabang writing group
Pearl River

The Fiery Years *(Huohong de niandai)*
火红的年代
d: Fu Chaowu, Sun Yongping, Yu Zhongying
s: Ye Dan, Fu Chaowu and others
Shanghai

Sparkling Red Star *(Shanshan de hongxing)*
闪闪的红星
d: Li Jun, Li Ang
s: Wang Yuanjian, Lu Zhuguo and others
August First

The Scout *(Zhencha bing)*
侦察兵
d,s: Li Wenhua
Beijing

Fighting North and South *(Nanzheng beizhan)*
南征北战
d: Cheng Yin, Wang Yan
s: Shen Ximeng and others
Beijing

Guerrillas on the Plain *(Pingyuan youjidui)*
平原游击队
d: Wu Zhaodi, Chang Zhenhua
s: Guerrillas on the Plain writing group
Changchun

Scouting across the Yangzi *(Dujiang zhenchaji)*
渡江侦察记
d: Tang Huada, Tang Xiaodan
s: Ji Guanwu, Gao Xing, Meng Senhui, and others
Shanghai

Iron Giant *(Gangtie juren)*
钢铁巨人
d: Yan Gong
s: Iron Giant writing group
Changchun

The Pioneers *(Chuangye)*
创业
d: Yu Yanfu
s: Zhang Tianmin and others
Changchun

1975

Breaking with Old Ideas (*Juelie*)
决裂
d: Li Wenhua
s: Chun Chao, Zhou Jie
Beijing

The New Doctor (*Hongyu*)
红雨
d: Cui Wei
s: Yang Xiao
Beijing

The Second Spring (*Di'erge chuntian*)
第二个春天
d: Sang Hu, Wang Xiuwen
s: Liu Chuan, He Baoxian and others
Shanghai

The Red Lantern (*Hongdeng ji*), Uighur version
红灯记
d: Cheng Yin
s: Adapted by the Xinjiang Uighur Autonomous Region Song and Dance
Troupe
August First

The Golden Road (*Jinguang dadao*), Part I
金光大道（上集）
d: Lin Nong, Sun Yu
s: Collectively adapted from the Hao Ran novel
Changchun

Haixia (*Haixia*)
海霞
d: Qian Jiang, Chen Huaikai, Wang Haowei
s: Xie Tieli
Beijing

1976

Counterattack (*Fanji*)
反击
d: Li Wenhua
s: Mao Feng and the Counterattack writing group
Beijing

1977

Youth (*Qingchun*)
青春
d: Xie Jin

s: Li Yunliang, Wang Lian
Shanghai

1978

Battle of Leopard Valley (*Baoziwan zhandou*)
豹子湾战斗
d: Wang Jiayi, Jiang Shusen
s: Ma Jixing and others
Changchun
Spring Comes Early on the Southern Border (*Nanjiang chunzao*)
南疆春早
d: Guo Jun, Xiao Lang
s: Zhu Xuming
Beijing
The Great River Rushes On (*Dahe benliu*)
大河奔流
d: Xie Tieli, Chen Huaikai
s: Li Zhun
Beijing

1979

Reverberations of Life (*Shenghuo de chanyin*)
生活的颤音
d, s: Teng Wenji
Xi'an
Bitter Laughter (*Ku'naoren de xiao*)
苦恼人的笑
d: Yang Yanjin, Deng Yimin
s: Yang Yanjin, Xue Jing
Shanghai
Twins Come in Pairs (*Talia he talia*)
她俩和他俩
d: Sang Hu
s: Wang Lian, Sang Hu, Fu Jinggong
Shanghai

1980

Effendi (*Afanti*)
阿凡提
d: Xiao Lang
s: Wang Yuhu, Xiao Lang
Beijing

Legend of Tianyun Mountain (*Tianyunshan chuanqi*)
天云山传奇
d: Xie Jin
s: Lu Yanzhou
Shanghai

Unrequited Love (*Kulian*)
苦恋
d: Peng Ning
s: Bai Hua, Peng Ning
More correctly, *The Sun and the Man* (*Taiyang he ren*)
Changchun

The Stars Are Bright Tonight (*Jinye xingguang canlan*)
今夜星光灿烂
d: Xie Tieli
s: Bai Hua
August First

They're in Love (*Tamen zai xiang'ai*)
他们在相爱
d: Qian Jiang, Zhao Yuan
s: Yang Lingyan, Wang Qi
Beijing

Love and Inheritance (*Aiqing yu yichan*)
爱情与遗产
d: Yan Xueshu
s: Li Yunliang
Xi'an

Night Rain on the River (*Bashan yeyu*)
巴山夜雨
d: Wu Yigong, Wu Yonggang
s: Ye Nan
Shanghai

1981

The Alley (*Xiaojie*)
小街
d: Yang Yanjin
s: Xu Yinhua
Shanghai

Longing for Home (*Xiangqing*)
乡情
d: Hu Binliu, Wang Jin
s: Wang Yimin
Pearl River

Intimate Friends (*Zhiyin*)
知音
d: Xie Tieli, Chen Huaikai, Ba Hong

s: Hua Ershi
Beijing

1982

The Herdsman (*Muma ren*)
牧马人
d: Xie Jin
s: Li Zhun
Shanghai

1983

Bao Father and Son (*Baoshi fu zi*)
包氏父子
d, s: Xie Tieli
Beijing

Under the Bridge (*Daqiao xiamian*)
大桥下面
d: Bai Chen
s: Bai Chen, Ling Qiwei, Zhu Dian, Zhang Binhui
Shanghai

River without Buoys (*Meiyou hangbiao de heliu*)
没有航标的河流
d: Wu Tianming
s: Ye Weilin
Xi'an

1984

Gazing into My Eyes (*Kanzhe wode yanjing*)
看着我的眼睛
d: Bao Zhifang
s: Wang Lian, Xu Wenyuan, Li Wen
Shanghai

Life (*Rensheng*)
人生
d: Wu Tianming
s: Lu Yao
Xi'an

Yellow Earth (*Huang tudi*)
黄土地
d: Chen Kaige
s: Zhang Ziliang
Guangxi

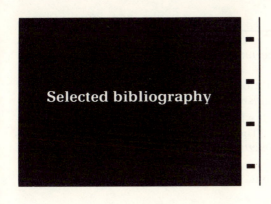

Selected bibliography

Bashan yeyu: cong juben dao yingpian [*Night Rain on the River:* From script to film], Beijing, Zhongguo dianying chubanshe, 1982.

Bai Hua and Peng Ning, *Kulian / Unrequited Love*, (Chinese–English ed.), Taibei, Institute of Current China Studies, 1981.

Bergeron, Régis, *Le cinéma chinois: I, 1905–1949* [Chinese film: I, 1905–1949], Lausanne, Alfred Eibel, Editeur, 1977.

———*Le cinéma chinois, 1949–1983* [Chinese film, 1949–1983], 3 vols., Paris, L'Harmattan, 1983–4.

Berry, Chris, "Stereotypes and ambiguities: An examination of the feature films of the Chinese Cultural Revolution," *Journal of Asian Culture* VI:37–72 (1982).

———"Sexual difference and the viewing subject in *Li Shuangshuang* and *The In-Laws*," in Berry, ed. (1985, pp. 32–46).

———"The sublimative text: Sex and revolution in *Big Road* [The Highway]," *East-West Film Journal*, 2:2 (June 1988), forthcoming.

———ed., *Perspectives on Chinese Cinema*, Ithaca, Cornell University East Asia Papers No. 39, 1985.

Burton, Wilbur, "Chinese reactions to the cinema," *Asia* 34(10):594–600 (October 1934).

Cai Chusheng et al., *Lun dianying juben chuangzuo de tezheng* [The characteristics of film script writing], Beijing, Zhongguo dianying chubanshe, 1956.

Chen Bo'er, "Gushipian: cong wu dao you biandao gongzuo," [Work on making the first feature films], *Wenyi bao* 1:3–5 (March 1950).

———et al., *Zhongguo dianying pinglun ji* [Collection of Chinese film reviews], Beijing, Zhongguo dianying chubanshe, 1957.

Cheng Bugao, *Yingtan yihui* [Movie memoirs], Beijing, Zhongguo dianying chubanshe, 1983.

Cheng Jihua, Li Shaobai, Xing Zuwen, eds., *Zhongguo dianying fazhanshi* [History of the development of Chinese film], 2 vols., Beijing, Zhongguo dianying chubanshe, 1963. Reprinted, with an introduction by Chen Huangmei, 1980.

China's Screen, Beijing, China Film Export and Import Corp., 1981 –

Chinese Literature, Beijing, Foreign Languages Press, 1951 –

Chou Yang, *A Great Debate on the Literary Front*, Beijing, Foreign Languages Press, 1965.

"Chuangxin dubai" yu Qu Baiyin ["Monologue on innovation" and Qu Baiyin], Beijing, Zhongguo dianying chubanshe, 1982.

Clark, Paul, "La Rivoluzione culturale e le sue consequenze sulla produzione cinematografica cinese (1966–1981) [The Cultural Revolution and its results in Chinese filmmaking"] in *Ombre elettriche: Saggi e ricerche sul cinema cinese* (1982, pp. 99–118).

————"Film-making in China: From the Cultural Revolution to 1981," *The China Quarterly* 94:304–22 (June 1983).

————"The film industry in the 1970s," in McDougall, ed. (1984, pp. 177–96).

————"Two hundred flowers on China's screens," in Berry, ed. (1985,pp. 66–96).

————"The Cultural Revolution and generational succession in Chinese filmmaking," paper presented at "New Perspectives on the Cultural Revolution" conference, Harvard University, May 1987.

————"Ethnic minorities in Chinese films: cinema and the exotic," *East–West Film Journal* 1(2):15–31 (June 1987).

Dahe benliu: cong juben dao yingpian [*The Great River Rushes On*: From script to film], Beijing, Zhongguo dianying chubanshe, 1980.

Dangdai dianying [*Contemporary Film*], 1984– .

Dangdai Zhongguo yanjiusuo, *Zhonggong dianyingjie wenhua dageming ziliao zhuanji (1964–1971)* [Collected materials on the Cultural Revolution in Chinese Communist film circles, 1964–1971], Hong Kong, Contemporary China Institute, [1971].

Dazhong dianying [*Popular Film*], 1951–66, 1979– .

Dianying chuangzuo [*Film Writing*], 1959–60, 1962, 1980– .

Dianying daoyan de tansuo [Explorations in film directing], Beijing, Zhongguo dianying chubanshe, 1981.

Dianying wenhua [*Film Culture*], 1980–2.

Dianying wenxue [*Film Literature*], 1959, 1962, 1964, 1979 – .

Dianying xinzuo [*New Film Writing*], 1979– .

Dianying yishu [*Film Art*], 1959–66, 1979– .

Dianying yishu cidian [Dictionary of film art], Beijing, Zhongguo dianying chubanshe, 1986.

Dianying yishu de canlan xinhua. "Shanshan de hongxing" pinglunji [A bright new flower of film art: collected reviews of "Sparkling Red Star"], Beijing, Renmin wenxue chubanshe, 1975.

Dianying yu guanzhong [*Films and Audiences*], 1955–6.

Ding Wang, *Wenhua dageming pinglunji* [Collected criticisms from the Cultural Revolution], Hong Kong, Contemporary China Institute, 1967.

Du Yunzhi, *Zhongguo dianying shi* [History of Chinese Films], 3 parts, Taibei, Commercial Press, 1972.

Duan Chengze, *Wu Xun xiansheng huazhuan* [Pictorial biography of Mr. Wu Xun], Chongqing, Shenghuo jiaoyushe, 1938 and 1944.

Eberhard, Wolfram, *The Chinese Silver Screen: Hong Kong and Taiwanese Motion Pictures in the 1960s*, Taibei, Orient Cultural Service, 1972.

Feng Xuefeng et al., *Dianying bian dao yan suitan* [Notes on film writing, directing and acting], Beijing, Zhongguo dianying chubanshe, 1957.

Fokkema, D. W., *Literary Debates in China and Soviet Influence, 1959–1960*, The Hague, Mouton, 1965.

Garside, Roger, *Coming Alive: China after Mao*, New York, McGraw-Hill, 1981.

Goldblatt, Howard, ed., *Chinese Literature for the 1980s. The Fourth Congress of Writers and Artists*, Armonk, N.Y., M. E. Sharpe, 1982.

Goldman, Merle, *Literary Dissent in Communist China*, Cambridge, Mass., Harvard University Press, 1967.

——*China's Intellectuals: Advise and Dissent*, Cambridge, Mass., Harvard University Press, 1981.

——ed., *Modern Chinese Literature in the May Fourth Era*, Cambridge, Mass., Harvard University Press, 1977.

Gray, Jack, and Patrick Cavendish, *Chinese Communism in Crisis: Maoism and the Cultural Revolution*, New York, Praeger, 1968.

Guangming ribao [*Guangming Daily*], 1948– .

Hong Shen, *Dianying xiju de bianju fangfa* [Methods for writing films and plays], Nanjing, Zhengzhong shuju, 1935.

Hongqi [*Red Flag*], 1958– .

Hongse niangzijun: cong juben dao yingpian [*The Red Detachment of Women*: From script to film], Beijing, Zhongguo dianying chubanshe, 1962.

Hsü, Tao-Ching, *The Chinese Conception of the Theatre*, Seattle, University of Washington Press, 1985.

Hu Chang, *Xin Zhongguo dianying de yaolan* [The cradle of new China's film], Changchun, Jilin wenshi chubanshe, 1986.

Hua'nan renmin chubanshe bianjibu [South China People's Publishing House], ed., *Wu Xun yu 'Wu Xun zhuan' pipan* [Wu Xun and the criticism of "The Life of Wu Xun"], Guangzhou, Hua'nan renmin chubanshe, 1951.

Huang Gang, *Zai dianying gongzuo gangwei* [At the film work post], Shanghai, Xinwenyi chubanshe, 1952.

——*Dianying piping yu chuangzuo wenti* [Film criticism and problems of writing], Shanghai, Xinwenyi chubanshe, 1954.

Huang, Joe C., *Heroes and Villians in Communist China: The Contemporary Chinese Novel as a Reflection of Life*, New York, Praeger, 1973.

Huashuo "Huang tudi" [Talking about *Yellow Earth*], Beijing, Zhongguo dianying chubanshe, 1986.

Ivens, Joris, *The Camera and I*, New York, International Publishers, 1970.

Jarvie, Ian C., *Window on Hong Kong: A Sociological Study of the Hong Kong Film Industry and Its Audience*, Hong Kong, Center of Asian Studies, University of Hong Kong, 1977.

Jiang Qing tongzhi jianghua xuanbian [Selected speeches of comrade Jiang Qing], Beijing, Renmin chubanshe, 1968.

Ke Ling, *Dianying wenxue congtan* [Collected essays on film writing], Beijing, Zhongguo dianying chubanshe, 1979.

Lee, Leo Ou-fan, and Andrew J. Nathan, "The beginnings of mass culture: Journalism and fiction in the late Ch'ing and beyond," in David Johnson, Andrew J. Nathan, and Evelyn Rawski, eds., *Popular Culture in Late Imperial China*, pp. 360–95, Berkeley, University of California Press, 1985.

Leyda, Jay, *Dianying: Electric Shadows: An Account of Films and the Film Audience in China*, Cambridge, Mass., Massachusetts Institute of Technology Press, 1972. Suppl. ed. [1978?].

Li Hui et al., *Zhongguo xiandai xiju dianying yishujia zhuan* [Biographies of modern Chinese theater and film artists], 2 vols., Nanchang, Jiangxi renmin chubanshe, 1981, 1984.

Li Shizhao, ed., *Wu Xun xiansheng de zhuanji* [Biography of Mr. Wu Xun], Shanghai, Shanghai jiaoyu shudian, 1948.

Li Shuangshuang: cong xiaoshuo dao yingpian [*Li Shuangshuang*: From short story to film], Beijing, Zhongguo dianying chubanshe, 1963.

Liehm, Mira, and Antonin J. Liehm, *The Most Important Art: Soviet and Eastern European Film after 1945*, Berkeley, University of California Press, 1976.

Lin Zexu: cong juben dao yingpian [*Lin Zexu*: From script to film], Beijing, Zhongguo dianying chubanshe, 1962.

Link, E. Perry, Jr., *Mandarin Ducks and Butterflies: Popular Fiction in Early Twentieth-Century Chinese Cities*, Berkeley, University of California Press, 1981.

Liu, Alan P., *The Film Industry in Communist China*, Cambridge, Mass., Center for International Studies, Massachusetts Institute of Technology, 1965.

———*Communications and National Integration in Communist China*, Berkeley, University of California Press, 1971.

Liu Binyan, "Meishang yinmu de gushi: ji Xi'an dianying zhipianchang changzhang, daoyan Wu Tianming" [A story that has not reached the screen: On Wu Tianming, head and a director of the Xi'an Film Studio], *Renmin ribao*, 7 and 8 August 1986, p. 8.

Liu Xiaoqing, *Wode lu* [My way], Hong Kong, Dongfang chubanshe, 1983.

Loh, Wai-fong, "From romantic love to class struggle: Some reflections on the film *Liu Sanjie*," in McDougall, ed. (1984, pp. 165–76).

Löwenthal, Rudolf, "Public communications in China before July, 1937," *The Chinese Social and Political Science Review* 22(1):47–50 (April–June 1938).

Lu Ren, " 'Li Shuangshuang' de daoyan fenxi he gousi" [Concept and analysis in directing "Li Shuangshuang"], in *Li Shuangshuang: cong xiaoshuo dao yingpian*, pp. 217–32.

Luo Dou, "Changying de diyige shengyin" [First sound from the Changchun Film Studio], *Wenyi bao* 11:1–2 (June 1957).

The Lute: Kao Ming's "P'i-p'a chi", trans. Jean Mulligan, New York, Columbia University Press, 1980.

McDougall, Bonnie S., trans. and ed., *Mao Zedong's "Talks at the Yan'an Conference on Literature and Art:" A Translation of the 1943 Text with Commentary*, Ann Arbor, Center for Chinese Studies, University of Michigan, 1980.

———ed., *Popular Chinese Literature and Performing Arts in the People's Republic of China, 1949–1979*, Berkeley, University of California Press, 1984.

———"Writers and performers, their works, and their audiences in the first three decades," in McDougall, ed. (1984, pp. 269–304).

MacFarquhar, Roderick, *The Origins of the Cultural Revolution. 1: Contradictions among the People 1956–1957*, New York, Columbia University Press, 1974.

———*The Origins of the Cultural Revolution. 2: The Great Leap Forward 1958–1960*, New York, Columbia University Press, 1984.

Mackerras, Colin, *The Chinese Theatre in Modern Times: From 1840 to the Present Day*, London, Thames and Hudson, 1975.

———*The Performing Arts in Contemporary China*, London, Routledge and Kegan Paul, 1981.

Mao Zedong, *Selected Works*, 5 vols., Beijing, Foreign Languages Press, 1965–77.

Mingbao yuekan [Mingbao Monthly], Hong Kong, 1981.

Moody, Peter R., *Opposition and Dissent in Contemporary China*, Stanford, Hoover Institution Press, 1977.

"Motion pictures in the Far East," *The Far Eastern Review. Engineering. Finance. Commerce* 28(11):532, 535 (November 1932).

Nathan, Andrew J., *Chinese Democracy*, New York, Alfred A. Knopf, 1985.

Ni Zhenliang, *Mingyun jiaoxiangqu – Zhao Dan zhuan* [The symphony of life: A biography of Zhao Dan], Beijing, Zhongguo wenlian chubangongsi, 1986.

Nongnu: cong juben dao yingpian [Serfs: From script to film], Beijing, Zhongguo dianying chubanshe, 1965.

North, C. J., "The Chinese motion picture market," U.S. Department of Commerce. Bureau of Foreign and Domestic Commerce. *Trade Information Bulletin, No. 467*, 1927.

Ombre elettriche: Saggi e ricerche sul cinema cinese [Electric shadows: History and research on Chinese film], Milan, Electa, 1982.

Pei Wenzhong et al., *Wode sixiang shi zenmeyang zhuanbian guolai de* [How my thinking was transformed], Beijing, Wushinian chubanshe, 1952.

Pipan ducao dianying ji, 2 [Critiques of poisonous weed films, Part 2], Shanghai, Shanghai renmin chubanshe, 1971.

Pollard, D. E., "The controversy over modernism, 1979–1984," *The China Quarterly* 104:641–56 (December 1985).

Qishi niandai [The Seventies], changed title to *Jiushi niandai [The Nineties]* in May 1984, Hong Kong, 1978–

Qu Baiyin, "Guanyu dianying chuangxin wenti de dubai" [Monologue on the problem of innovation in films], *Dianying yishu* 3:50–7 (June 1962).

Quanguo baokan dianying wenzhang mulu suoyin, 1949–1979 [Index to articles on film in Chinese newspapers and periodicals, 1949–1979], Beijing, Zhongguo dianying chubanshe, 1983.

Quiquemelle, Marie-Claire, and Jean-Loup Passek, eds., *Le cinéma chinois* [Chinese film], Paris, Centre Georges Pompidou, 1985.

Ragvald, Lars, *Yao Wenyuan as Literary Critic and Theorist: The Emergence of Chinese Zhdanovism*, Stockholm, University of Stockholm, 1978.

Rayns, Tony, *More Electric Shadows: Chinese Cinema 1922–1984* (Programme notes), London, British Film Institute, 1985.

———and Scott Meek, eds., *Electric Shadows: 45 Years of Chinese Cinema*, London, British Film Institute, 1980.

Renmin dianying [People's Film], 1976–8.

Renmin ribao [People's Daily], 1949– .

Sato Tadao, "Il cinema di Shanghai sotto l'occupazione giapponese (1939–1945)" [Shanghai film under the Japanese occupation], in *Ombre elettriche: Saggi e ricerche sul cinema cinese*, pp. 72–80.

———and Karima Fumitoshi, *Shanghai: kinema pōto. Yomigairu Chugoku eiga* [Shanghai: cinema port: Reviving Chinese film], Tokyo, Kaifusha, 1985.

Schneider, Laurence A., *A Madman of Ch'u: The Chinese Myth of Loyalty and Dissent*, Berkeley, University of California Press, 1980.

Scott, A. C., *Literature and the Arts in Twentieth Century China*, London, George Allen and Unwin, 1965.

Semsel, George S., ed., *Chinese Film: State of the Art*, New York, Praeger, 1987.

Shanghai dianying [Shanghai Film], 1960, 1962.

Shao Mujun, "Chinese film amidst the tide of reform," *East–West Film Journal* I(1):59–68 (December 1986).

Sidane, Victor, and Wojtek Zafanolli, eds., *Procès politiques à Pékin: Wei Jingsheng, Fu Yuehua* [Political trials in Beijing: Wei Jingsheng and Fu Yuehua], Paris, Maspero, 1981.

'Siren bang' shi dianying shiye de sidi. Wenhuabu dianying xitong jiepi 'siren bang' zuixing dahui fayan huibian [The Gang of Four is the deadly enemy of the film industry: Collection of speeches at a conference of the Ministry of Culture's film system exposing and criticizing the Gang of Four], Beijing, Zhongguo dianying chubanshe, 1978.

Sun Yu, "Biandao 'Wu Xun zhuan' ji" [Directing *The Life of Wu Xun*], *Guangming ribao*, 26 February 1951, p. 4.

———"Dui biandao dianying 'Wu Xun zhuan' de jiantao" [Self-criticism on making *The Life of Wu Xun*], in Pei Wenzhong et al. (1952, pp. 177–95).

———"Huiyi 'Wusi' yundong yingxiang xia de sanshi niandai dianying" [Recollection of 1930s film under the influence of the May Fourth movement], *Dianying yishu* 3:7–9, 36 (March 1979). English translation in Rayns and Meek, (1980, pp. T2–T7).

Taylor, Richard, *The Politics of the Soviet Cinema, 1917–1929*, Cambridge, Cambridge University Press, 1979.

Tian Han, *Yingshi zhuiyi lu* [Film memoirs], Beijing, Zhongguo dianying chubanshe, 1981.

Tianyunshan chuanqi: cong xiaoshuo dao dianying [*Legend of Tianyun Mountain*: From novel to film], Beijing, Zhongguo dianying chubanshe, 1983.

Toroptsev, Sergai A., *Trudnye gody kitaiskogo kino* [Difficult years of Chinese film], Moscow, Iskusstvo, 1975.

––––––*Ocherk istorii kitaiskogo kino, 1896–1966* [Essays on the history of Chinese film], Moscow, Nauka, 1979.

Wang Chao, *Guangzhou dianyingjie de zaofanzhe: Zhuying 'Dongfang hong'* [Rebels in Guangzhou film circles: Pearl River studio's "East is Red" faction], Hong Kong, Zhongbao zhoukan, 1969.

Way, E. T., "Motion pictures in China," U.S. Department of Commerce. Bureau of Foreign and Domestic Commerce. *Trade Information Bulletin, No. 722*, 1930.

Wenyi bao [*Literary Gazette*], 1949–66, 1978– .

Womack, Brantly, ed., "Media and the Chinese public: A survey of the Beijing media audience," *Chinese Sociology and Anthropology: A Journal of Translations* 18:3–4 issue (Spring–Summer 1986).

Wusi yilai dianying juben xuanji [Selected film scripts since May Fourth], 2 vols., Beijing, Zhongguo dianying chubanshe, 1979.

Xia Yan, "Cong 'Wu Xun zhuan' de piping jiantao wo zai Shanghai wenhua yishujie de gongzuo" [Self-criticism of my work in Shanghai cultural and artistic circles in the light of the criticism of *The Life of Wu Xun*], *Renmin ribao*, 26 August 1951, p. 3.

––––––"Jiuzheng cuowu, gaijin lingdao, jianjue guanche Mao zhuxi de wenyi fangzhen" [Solicit criticism of our mistakes, reform our leadership, and firmly implement Chairman Mao's policy on literature and art], *Wenyi bao* 11–12:8–10 (June 1952).

––––––*Xie dianying juben jige wenti* [Some problems in writing film scripts], Beijing, Zhongguo dianying chubanshe, 1959.

––––––"Zatan gaibian" [Notes on adaptation], in *Zhufu: cong xiaoshuo dao dianying* (1959, pp. 115–24).

––––––*Dianying lunwenji* [Essays on films], Beijing, Zhongguo dianying chubanshe, 1963.

––––––*Jiehou ying tan* [Talks on films since the Cultural Revolution], Beijing, Zhongguo dianying chubanshe, 1980.

––––––*Lanxun jiumeng lu* [Languid recollections of old dreams], Beijing, Sanlian shudian, 1985.

Xiang Sulian dianying xuexi [Learn from Soviet films], Hankou, Zhongnan renmin wenxue yishu chubanshe, 1952.

Xie Jin, "Daoyan chanshu" [Explanations of a director], in *Hongse niangzijun: cong juben dao yingpian* (1962, pp. 251–64).

––––––" 'Hongse niangzijun' daoyan chuangzuo zhaji" [Notes on directing *The Red Detachment of Women*], in *Hongse niangzijun: cong juben dao yingpian* (1962, pp. 265–97).

Xue Yan and Li Tao, "Zhongguo dianyingshi gailun" [An outline history of Chinese film], *Nanbeiji* [*The Perspective*], 81–95 (1977–8).

Yang Cun, *Zhongguo dianying sanian* [Thirty years of Chinese films], Hong Kong, Shijie chubanshe, 1954.

Yang, Daniel Shih-P'eng, "The traditional theatre of China in its contemporary setting: An examination of the pattern of change within the Peking theatre since 1949," unpublished dissertation, University of Wisconsin, 1968.

Yang Hansheng, "Guotongqu jinbu de xiju dianying yundong" [The progressive theater and film movement in the Guomindang-controlled regions], in *Zhonghua quanguo wenxue yishu gongzuozhe daibiao dahui jinian wenji* (1950, pp. 248–72).

———*Yang Hansheng dianying juben xuanji* [Selected film scripts of Yang Hansheng], Beijing, Zhongguo dianying chubanshe, 1981.

Yang Sheng, *Zhongguo dianying yanyuan bairen zhuan* [One hundred Chinese film actors], Changjiang wenyi chubanshe, 1984.

Yu Shan, *Jingxian dianying chutan* [A preliminary exploration of suspense films], Beijing, Qunzhong chubanshe, 1981.

Yuan Muzhi, "Guanyu jiefangqu dianying gongzuo" [On film work in the liberated regions], in *Zhonghua quanguo wenxue yishu gongzuozhe daibiao dahui jinian wenji* (1950, pp. 200–4).

———*Jiefangqu de dianying* [Film in the liberated regions], Beijing, Zhongguo dianying chubanshe, 1963.

Yuan Wenshu, *Dianying qiusuo lu* [In search of film], Beijing, Zhongguo dianying chubanshe, 1963.

Zhang Junxiang, Sang Hu, et al., *Lun xiqu dianying* [On opera films], Beijing, Zhongguo dianying chubanshe, 1959.

Zhang Mosheng, *Wu Xun zhuan* [Life of Wu Xun], Shanghai, Dongfang shushe, 1946.

Zhao Cong, *Zhongguo dalu de xiqu gaige* [The reform of opera in mainland China], Hong Kong, Chinese University of Hong Kong Press, 1969.

Zhao Dan, *Diyu zhi men* [The gate of hell], Shanghai, Shanghai wenyi chubanshe, 1980.

———*Yinmu xingxiang chuangzao* [Creating screen characters], Beijing, Zhongguo dianying chubanshe, 1980.

Zheng Junli, *Huawai yin* [Sounds off-screen], Beijing, Zhongguo dianying chubanshe, 1979.

———*Juese de dansheng* [Birth of a role], Beijing, Zhongguo dianying chubanshe, 1981.

Zhengming [*Debate*], Hong Kong, 1977–

[Zhong Dianfei], "Dianying de luogu" [Gongs and drums at the movies], *Wenyi bao* 23:3–4 (December 1956).

———ed., *Dianying meixue: 1984* [Film aesthetics: 1984], Beijing, Zhongguo dianying chubanshe, 1985.

Zhongguo dianying [*China's Films*], 1956–8.

Zhongguo dianying juben xuanji [Selected Chinese film scripts], Beijing, Zhongguo dianying chubanshe, 1959–63, 1979–83.

Zhongguo dianying nianjian, 1981, 1982, 1983, 1984, 1985 [China film year-
books, 1981–1985], Beijing, Zhongguo dianying chubanshe, 1982, 1983, 1984,
1985, 1987.

Zhongguo dianying ziliaoguan, Zhongguo yishu yanjiuyuan dianying yanjiusuo
[China Film Archive, and Film Research Institute of the China Art Research
Academy], eds., *Zhongguo yishu yingpian bianmu (1949–1979)* [Catalogue of
Chinese feature films, 1949–1979], 2 vols., Beijing, Wenhua yishu chubanshe,
1981.

Zhongguo dianyingjia xiehui [China Film Association], ed., *Zhongguo dianyingjia liezhuan* [Biographies of Chinese film artists], 7 vols., Beijing, Zhongguo
dianying chubanshe, 1982–6.

Zhongguo wenxue yishujie lianhehui [Chinese Federation of Literary and Art
Circles], ed., *Kaipi shehuizhuyi wenyi fanrong de xin shiqi* [Open up a glorious
new age in socialist literature and art], Chengdu, Sichuan renmin chubanshe,
1980. Partial English translation in Howard Goldblatt, ed., *Chinese Literature
for the 1980s: The Fourth Congress of Writers and Artists.*

Zhongguo yingtan xinren lu [New faces in the Chinese film world], Beijing,
Zhongguo dianying chubanshe, 1984.

Zhongguo yishujia cidian–xiandai [Biographical dictionary of Chinese artists–
modern], 4 vols., Changsha, Hunan renmin chubanshe, 1981–4.

Zhonghua quanguo wenxue yishu gongzuozhe daibiao dahui jinian wenji [Docu-
ments from the First National Writers and Artists Congress], Beijing, Xinhua
shudian, 1950.

Zhonghua renmin gongheguo dianying shiye sanshiwunian, 1949–1984 [Thirty-
five years of the Chinese film industry, 1949–1984], Beijing, Zhongguo dianying chubanshe, 1985.

Zhou Yang, "Xin min'ge kaituo le shige de xin daolu" [New folksongs open up a
new pathway for poetics], *Hongqi* 1:33–8 (June 1958).

———"Jianli Zhongguo ziji de Makesizhuyi de wenyi lilun he piping" [Establish
China's own Marxist literary and artistic theory and criticism], *Wenyi bao*
17:7–12 (September 1958).

———et al., *Wenyi zhanxianshang de yichang dabianlun* [A great debate on the
literary and art front], Beijing, Zuojia chubanshe, 1958. English translation in
Chou Yang (1965).

Zhufu: cong xiaoshuo dao dianying [*The New Year's Sacrifice*: From short story
to film], Beijing, Zhongguo dianying chubanshe, 1959.

Zhuo Geyun, *Tantan kan dianying* [About watching movies], Guangzhou, Guangdong renmin chubanshe, 1956.

Index

Note: Page numbers in italics refer to illustrations.

Ai Qing, 35
All-China Federation of Literary and Art
    Circles, 48
Alley, 163–4
Along the Sungari River, 17
American films, 4, 7, 10, 20, 38, 39–40, 53,
    157
animated films, 60, 207n19
Anti-Rightist campaign, 56, 76–9, 80, 143,
    158
April 5, 1976 demonstrations, 128, 162, 167
Ashma, 99, *122*
audiences, 2, 3, 8, 60, 65; in Cultural Revo-
    lution, 144–5, 148; Communist Party's
    view of, 27, 28, 30, 118; 1950s growth
    of, 36–7, 38–41, 57, 61–2, 64; pre-
    1949, 5, 8, 10, 15, 19–20, *20;* since
    1976, 161, 164, 167, 184; *see also*
    worker/peasant/soldier audiences
August First studio, 60, 80, 81, 132, 136,
    140, 141, 142

Bai Hua, 159, 160, 167, 169, 170–2
Bai minority, 95, 99
Bai Yang, 19
ballet, 128, 132; *see also* model perfor-
    mances
Bao Father and Son, 176
Battle of Leopard Valley, 145
Before the New Director Arrives, 75, 77, *90*
Beijing, 6, 7, 30, 31
Beijing Evening News, 170
Beijing Film Academy, 63, 156–7, 163, 179,
    206n3
Beijing opera, 108; *see also* opera
Beijing studio, 31, 41, 53, 63, 80, 81,
    197n87; in Cultural Revolution, 140–1,
    142

Big Li, Little Li, and Old Li, 66, *119*
Big Wave, 81
Bitter Laughter, 163
Blue Shirt faction, 11, 12, 17
Boundless Light, 43
bourgeois liberalization, 184
box office, 74; *see also* audiences
Braving Wind and Waves, 78
Breaking with Old Ideas, 135, 142
Bridge, 24, 42

Cai Chusheng, 15, 19, 77, 81, 133
Cai E, 164
Cantonese, 58, 59, 60, 108, 194n3, 204n64;
    see also language
Cao Yu, 35
Cen Fan, 108, 201n37
censorship, 28, 44, 75, 94–5, 155, 166, 174;
    before 1949, 14, 17, 18, 31; Communist
    Party directives on, 30, 34–5, 85
Central Film Enterprises, 32
Central Film Management Agency, 32
Central Film Management Bureau, *see* Film
    Bureau
Central Film Services Agency, 31
Changchun studio, 17, 157, 195n24; assists
    other studios, 60, 80; creative groups
    at, 72, 85; in Cultural Revolution, 139,
    140, 141, 143; before 1955, *see* North-
    east studio; in late 1950s, 73, 74, 77,
    197n87
Changsha, 36, 58–9, 60
Chen Baichen, 32
Chen Bo'er, 29, 42, 43, 52–3
Chen Huaikai, 147, 205n74, 209n49
Chen Huangmei, 73, 79, 83, 198n94
Chen Kaige, *153,* 179, 180, 181
Chen Qiang, 103, 205n75